DATE DUE

DEMCO, INC. 38-2931

HANDBOOK FOR DIRECTORS OF FINANCIAL INSTITUTIONS

Jean, Andy and Carol, Jeremy and Lincoln

Handbook for Directors of Financial Institutions

Edited by

Benton E. Gup

University of Alabama, USA

Edward Elgar
Cheltenham, UK • Northampton, MA, USA

Published by
Edward Elgar Publishing Limited
The Lypiatts
Lansdown Road
Cheltenham
Glos GL50 2JA
UK

Edward Elgar Publishing, Inc.
William Pratt House
9 Dewey Court
Northampton
Massachusetts 01060
USA

A catalogue record for this book
is available from the British Library

Library of Congress Cataloging in Publication Data

Handbook for directors of financial institutions / edited by Benton E. Gup.
  p. cm. — (Elgar original reference series)
  Includes bibliographical references and index.
  1. Financial institutions—Management—Handbooks, manuals, etc. 2. Bank management—Handbooks, manuals, etc. 3. Financial institutions—United States—Management—Handbooks, manuals, etc. 4. Bank management—United States—Handbooks, manuals, etc. I. Gup, Benton E.
  HG173.H32 2008
  332.1068′4—dc22

                                                          2007050564

ISBN 978 1 84720 469 1

Printed and bound in Great Britain by MPG Books Ltd, Bodmin, Cornwall

Contents

Preface
Benton E. Gup

Directors are responsible for good corporate governance. Corporate governance is a hot topic because of Enron, Tyco, WorldCom, and dozens of
other corporate scandals. In response to these scandals, Congress passed
the Sarbanes-Oxley Act of 2002 (SOX), which imposed additional pressures and costs on firms. In addition, the USA PATRIOT Act (2001)
increased the regulatory burden and costs on all financial institutions.
Financial institutions, in the context of the Bank Secrecy Act and anti-
money laundering laws, include but are not limited to commercial banks,
all subsidiaries of bank holding companies, US branches and agencies of
foreign banks, savings and loan associations, credit unions, federally regulated securities brokers, dealers, and investment companies, money service
businesses, casinos, card clubs, futures commission merchants, insurance
companies offering selected products, and mutual funds.

The motivation for this book came when I interviewed some of the directors of a financial institution that had suffered serious problems due to lack
of proper oversight. The directors were intelligent, and very successful in
their own professions. However, they had little or no background in
financial institutions, which can be extraordinarily complex. Accordingly,
this book differs significantly from other sources of information about corporate governance because it contains advice from existing directors of
banks, credit unions, and insurance companies, regulators, lawyers, and
academics from the US, Europe, and Australia about what directors of
financial institutions need to know in order to perform their duties. It
covers a wide range of subjects, including corporate social responsibility,
directors' and officers' liability insurance, directing credit unions, forces of
change in financial markets, Islamic banking, regulatory compliance, starting a new bank, subprime lending, and other essential topics for directors
of financial institutions.

The bottom line is that there are increased pressures on boards of directors to protect shareholder and public interests. Failure to do so can have
unfortunate consequences for both the directors and their companies.
Enron is only one example.

Contributors

Mohamed Ariff held a chair in finance and headed the finance faculty in Monash University, Melbourne, Australia, before moving to Bond University in 2007 where he is a Professor of Finance. His research interest is mostly on capital markets, particularly in the Asia-Pacific region. In addition, he is doing research on the consolidation of Islamic banking and finance principles within the broader framework of modern banking and finance concepts. He and two others won a large Australian Research Council grant to work on Islamic banking. Ariff was the president of the Asian Finance Association in 2004–06.

David L. Bickelhaupt is a Professor Emeritus of Insurance, Ohio State University, where he taught courses in insurance and risk management for almost 30 years. He also taught at the Wharton School of the University of Pennsylvania, Skidmore College, Georgia State University, and the University of Arizona. His BSc and PhD are from Penn, and his MSc is from Columbia. In addition, he holds various professional designations, including ChFC, CLU, CPCU, and ARM. He is the author of two books, and has contributed chapters and sections to six others. In addition, he has published almost 100 articles that have appeared in professional publications and leading journals. He served on the board of directors for six companies of the State Automobile Insurance Group, as well as other boards.

Ben S. Branch is a Professor of Finance at the University of Massachusetts, Amherst, where he has taught finance, investment, banking, and industrial organization for over 30 years. He has previously taught at Dartmouth College, the University of Michigan, and the University of Texas, and has served on the boards of several corporations, including the First Republic Bank, BankEast, Bank of New England, and Proactive Technologies. He is currently an associate editor of the *International Review of Financial Analysis*. He has published dozens of journal articles and book reviews and three books.

Irv Burling served as the CEO of Century Companies of America for 17 of the 23 years he was associated with that company. He also worked at Lutheran Brotherhood Insurance Company and Investors' Syndicate Life Insurance Companies. Irv served on the boards of Wartburg College, Wartburg Seminary, ELCA Board of Pensions, and LOMA. He acted as a "Life Coach for CEOs" for five years. He is a graduate of the University of

Minnesota, Harvard Business School, Advanced Management Class, and a fellow of the Society of Actuaries. Irv is the author of three books.

Ronald Dulek is the John R. Miller Professor of Management at the University of Alabama. He has published eight books and more than 40 refereed journal articles. Ron is the 2006 recipient of the Kitty Locker Outstanding Researcher Award from the Association for Business Communication. He served as Head of the Management and Marketing Department from 1988 to 2005. He also serves and has served on a number of community and civic boards, including the Alabama Credit Union, the West Alabama Red Cross, the YMCA, and the University of Alabama Press.

Benton E. Gup holds the Robert Hunt Cochrane-Alabama Bankers Association Chair of Banking at the University of Alabama. He also held banking chairs at the University of Tulsa and the University of Virginia. Dr Gup is the author or editor of 26 books and more than 90 articles on banking and financial topics. He was an economist at the Federal Reserve Bank of Cleveland, and visiting economist at the Office of the Comptroller of the Currency. Dr Gup has lectured in Australia, Latin America, South Africa, and New Zealand. He serves as a consultant to government and industry.

Warren Hogan is Emeritus Professor of Economics at the University of Sydney (Australia), and an Adjunct Professor at the University of Technology, Sydney. He previously served as Professor of Economics and Dean of the Faculty of Economics and Commerce in the University of Newcastle. From August 1986 to December 2001 he was a member of the Board of Directors of Westpac Banking Corporation. He was a member of the board of the Australian Mutual Provident Society between 1993 and 1995. In recent years his predominant academic and professional research interests have been with domestic and international banking and finance.

Júlia Király is Deputy Governor of the National Bank of Hungary. After graduating from the Budapest University of Economics Ms Kiraly was an applied econometrician at the Planning Office. In 1988, after having defended her PhD thesis, she joined ITCB Consulting & Training. Between 1999 and 2007 she was one of the CEOs and one of the owners from 2003. Ms Kiraly took part in the privatization of large Hungarian commercial banks: the MHB (1996) and K&H (2000) as member of the board, and in the privatization of the Postabank in 2003 as the chairwoman of the board. She has lectured at the Budapest University of Economics since 1989. Her studies have been published in Hungarian and in English in various journals and books.

Cathy Lemieux is Senior Vice President in charge of Supervision and Regulation at the Federal Reserve Bank of Chicago. Cathy directs the supervision and regulation of more than 1000 banking organizations within the Seventh Federal Reserve District. Additionally, she chairs the System's Regional Banking Organization (RBO) group, serves as the chair of the Federal Reserve System Subcommittee implementing Basel II training, and is a member of the Basel Implementation Council. Cathy has over 30 years' experience in the industry, serving as a lender, professor, policy analyst, and bank regulator. She holds a PhD from Texas A&M University.

Katalin Mérö is Managing Director of the Hungarian Financial Supervisory Authority's Economics, Risk Assessment and Regulatory Directorate. Previously she was the deputy head of the Financial Stability Department of the National Bank of Hungary. From 1990 to 1997 she was Director of Strategy and Economic Analysis at K&H, a large Hungarian commercial bank. Prior to her banking career she worked as a researcher at the Economic Research Institute and Research Institute for Labour. Ms Mérö graduated from the Budapest University of Economics and received her PhD from Budapest University of Technology and Economics.

Barbara Parker is a Professor of Management in the Albers School of Business and Economics, Seattle University. She conducts research on cross-sector partnerships, strategic management of diversity, joint venture management, and globalization; the results appear in a wide range of books and journals. She is the author of two books on globalization *Globalization and Business Practices: Managing across Boundaries* (1996), and *Introduction to Globalization and Business: Relationships and Responsibilities* (2005).

Laurence Pettit is Professor Emeritus of Commerce in the McIntire School of Commerce at the University of Virginia, where he specializes in corporate finance and banking. Larry specializes in consulting with financial institutions' management in the areas of strategic planning, credit, and feasibility studies for products and branches. He also serves as a consultant to middle market and industrial firms. Larry's consulting assignments have included international, national, and regional banking firms. In addition to his strategy and credit activities with existing banks, Larry has been involved in forming and advising more than 20 new community banks.

Robin Russell is a partner in the Houston office of Andrews LLP. Her law practice in more than 100 Chapter 7 and Chapter 11 bankruptcy proceedings included the Bank of New England Corporation, BankEast Corporation, and the OneBancorp. She received her BSc degree from Texas Tech University and her law degree from Baylor. Her LLM in Banking Law, *cum* *laude* is from Boston University. She is the author of the Texas Bankers Association *Texas Secured Lending Guide* and *Problem Loan Guide*. She co-authored several books including *Last Rights: Liquidating a Company* (with Ben Branch and Hugh Ray). She was named a 2006 Texas Super Lawyer.

Rowan Trayler is a Senior Lecturer in the School of Finance and Economics at the University of Technology, Sydney. Prior to joining the faculty at the University of Technology, Sydney, he worked for 16 years in the banking and finance industry. Rowan spent 11 years at Barclays Bank Australia Ltd, where he helped establish the new bank in Australia, when Barclays was granted a banking license. Since joining the University of Technology Rowan has been closely involved in the development and co-ordination of the postgraduate Masters of Business in Finance as well as being responsible for the banking stream.

Steven VanBever is a Lead Supervision Analyst at the Federal Reserve Bank of Chicago. Since 1981, he has worked in various areas of bank supervision within the Federal Reserve System, including projects on corporate governance and operational risk management. He holds a BA degree from the University of Michigan and an MBA degree from Wayne State University in Detroit, Michigan.

1 Introduction to financial institutions
Benton E. Gup

Financial institutions defined

In general terms, financial institutions are organizations whose principal function is managing the financial assets of business concerns and individuals. They bring savers and borrowers together by selling securities and services to savers, and then lending (or investing) those funds to borrowers. It is obvious that banks are financial institutions. But it is not obvious that casinos or card clubs are considered financial institutions under the Bank Secrecy Act and anti-money laundering (BSA/AML) laws in the United States.[1] This book is not about money laundering, but the BSA/AML laws provide another definition of financial institutions.

The term "banks" is used in the broad sense of the word. It includes commercial banks, all of the subsidiaries of Bank Holding Companies, Edge and Agreement corporations, US branches and agencies of foreign banks, savings and loan associations, and credit unions.

Other types of financial institutions include, but are not limited to:

- All federally regulated securities brokers, dealers, and investment companies.
- Insurance companies offering selected products.
- Money service businesses (MSBs, currency dealers or exchangers; check cashers, issuers of travelers' checks, money orders, or stored value; sellers or redeemers of travelers' checks, money orders, or stored value; and funds transmitters), the United States Postal Service is considered an MSB because it issues money orders.
- Persons subject to supervision by state or federal bank supervisory authority.
- Casinos.
- Card clubs.
- Futures commission merchants, including brokers, commodity pool operators, and commodity trading advisers.
- Individuals or groups engaged in conducting, controlling, directing or owning informal value transfer systems (IVTS) in the United States.

Some firms are considered "financial services firms," but they are not financial institutions in the traditional sense of the word. For example, GE

Table 1.1   FDIC-insured commercial banks, September 2006

	Asset size				
	All insured institutions	Less than $100 million	$100 million to $1 billion	$1 billion to $10 billion	Greater than $10 billion
Number of institutions	7450	3331	3631	401	87
Total assets ($billion)	$9765.4	$173.9	$1031.9	$1095.3	$7464.3
Percentage	100%	1.8%	10.6%	11.2%	76.4%

Source: FDIC-Quarterly Banking Profile, Table III-A, First Three Quarters 2006, FDIC-Insured Commercial Banks, 2007.

Commercial Finance is one of the largest financial services firms in the world, with total assets of over $206 billion.[2] It provides a wide variety of finance and insurance products. This includes financing corporate aircraft, trucks and trailers, health care equipment, and so on. In addition, GE provides credit cards, personal loans, mortgage loans, and other consumer financial products.

In summary, there are various definitions of financial institutions. The exact definition is not important for our purpose, which is to help directors of financial institutions do their jobs better.

Banks
Commercial banks are the largest financial institutions in terms of total assets. As shown in Table 1.1, there were 7450 commercial banks used by the Federal Deposit Insurance Corporation (FDIC) in 2006. The overwhelming majority of commercial banks are small, with total assets of less than $1 billion. At the other end of the spectrum, 87 large banks with total assets of $10 or more accounted for 76.4 per cent of the total assets of all banks. In this group of large banks, the five banks listed in Table 1.2 account for 40 per cent of the total assets of all the FDIC-insured commercial banks. The data from Tables 1.1 and 1.2 show that we have a large number of small commercial banks; but that most of the assets are concentrated in a few large ones.

The banks listed in Table 1.2 are parts of bank and financial holding companies – companies that own one or more banks and engage in other permissible activities. For example, JP Morgan Chase Bank NA is part of JP Morgan Chase & Co. which operates in the USA and overseas. Management operations are divided into six reporting segments: asset

Table 1.2   Total assets and derivatives of selected banks, September 2006

Bank	Total assets ($ million)	Total derivatives ($ million)
JP Morgan Chase Bank NA	1 173 732	62 634 961
Bank of America NA	1 185 581	25 473 719
Citibank NA	816 362	24 476 944
Wachovia Bank NA	517 174	5 245 300
HSBC Bank USA NA	166 632	4 167 509
Total	3 859 481	121 998 442

Source: Office of the Comptroller of the Currency (2006b), "OCC's Quarterly Report on Bank Derivatives Activities," Third Quarter 2006, Press Release 2006-137, Table 10.

and wealth management, card services, commercial banking, corporate (including private equity and treasury businesses, as well as corporate support functions), investment banking, retail financial services, and treasury and securities services.[3]

Table 1.2 also shows that the top five banks hold about $122 trillion in derivatives. There are 908 other banks and trust companies that hold an additional $4 trillion in derivatives. Thus, the top five banks control the overwhelming majority of both bank assets and derivatives. Interest rate contracts (swaps, options, futures and forwards, and credit derivatives) account for about 82 per cent of the total derivatives contracts.

Asset concentration groups   The FDIC recognizes that not all banks do the same things. Some banks' assets are concentrated in particular types of loans or activities. Thus, consumer-oriented credit-card banks are going to have a different focus and methods of operation than commercial lenders. The following are the FDIC definitions of asset concentration groups.[4]

- *International banks*   Banks with assets greater than $10 billion and more than 25 per cent of total assets in foreign offices.
- *Agricultural banks*   Banks whose agricultural production loans plus real estate loans secured by farmland exceed 25 per cent of total loans and leases.
- *Credit-card lenders*   Institutions whose credit-card loans plus securitized receivables exceed 50 per cent of total assets plus securitized receivables.
- *Commercial lenders*   Institutions whose commercial and industrial loans, plus real estate construction and development loans, plus loans secured by commercial real estate properties exceed 25 per cent of total assets.

- *Mortgage lenders* Institutions with residential mortgage loans, plus mortgage-backed securities, exceeding 50 per cent of their total assets.
- *Consumer lenders* Institutions with residential mortgage loans, plus credit-card loans, plus other loans to individuals, that exceed 50 per cent of their total assets.
- *Other specialized < $1 billion* Institutions with assets less than $1 billion, whose loans and leases are less than 40 per cent of total assets.
- *All other < $1 billion* Institutions with assets less than $1 billion that do not meet any of the definitions above; they have significant lending activity with no identified asset concentrations.
- *All other > $1 billion* Institutions with assets greater than $1 billion that do not meet any of the definitions above; they have significant lending activity with no identified asset concentrations.

Bank holding companies

Table 1.3 lists the top 10 bank holding companies in the USA. Some of these institutions are considered large complex banking organizations (LCBOs) because of their size, the complex composition of their organizations, and their international operations. Citigroup, for example, has operations in more than 100 countries. As shown in Table 1.3, Citigroup has 1642 affiliated entities in their organizational hierarchy.[5] They are located in the US and abroad. The individual entities, such as Citicorp Holdings Inc., may have sub-units as well. Thus, the total number of entities is greater than 1642.

HSBC Holdings plc (London) is the largest banking organization in the world by asset size. It has more than 9500 offices in 76 countries and territories. HSBC's operating unit in the United States, HSBC North America Holdings Inc., has 360 affiliated entities in the US and overseas.[6]

LCBOs are involved in banking, but they are also engaged in a wide range of other activities through their affiliated entities. Citigroup is an example of an LCFO. It offers consumer and commercial banking, insurance, brokerage services, corporate and investment banking, wealth management, and alternative investments including hedge funds.[7] It recently bought a mortgage servicing business.[8] It is also part of a consortium of nine large banks that want to build a European stock-trade-reporting system to compete with existing regional stock exchanges.[9] In addition, Citigroup was considering buying into China's Spring Airlines.[10] In 2003, Citigroup spun off its property/casualty insurance unit of Travelers Insurance Group. In 2005, it sold its life insurance unit to MetLife. Thus, it is a dynamic organization that buys and sells various lines of business.

Table 1.3   Top 10 bank holding companies in the USA, third quarter, 2006

Rank	Institution	Location	Total assets $000s (30 Sept. 2006)	Affiliated entities
1	Citigroup Inc	New York, NY	$1 746 248 000	1642
2	Bank of America Corporation	Charlotte, NC	$1 451 603 528	2191
3	JP Morgan Chase & Co.	New York, NY	$1 338 029 000	1506
4	Wachovia Corporation	Charlotte, NC	$559 922 000	1667
5	Wells Fargo & Company	San Francisco, CA	$483 441 000	1153
6	HSBC North America Holdings Inc.	Prospect Heights, IL	$473 711 105	360
7	Taunus Corporation	New York, NY	$430 384 000	504
8	US Bancorp	Minneapolis, MN	$216 855 000	20
9	Countrywide Financial Corporation	Calabasas, CA	$193 194 572	118
10	Suntrust Banks, Inc.	Atlanta, GA	$183 104 553	401

Source: Federal Financial Institutions Examination Center (FFIEC), National Information Center, "Top 50 bank holding companies," http://www.ffiec.gov/nicpubweb/nicweb/Top 50Form.aspx.

Similarly, Bank of America offers various banking and non-banking financial services and products in the US and throughout the world. It received permission to build and own a Ritz-Carlton Hotel at its corporate headquarters in Charlotte, North Carolina.[11] Finally, Union Bank of California NA received permission from bank regulators to operate a "wind energy project" where wind turbines are used to generate electricity that will be sold.[12]

The key point is that LCBOs are more than just "banks." They engage in a very wide range of activities that are not traditionally associated with banks. Today banks, insurance companies, and securities firms can be included in an LCBO. For example, Macquarie Bank Group (Sydney, Australia) operates investment banking, commercial banking, and selected retail financial services markets in Australia and 23 other countries.[13] In addition, Macquarie Global Infrastructure Fund acquired PCAA/Avistar, the largest provider of off-airport parking services in the United States. Macquarie Infrastructure Group/Cintra consortium operates and manages the Chicago Skyway toll road. In Europe, its acquisitions include an airport in Denmark, a toll road in France, a tank storage business in Germany, a gas and electric network in the Netherlands. In the UK it acquired two ferry services in addition to other businesses. The front page of its 2006 Annual Report shows an explosive device, because Macquarie

Group led a consortium to buy the international explosives company, Dyno Nobel, headquartered in Norway.[14]

Savings institutions

In addition to commercial banks, there were 1293 FDIC-insured savings (thrift) institutions in 2006.[15] FDIC-insured savings banks and savings and loan institutions operate under state or federal banking laws. Qualified thrift lenders (QTL) must have 65 per cent or more of their assets in housing related loans (including mortgage backed securities) and other permissible loans such as educational and small business loans. They also qualify for low-cost advances from its Federal Home Loan Bank. Historically, many thrifts were depositor owned (that is, mutual savings banks), but they converted to stock ownership after the passage of the Garn-St Germain Depository Institutions Act of 1982. Most thrifts are located in the northeastern states.

Credit unions

Credit unions are nonprofit, cooperative financial institutions that are owned and run by their members. The term "nonprofit" is misleading because, like other financial institutions, they cannot operate for long periods at a loss, and they require adequate capitalization. There were 8695 credit unions as of 31 December 2005.[16] Like banks, there are a few very large credit unions, but the majority of them are relatively small. The largest credit union is the Navy Credit Union (Merrifield, VA) with $24.6 billion in assets. State Employees Credit Union (Raleigh, NC) with $12.9 billion is the second largest, and the Pentagon Credit Union (Alexandria, VA) with $8 billion is in third place.

Insurance companies

The two largest groups in the insurance industry in the USA are life/health insurance companies and property/casualty companies. There were 4009 life/health and property/casualty insurance companies at the end of 2004.[17] In addition, there are health insurance companies (for example, Blue Cross/Blue Shield), fraternal groups that provide insurance for their members, title insurance companies, limited benefit plans, risk retention groups, and others. Finally, reinsurance companies provide products that allow other insurance companies better to manage some of their risks.

Many large insurance companies offer a wide array of insurance policies as well as other financial services. For example, Metropolitan Life Insurance Company (MetLife), the largest life insurance company in North America, also offers non-medical health and property and casualty insurance, as well as banking (MetLife Bank NA), brokerage services

(MetLife Securities, Inc.), mutual funds and other financial products and services.[18]

Some insurance companies also own thrifts that are regulated by the Office of Thrift Supervision (OTS). For example, State Farm Mutual Auto Insurance Company owns State Farm Bank, FSB (Federal Savings Bank).[19] State Farm's bank focuses on consumer-oriented financial products. It operates mainly through its insurance agents, call centers and the internet. Like other large insurance companies, State Farm Investment Management Corp. offers mutual funds.

Corporate governance issues

Regulatory concerns
LCBOs and non-traditional banking activities provide special challenges to managers, directors, and bank regulators. Federal Reserve Governor Susan Schmidt Bies said:

> the complexity of these organizations makes it more difficult for executive management to view risk in a comprehensive way, both in terms of aggregating similar and correlated risks, but also in identifying potential conflicts of interest between the growth of a line of business and the reputation, legal, and compliance risks of the firm as a whole. In recent years, large financial institutions have reported losses from breaks in these operating controls that in some cases have exceeded those in credit or market risk.[20]

For example, JP Morgan Chase & Co. agreed to pay the Securities and Exchange Commission $135 million to settle allegations that it helped Enron to commit fraud. Similarly, Citigroup agreed to pay $120 million to settle SEC allegations that it helped Enron and Dynegy commit fraud.[21] Part of the problem involved complex structured finance transactions (CSFTs).[22] These have become widely used in both international and domestic capital markets. However, they have also been used to misrepresent the financial condition of firms to investors and regulators, and they have been used in illegal schemes. Therefore CSFTs may involve substantial legal and reputational risks such as those faced by JP Morgan Chase and Citigroup.

Other Citigroup problems included:

- *Japan*   In 2001, Japan's Financial Services Agency (FSA) had concerns about Citibank's Japan Branch (the Marunouchi Branch of Citibank). In 2004, the FSA took administrative actions to close four offices of the Japan branch because several of the bank officers misled customers into investing in structured bonds and complex securities in violation of Japan's security laws, as well as numerous other violations.[23]

- *Germany* Citigroup bond traders were accused of "market manipulation" using the "Dr Evil Strategy". But that strategy did not violate Germany's laws, and the charges were dropped.[24]
- *Brazil* It is alleged that a Citigroup private equity manager tried to coerce a large investor into selling shares in a Brazilian telecom at below market prices. The manager was fired.[25]
- *Australia* Citigroup faced a $715 million fine in Australia for insider trading in connection with a takeover bid of a large company.[26]
- *New York* Citigroup settled Enron class action law suit for $2 billion.[27]
- *Chicago* The headline in the *Chicago Tribune* online edition stated "Even big boys get scammed: A tense corporate drama unfolds when one of the nation's major lenders finds its Chicago Operation enmeshed in mortgage fraud."[28] The major lender was part of Citigroup.

Collectively, these problems illustrate the fact that it is very difficult to manage LCBOs. They also reveal that these problems occurred at locations that were far from the corporate headquarters in New York. Stated otherwise, it is difficult to manage and supervise operations at distant locations

A board that failed
Enron was considered an innovative and growing company with revenues of over $111 billion. The 2000 Annual Report said that "Enron's performance was a success by any measure, as we continued to outdistance the competition."[29] On 2 December 2001 Enron declared bankruptcy. It was the seventh largest publicly traded company in the USA. The bankruptcy and scandal that followed caused shock waves throughout the financial community.

The Enron scandal was followed by bankruptcies and scandals at Tyco International, Peregrine Systems, and WorldCom that collectively contributed to the passage of the Sarbanes-Oxley Act of 2002. It is also known as the Public Company Accounting Reform and Investor Protection Act of 2002, or SOX. It provided for new and improved standards for all US public company boards, management, and public accounting firms.

Enron was very focused on its credit ratings, cash flows, and its debt burden. Enron also had an "asset light" strategy which means that it moved millions of dollars off its balance sheet into affiliated companies. Similarly, it made extensive use of complex accounting structures and derivatives. In

Table 1.4   Enron's outside directors

Name	Location and occupation
Robert A. Belfer	New York, NY, Chairman, Belco Oil & Gas Corp.
Norman P. Blake, Jr	Colorado Springs, CO, Chairman, President and CEO, Promus Hotel Corp.
Ronnie C. Chan	Hong Kong, Chairman, Han Lung Group
John H. Duncan	Houston, TX, Former Chairman of the Executive Committee of Gulf & Western Industries
Dr Wendy L. Gramm	Washington, DC, Director of the Regulatory Studies Program, George Mason University. Former Chairman, US Commodity Futures Trading Commission
Ken L. Harrison	Portland, OR, Former Chairman and CEO, Portland General Electric Company
Dr Robert K. Jaedicke	Stanford, CA, Professor of Accounting (Emeritus) and former Dean, Graduate School of Business, Stanford University
Dr Charles A. LeMaistre	San Antonio, TX, President Emeritus, University of Texas M.D. Anderson Cancer Center
Dr John Mendelsohn	Houston, TX, President, University of Texas M.D. Anderson Cancer Center
Jerome J. Meyer	Wilsonville, OR, Chairman, Tektronix, Inc.
Paulo V. Ferraz Pereira	Rio de Janeiro, Brazil, Executive Vice President of Groupo Bozano, Former President and COO, Meridonal Financial Group, and Former President and CEO, State Bank of Rio de Janeiro, Brazil
John A. Urquhart	Fairfield, CT, President, John A. Urquhart Associates, and Former Senior Vice President of Industrial and Power Systems, General Electric
Lord John Wakeham	London, England, President, Winokur Holdings, Inc., and Former Senior Executive Vice President, Penn Central Corp.

Source: Enron Annual Report 2000, pp. 64–5.

this sense Enron is similar to the LCBOs that were discussed previously. This does not imply that the LCBOs have done or are doing anything wrong – but there are some structural similarities. Size and complexity make it more difficult for directors to do their jobs.

Enron's Board of Directors had 15 members, including two insiders, Kenneth L. Lay (Chairman) and Jeffrey K. Skilling (President and CEO). The 13 outside directors listed in Table 1.4 included very successful and high profile individuals. But they failed miserably in their duties as Enron's board of directors. In legal jargon, directors have a fiduciary duty to the shareholders. This means that they are accountable to the shareholders for their actions. In the case of financial institutions, they are also accountable to regulators.

The legal duties of directors are the duties of obedience, loyalty, and care.[30] The duty of obedience requires directors to avoid committing acts beyond the scope of powers defined by the corporate charter or the laws of the state of incorporation. The duty of loyalty prohibits directors from putting their personal or business interests above the interest of the firm they are directing. The duty of care requires directors to act in good faith and carry out their duties diligently and prudently.

A US Senate Committee report, "The Role of The Board of Directors in Enron's Collapse," examined more than one million pages of documents and interviewed 13 Enron Board members.[31] The report found the following:[32]

1) **Fiduciary Failure.** The Enron Board of Directors failed to safeguard Enron shareholders and contributed to the collapse of the seventh largest public company in the United States, by allowing Enron to engage in high risk accounting, inappropriate conflict of interest transactions, extensive undisclosed off-the-books activities, and excessive executive compensation. The Board witnessed numerous indications of questionable practices over several years, but chose to ignore them to the detriment of Enron shareholders, employees and business associates.

2) **High Risk Accounting.** The Enron Board of Directors knowingly allowed Enron to engage in high-risk accounting practices.

3) **Inappropriate Conflicts of Interest.** Despite clear conflicts of interest, the Enron Board of Directors approved an unprecedented arrangement allowing Enron's chief financial officer to establish and operate LJM private equity funds which transacted business with Enron and profited at Enron's expense. The Board exercised inadequate oversight of LJM transactions and compensation controls and failed to protect Enron shareholders from unfair dealing.

4) **Extensive Undisclosed Off-the-Books Activity.** The Enron Board of Directors knowingly allowed Enron to conduct billions of dollars in off-the-books activity to make its financial condition appear better than it was and failed to ensure adequate public disclosure of material off-the-books liabilities that contributed to Enron's collapse.

5) **Excessive Compensation.** The Enron Board of Directors approved excessive compensation for the company executives, failed to monitor the cumulative cash drain caused by Enron's 2000 annual bonus and performance unit plans, and failed to monitor or halt abuse by Board Chairman and Chief Executive Officer Kenneth Lay of a company-financed multi-million dollar personal credit line.

6) **Lack of Independence.** The independence of the Enron Board of Directors was compromised by financial ties between the company and certain Board members. The Board also failed to ensure the independence of the company's auditor, allowing Arthur Andersen LLP to provide internal audit and consulting services while serving as Enron's outside auditor.

Industry concentration and stock returns

The data reveal that the banking industry is highly concentrated in a few large firms. Their size can be both an advantage and disadvantage. On the advantage side of the argument, they can have diversified portfolios, which allows them to withstand economic shocks better than smaller firms. In addition, they are of sufficient size and have the resources to invest in new areas and acquire other firms. For example, Wachovia Bank acquired SouthTrust bank in 2005.

On the other side of the coin, a study by Hou and Robinson[33] found that firms in concentrated industries earned lower returns than firms in competitive industries. They argue that firms in highly concentrated industries engage in less innovation and therefore they command lower expected returns. They also argue that barriers to entry insulated some firms from aggregate demand shocks, while exposing other firms to the distress risk. Industries with high barriers to entry are associated with lower stock returns. Hou and Robinson's data revealed that firms in the highest quintile in the most competitive industries earned nearly 4 per cent more than those in the highest quintile of the most concentrated industries.

Small banks are not immune from management problems

As shown in Table 1.1, 6962 banks in the US have assets of less than $1 billion. Small banks can have management problems too. Consider the case of First Southern Bank.[34] In March 2002, the FDIC and the Alabama State Banking Department issued a cease and desist order (C&D) to First Southern Bank, Florence, AL.[35] According to the C&D, the bank had inadequate management, a large volume of poor quality loans following hazardous lending and lax collection practices, and so on.

The story behind these losses provides important insights about the corporate governance of small thrifts that convert into banks. Some parts of this lesson may be applicable to credit unions when they attempt to act like banks.

First Federal Savings & Loan Association was chartered in Florence in 1935. It was a successful savings and loan (S&L). Sixty years later in 1995, management decided to convert from an S&L into a bank holding company and a state-chartered commercial bank – First Southern Bank. One reason for the change was because a bank could provide a wider range of loans and services to the communities served.

On the surface, First Southern Bank appeared to be a well-functioning organization. However, there were significant corporate governance problems that almost resulted in the demise of the bank.

The CEO of the bank made statements to the effect that he would run the bank just like he ran the S&L. The problem is that banks are significantly different to S&Ls, and neither he nor his staff had experience in making, monitoring, or collecting commercial loans. Moreover, the CEO had an "alpha male personality," that can be interpreted to mean "I'm the boss, I know how to run this shop, and I don't like to be questioned." The board must have thought that he did an excellent job, because he was one of the highest paid CEOs in banks of equivalent size.

The CEO was not a lender. He delegated the lending to his second in command. The loan committee rubber stamped most of the loans that were made. The bank's outside audits were done by a local accounting firm that had little experience in banking. But they were socially close with the CEO.

The board of directors of the bank, like that of many small banks, consisted of successful people in the local community. The board of directors included the CEO, the second in command, and eight outside directors. However, the outside directors had little or no formal training concerning their roles as bank directors. They participated in various committees, audit, personnel, and the like. However, the outside directors passively followed the agenda set by senior management and did not fulfill their role to establish bank policies, to set strategic bank direction, and to oversee bank management. That was the CEO's job, or so he told them.

The board members were given "board packets" as they entered the board of directors meetings. The board packets consisted of a few pages of information, simple financial statements, and other items that were on the agenda. This is the way it was always done. In hindsight, the outside directors did not have an accurate picture of the bank's business or financial situation.

Everything appeared to be going well. The bank grew from $160 million in assets at the time of conversion to about $190 million in 2000. In management's opinion the bank was overcapitalized, and they paid large dividends.

Shortly before a senior loan officer died in 2000, board members became suspicious that something was wrong with the loan portfolio. A number of problem loans began to appear, and provisions for loan losses were needed. Bad credit was a ticking bomb that was about to explode. The bottom line is that there was no control over the commercial loan portfolio and the bad loans almost wiped out the bank.

In order to save the bank, assets were sold, additional capital was raised, management was changed, and a qualified attorney was retained. By 2006, the bank was out from under the regulators' umbrella because of their much improved financial condition.

The outside directors learned some important lessons about corporate governance. One of the outside directors said that there were three things that directors had to know – capital and management, capital and management, and capital and management. The outside directors also learned the importance of qualified auditors, and director training and responsibilities. With such training, they might have recognized obvious red flags. For example, the senior loan officer who died never took vacation time. The outside directors had no real oversight; they should control the audit committee and have meaningful contact with the outside auditing firm. Now the outside directors are in charge of the bank. It is not likely that they will make the same mistakes again. The cultures and operations of S&Ls and banks are quite different.

Corporate culture and mergers

Every organization has a corporate culture that can be defined as "the way we do things around here." Corporate cultures are analogous to people's personalities. Some personalities get along well together, and some don't. Thus, corporate culture is an important issue in mergers, just as personalities are important in the case of marriage. About 50 per cent of marriages fail, and about the same number of corporate mergers fail – and one of the reasons for the failures is different corporate cultures.

Differences in corporate culture was the theme of a front page story in the *Wall Street Journal* – "Bank of America hits snag in bid to woo the rich."[36] Bank of America, a retail-oriented bank, acquired US Trust, a private-banking wealth management operation from Charles Schwab. The chief executive officer of US Trust quit after "disagreements over how the combined operation should be run." The issues involved personal services to high net-worth clients versus the mass market.

In general terms, private banking and trust operations cater to high net-worth individuals who want to be pampered. US Trust requires a minimum of $2 million to open an account. A key point here is that trust departments have a fiduciary duty to act in the best interest of their clients.

In contrast, Bank of America is a financial supermarket. It wants its employees to cross-sell and promote all of their financial products and automated services.

Some of the differences between trust departments and retail banking center on the treatment of high net-worth clients. Should high net-worth clients accustomed to personal bankers should steered to toll-free telephone numbers for service? Should clients who entrust millions of dollars to their bankers now pay automated teller machine (ATM) fees? Should the bankers acting in the best interest of their clients be required to cross-sell the bank's products?

Corporate culture and operational risk

Operational risk is defined as the losses resulting from inadequate or failed internal processes, people and systems, and from external events.[37]

Operational risk includes accounting issues, damage to physical assets, fraud, legal issues, and so on. Corporate culture plays an important role in operational risk. Operational risks are commonly associated with corporate culture, lax internal controls, asset size, complex transactions, and compensation. Consider the case of General Re, a property/casualty insurance company that lost $173 million. Warren Buffet's Berkshire Hathaway Inc. bought General Re. Warren Buffet's (2003) letter to the stockholders explained the losses.[38] He said that General Re's culture and practices had changed and they were grossly mispricing their business. Buffet went on to say that "the reinsurance business and derivatives are similar: Like Hell, both are easy to enter and almost impossible to exit . . . Once you write a contract . . . which may require large payments decades later . . . you are usually stuck with it." Another commonality of reinsurance and derivatives is that both generate reported earnings that are often wildly overstated. That's true because today's earnings are in a significant way based on estimates whose inaccuracy may not be exposed for many years. Finally, Buffet said that "derivatives are financial weapons of mass destruction, carrying the dangers that while now latent, are potentially lethal."

Financial incentives are another hotspot. Executive compensation, and compensation to securities traders have frequently been associated with large losses. In 2002, Freddie Mac got into trouble for smoothing earnings in order to meet earnings targets.[39] Finally, Barings Bank in England went bankrupt when a securities trader in its Singapore office bet more than $1 billion on the direction of the Japanese stock market and he and the bank lost.[40] Barings had weak internal controls and rewarded the trader for his speculative gains.

Notes

1. For a detailed discussion of the definition of financial institution, see *Federal Register*, **71** (2), 4 January 2006, 31 CFR Part 103, Financial Crimes Enforcement Network: Anti-Money Laundering Programs; Special Due Diligence Programs for Certain Foreign Accounts: Final Rule and Proposed Rule.
2. See GE's web pages for additional details: www.gecommercialfinance.com; http://www.ge.com/en/financial/business.htm; http://www.ge.com/en/financial/personal.htm.
3. CNN Money.com, JP Morgan Chase & Co., Snapshot, http://money.cnn.com/quote/snapshot/snapshot.html?symb=JPM, accessed 8 February, 2007.
4. FDIC, Glossary, http://www2.fdic.gov/qbp/Glossary.asp?menuitem=GLOSSARY.
5. FFEIC, National Information Center, "Top 50 bank holding companies, organization hierarchy," http://www.ffiec.gov/nicpubweb/nicweb/OrgHierarchySearchForm.aspx?parID_RSSD=1951350&parDT_END=99991231, accessed 9 February, 2007.
6. Ibid.
7. See Citigroup's web page, "How Citigroup is organized", http://www.citigroup.com/citigroup/business/index.htm, accessed 9 February, 2007.
8. Michael Hudson and James R. Hagerty (2007), "Citigroup is expanding mortgage-service arm," *Wall Street Journal*, 23 January, C2.

9. Carrick Mollenkamp and Alistair MacDonald (2007), "Banks work to build Europe stock system," *Wall Street Journal*, 23 January, C3.
10. "Citigroup may buy into Chinese airlines," MSNBC.com, 28 December 2006, http://www.msnbc.msn.com/id/16379457/.
11. Rick Rothacker (2007), "Bank of America receives permission from Federal Bank regulators to build and own a $60 million Ritz-Carlton hotel next to its Charlotte headquarters," Hotel Online, 10 January, http://www.hotel-online.com/News/PR2006_1st/Jan06_RitzBofA.html.
12. Office of the Comptroller of the Currency (2006a), Interpretive Letter #1048, January (Re Union Bank of California NA). Union Bank of California is part of Unionbancal Corporation, the 28th largest bank holding company in the US as of 30 September 2006.
13. See Macquarie Bank's web page, http://www.macquarie.com.au, accessed 13 February, 2007.
14. Macquarie Bank 2006 Annual Review (available on Macquarie Bank's web page).
15. FDIC-Quarterly Banking Profile, "Statistics at a glance," 30 September 2006.
16. National Credit Union Administration (2006), "2005 yearend statistics for federally insured credit unions," http://www.ncua.gov/ReportsAndPlans/statistics/Yearend 2005.pdf.
17. "The Financial Services Fact Book" (2007), Insurance Information Institute and the Financial Services Roundtable, p. 67.
18. For additional information, see www.metlife.com.
19. For additional information, see http://www.statefarm.com/about/companie.asp.
20. Bies, Susan Schmidt (2005), Testimony of Governor Susan Schmidt Bies *Basel II implementation and revisions to Basel I* Before the Committee on Banking, Housing, and Urban Affairs, US Senate, 10 November.
21. "SEC settles enforcement proceedings against JP Morgan Chase and Citigroup," Securities and Exchange Commission (2003), Press Release, 2003–87, 28 July.
22. Office of the Comptroller of the Currency (2007), OCC Bulletin, "Complex structured finance transactions"; *Federal Register* (2007), "Interagency statement on sound practices concerning elevated risk complex structured finance activities," **72** (7), 1372–80.
23. Mayumi Negishi (2004), "Citibank Japan ordered to close four offices over legal breaches," *Japan Times*, Japan Times Online, 18 September; Financial Services Agency (2004), The Government of Japan, "The administrative action against Citibank, N.A., Japan branch," Provisional Translation, 17 September, http://www.fsa.go.jp.
24. Edward Taylor and Oliver Biggadike (2005), "Germany won't charge Citigroup bond trader," *Wall Street Journal*, 22 March, C3.
25. Geraldo Samor (2005), "Citigroup parts ways with manager in Brazil, Dantas, focus of dispute, ran bank's private equity; cleaning up ethical issue," *Wall Street Journal*, 11 March, C3.
26. "Citigroup facing $715 m fine for insider trading," CNNMoney.com, 31 March 2006.
27. "Citigroup settles Enron class action suit for $2 billion" (2005), *Banking Legislation & Policy*, Federal Reserve Bank of Philadelphia, April–June.
28. David Jackson (2005), "Even big boys get scammed: a tense corporate drama unfolds when one of the nation's major lenders finds its Chicago operation enmeshed in mortgage fraud," *Chicago Tribune* Online Edition, 8 November.
29. Enron Annual Report 2000, p. 2.
30. US Senate, "The role of the board of directors in Enron's collapse" (2002), report prepared by the Permanent Subcommittee on Investigations of the Committee on Governmental Affairs, United States Senate, Report 107-70, 107th Congress, 2nd Session, 8 July, p. 5.
31. Ibid.
32. Ibid., p. 3.
33. Kewei Hou and David Robinson (2006), "Industry concentration and average stock returns," *Journal of Finance*, August, 1927–56.
34. This case study is based on publicly available information and information provided in a meeting at First Southern Bank on 20 April 2006, in Florence, AL, with several

members of the current board of directors. The author is indebted to J. Acker Rogers, Chairman of the Board of First Southern Bancshares, First Southern Bank, and part owner of Rogers, Carlton & Associates, Inc., Florence, AL; Robert "Bob" Walker, Baker Donelson, Bearman, Caldwell & Berkowitz, PC, Memphis, Tenn., for their helpful suggestions and comments. Any errors are mine.

35. FDIC Enforcement Decisions and Orders (2003), "In the matter of First Southern Bank, Florence, Alabama," Docket No. 02-023b, 15 March.
36. Robert Frank and Valerie Bauerlein (2007), "Bank of America hits snag in bid to woo the rich," *Wall Street Journal*, 4 April, A1.
37. Basel Committee on Banking Supervision (2001), "Operational risk: supporting document to the new Basel Capital Accord," Consultative Document, January, www.bis.org.
38. Warren E. Buffet (2003), "To the shareholder of Berkshire Hathaway, Inc.," Berkshire Hathaway Inc., 2002 Annual Report.
39. Freddie Mac Press Release (2003), "Freddie Mac releases board council's report," 23 July.
40. Benton E. Gup (1998), *Bank Failures in the Major Trading Countries of the World: Causes and Remedies*, Westport, CT: Quorum Books, Chapter 3.

References

Basel Committee on Banking Supervision (2001), "Operational risk: supporting document to the new Basel Capital Accord," consultative document, January, accessed at www.bis.org.

Bies, Susan Schmidt (2005), "Basel II implementation and revisions to Basel I", testimony of Governor Susan Schmidt Bies before the US Senate Committee on Banking, Housing, and Urban Affairs, 10 November.

Buffet, Warren E. (2003), "To the shareholders of Berkshire Hathaway, Inc.," in Berkshire Hathaway Inc. 2002 annual report.

CNNMoney.com (2006), "Citigroup facing $715 m fine for insider trading," 31 March.

Enron Corporation (2003), *Annual Report 2000*.

Federal Deposit Insurance Corporation (FDIC) (2003), enforcement decisions and orders, "In the matter of First Southern Bank, Florence, Alabama," docket no. 02-023b, 15 March.

FDIC (no date), glossary, accessed at www2.fdic.gov/qbp/Glossary.asp?menuitem=GLOSSARY.

FDIC (2006), "Statistics at a glance," in *Quarterly Banking Profile*, 30 September.

FDIC (2007), Table III-A, first three quarters 2006, FDIC-insured commercial banks, *Quarterly Banking Profile*.

Federal Financial Institutions Examination Center (FFEIC) (no date), "Top 50 bank holding companies, organization hierarchy," National Information Center, accessed 9 February, 2007 at www.ffiec.gov/nicpubweb/nicweb/OrgHierarchySearchForm.aspx?parID_RSSD=1951350&parDT_END=99991231.

Federal Register (2007), "Interagency statement on sound practices concerning elevated risk complex structured finance activities," **72** (7), 1372–80.

Federal Reserve Bank of Philadelphia (2005), "Citigroup settles Enron class action suit for $2 billion," *Banking Legislation & Policy*, April–June.

Financial Services Agency, Government of Japan (2004), "The administrative action against Citibank, N.A., Japan branch," provisional translation, 17 September, accessed at www.fsa.go.jp.

The Financial Services Fact Book (2007), Insurance Information Institute and the Financial Services Roundtable, p. 67.

Frank, Robert and Valerie Bauerlein (2007), "Bank of America hits snag in bid to woo the rich," *Wall Street Journal*, 4 April, A1.

Freddie Mac (2003), "Freddie Mac releases board council's report," press release 23 July.

Gup, Benton E. (1998), *Bank Failures in the Major Trading Countries of the World: Causes and Remedies*, Westport, CT: Quorum Books, Chapter 3.

Hou, Kewei and David Robinson (2006), "Industry concentration and average stock returns," *Journal of Finance*, August, 1927–56.

Hudson, Michael and James R. Hagerty (2007), "Citigroup is expanding mortgage-service arm," *Wall Street Journal*, 23 January, C2.

Jackson, David (2005), "Even big boys get scammed: a tense corporate drama unfolds when one of the nation's major lenders finds its Chicago operation enmeshed in mortgage fraud," *Chicago Tribune* online edition, 8 November.

Mollenkamp, Carrick and Alistair MacDonald (2007), "Banks work to build Europe stock system," *Wall Street Journal*, 23 January, C3.

MSNBC.com (2006), "Citigroup may buy into Chinese Airlines," 28 December, accessed at www.msnbc.msn.com/id/16379457/.

National Credit Union Administration (2006), "2005 yearend statistics for federally insured credit unions," accessed at www.ncua.gov/ReportsAndPlans/statistics/Yearend2005.pdf.

Negishi, Mayumi (2004), "Citibank Japan ordered to close four offices over legal breaches," *Japan Times*, online, 18 September.

Office of the Comptroller of the Currency (2006a), interpretive letter no. 1048 (re: Union Bank of California, NA), January.

Office of the Comptroller of the Currency (2006b), "OCC's Quarterly Report on Bank Derivatives Activities, Third Quarter 2006," press release 2006-137, Table 10.

Office of the Comptroller of the Currency (2007), "Complex Structured Finance Transactions," *OCC Bulletin*.

Rothacker, Rick (2007), "Bank of America receives permission from federal bank regulators to build and own a $60 million Ritz-Carlton hotel next to its Charlotte headquarters," *Hotel Online*, accessed at www.hotel-online.com/News/PR2006_1st/Jan06_RitzBofA.html, 10 January.

Samor, Geraldo (2005), "Citigroup parts ways with manager in Brazil, Dantas, focus of dispute, ran bank's private equity; cleaning up ethical issues," *Wall Street Journal*, 11 March, C3.

Securities and Exchange Commission (SEC) (2003), "SEC settles enforcement proceedings against JP Morgan Chase and Citigroup," press release, 2003-87, 28 July.

Taylor, Edward and Oliver Biggadike (2005), "Germany won't charge Citigroup bond traders," *Wall Street Journal*, 22 March, C3.

US Senate (2002), "The role of the board of directors in Enron's collapse," report prepared by the Permanent Subcommittee on Investigations of the Committee on Governmental Affairs, report 107-70, 107th Congress, 2nd Session, 8 July, p. 5.

2 Forces of change
Benton E. Gup

Some of the major factors that determine the success or failure of financial institutions are beyond their control. These forces include, but are not limited to laws, globalization, technology, competitors, activist investors, demographics, and changing business models that are discussed below.

Selected US federal legislation
Federal and state laws and regulations limit the activities of financial institutions. In this section, we examine three federal laws directly tied to financial institutions, and some of their consequences to illustrate how laws can bring about changes in the financial system.

Federal laws do not have to be directed at financial institutions in order to have an impact on them. As noted in Chapter 1, the Sarbanes-Oxley Act of 2002 (SOX) was enacted as a reaction to the scandals and bankruptcies of Enron, WorldCom, and other firms in order to deter financial misconduct. The law has resulted in such high compliance costs for publicly-traded companies that some firms are going private, or changing their listing to foreign stock exchanges. Robert Grady, who runs the venture capital arm of the Carlyle Group, argues that Intel, Cisco, and E*Trade probably would not have public offerings today because of SOX.[1]

Financial Executives International reported in 2005 that the average cost of complying with SOX Section 404 was $4.36 million.[2] "Going private" means that a company reduces its shareholders to fewer than 300, and is no longer required to report to the Securities and Exchange Commission.[3]

Many *de novo* financial institutions are privately held in order to avoid SOX. Some are "Subchapter S corporations" that have 75 or fewer shareholders, which allows them to enjoy the benefits of incorporation, but to be taxed as a partnership.

Riegle-Neal Interstate Banking and Branching Efficiency Act of 1994 The Riegle-Neal Interstate Banking and Branching Efficiency Act of 1994 allowed interstate mergers between adequately capitalized and managed banks subject to certain limits. This opened the door for consolidation of banks.

Consolidation   The number of commercial banks in the United States peaked at 14 451 in 1982. Subsequently, the number declined to 7450 in 2006, due mostly to a large number of mergers and a relatively small number of failures. As discussed in Chapter 1 (see Table 1.1), the system is dominated by 87 large banks, which control 76 per cent of the total assets of all commercial banks. The decline in the number of banks and the increased concentration of bank assets held by a relatively small number of banks is referred to as "consolidation."

Displaced bankers   One of the major benefits of mergers in the same line of business, such as banking, is cutting common costs. That means reducing personnel costs – retiring or firing bank managers, loan officers, and others. In some cases, these individuals start new banks, hoping to take their customers with them. Thus, large bank acquisitions stimulate an increase in *de novo* banks and other institutions. For example, in 2006, there were 342 mergers of FDIC-insured institutions, and 191 new charters.[4]

Gramm-Leach-Bliley Act   Similarly, the Gramm-Leach-Bliley Act of 1999 allowed for the creation of financial holding companies that can engage in underwriting and selling insurance and securities, conduct commercial and merchant banking, and invest in and develop real estate and other "complementary activities." This gave rise to convergence in the banking industry as banks, securities firms, and insurance companies operated as part of the same financial holding company. Under the Bank Holding Company Act (P.L. 84-511), bank holding companies may elect to be financial holding companies. Bank holding companies are permitted to own one or more banks and engage in other permissible activities that are closely related to banking. For example, Synovus is a bank holding company that also owns 81 per cent of TSYS, one of the world's leading processors of credit and debit card transactions.[5] TSYS processes about half of all credit card transactions in the US.

Consolidation and convergence is good for some firms and bad for others. TSYS is one of the largest credit card processors in the world. The TSYS 2005 Annual Report noted that as a result of Bank of America's acquisition of MBNA, Bank of America will switch MBNA's processing of its credit-card portfolio of about 49 million accounts from TSYS to an in-house service.[6] Bank of America gains and TSYS loses on this deal. However, globalization is another force of change that will be discussed shortly. Although TSYS lost the MBNA account, it is expanding its global operations in China, Europe, and Latin America.

USA PATRIOT Act of 2001   Following the 11 September 2001 terrorist attacks on the United States, Congress passed the USA PATRIOT Act (formally known as the Uniting and Strengthening America by Providing Appropriate Tools Required to Intercept and Obstruct Terrorism Act of 2001).[7] The intent of the law is to deter terrorists and others from using the US financial system anonymously to launder money, and to deter and punish terrorists acts in the US and around the world. Part of the Act made financing of terrorism a criminal activity, and it increased the civil and criminal penalties for money laundering. It expanded the anti-money laundering program requirements to all financial institutions, including broker-dealers, casinos, futures commission merchants, introducing brokers, commodity pool operators, and commodity trading advisers. Also included in the definition of financial institutions are any individual or groups engaged in conducting, controlling, directing or owning informal value transfer systems (IVTS) in the United States.[8]

Violations of these laws can be costly. The Federal Reserve Board issued a $100 million civil money penalty (CMP) against UBS, AG, Zurich Switzerland, a foreign bank. The CMP was issued in connection with "US dollar banknote transactions with counterparties in jurisdictions subject to sanctions under US law, specifically Cuba, Libya, Iran, and Yugoslavia."[9] UBS had a contract with the Federal Reserve and Treasury to act as a custodian for US currency overseas. It violated the terms of the contract which included obeying certain US laws.

Globalization

Globalization refers to the extent to which countries' economies and financial markets become integrated, and the development of a single world market. By way of illustration, Citigroup has more than 200 million customers in more than 100 countries.[10] As noted in Chapter 1, HSBC Holdings PLC of London, England, has offices in 76 countries and territories. In 2006, Royal Bank of Canada's RBC Centura expanded its footprint in the US by acquiring 39 bank branches from AmSouth bank in Alabama. And in 2007, Spanish–owned Banco Bilboa Vizcaya Argentaria SA (BBVA) acquired Compass Bancshares, whose primary market is in Texas and other Southwestern states. BBVA is one of the largest banks in Latin America.

Harmonization   Globalization requires uniform international banking regulations so that all financial institutions operate on a level playing field. This is referred to as "harmonization." The Basel Committee on Banking Supervision, located in Basel, Switzerland, has no regulatory authority but it has helped to harmonize certain banking standards and best practices. It is hoped that both member countries and other countries will implement the standards, taking into account their own needs.

The 1988 Basel Accord is one example of harmonization. It stated that internationally active banks should have a minimum of 8 per cent capital. The 8 per cent capital requirement was an arbitrary number. Moreover, it was not sufficiently risk-sensitive to credit, market, and operational risks.

The 1988 Basel Capital Accord is being revised, and the new Basel Capital Accord (Basel II) is a work in progress.[11] The amount of capital to be held by banks can be measured in a variety of ways. Holding too much capital means higher costs to borrowers and lower returns to investors. Equally important, the capital needs of banks in developed countries are different from those of developing countries. Thus, there is a lively debate about measurement issues and costs involved in implementing Basel II.

Markets in Financial Instruments Directive (MIFD)   The MIFD is part of the European Union's Financial Services Action Plan to have a single integrated market for securities and derivatives in its 25 member states. It is the harmonization of financial service regulation for the EU that is expected to come into effect in November 2007. The idea behind the MIFD is to facilitate cross-border trading and the integration of EU capital markets. The MIFD affects all financial service firms that deal in securities – asset managers, banks, brokers, data providers, stockbrokers, and so on.

Securitization and derivatives
Securitization   Asset securitization is the issuance of a debt instrument in which the promised payments are derived from revenues generated by a defined pool of loans. The pools include mortgages, credit cards, car loans, and loans to businesses.

In the past, banks made loans and retained them until they were paid off, refinanced, or defaulted. In recent years, an increasing number of loans have been securitized. The securitized loans are sold to a special purpose entity (SPE) that is part of the bank holding company (BHC). The BHC sells the securitized loans to pension plans, retirement funds, hedge funds, and other investors. The BHC earns fee income from servicing the loans. The SPEs issue multiple classes of the securities known as "tranches." The tranches are divided into senior tranches, which are the highest quality, mezzanine tranches, which are medium quality, and junior tranches, also called the residual or equity tranches, which are the lowest quality. The equity tranche is the first to sustain any losses. All or part of the equity tranche may be retained on the balance sheet of the originating bank in order to enhance the credit quality of the higher tranches.[12] In other words, banks get hit with losses first – therefore securitization does not eliminate all of the credit risk from the bank.

A study by Wenying et al. (2007) revealed that banks funded with securitization have higher profitability, higher leverage, and lower risk of insolvency than banks that make less extensive use of it.[13] The growth of securitized loans has increased the breadth and depth of investments in the capital markets.

Securitized loans range from high-quality loans to subprime loans. In early 2007, a large number of subprime loans that were securitized defaulted.[14] *Caveat emptor*.

Government actions   According to Federal Reserve Chairman Ben Bernanke, government actions had considerable influence in shaping the growth of securitization. In 1968, the Federal National Mortgage Association – "Fannie Mae" – was split into two agencies: the Government National Mortgage Association (Ginnie Mae) and the re-chartered Fannie Mae, which became a privately owned government-sponsored enterprise (GSE), authorized to operate in the secondary market for conventional as well as guaranteed mortgage loans. In 1970, to compete with Fannie Mae in the secondary market, another GSE was created – the Federal Home Loan Mortgage Corporation, or Freddie Mac. Also in 1970, Ginnie Mae issued the first mortgage pass-through security, followed soon after by Freddie Mac. In the early 1980s, Freddie Mac introduced collateralized mortgage obligations (CMOs), which separated the payments from a pooled set of mortgages into 'strips' carrying different effective maturities and credit risks. By the 1990s, increased reliance on securitization led to a greater separation between mortgage lending and mortgage investing even as the mortgage and capital markets became more closely integrated. About 56 per cent of the home mortgage market is now securitized, compared with only 10 per cent in 1980 and less than 1 per cent in 1970."[15]

Derivatives   Financial derivatives describe securities that derive their value from underlying financial assets such as futures contracts, options, interest rate swaps, and other types of contracts. Derivatives are used to hedge financial risks, such as interest rate risk, credit risk, foreign exchange risk, and liquidity risk. Simply stated, banks can reduce these risks through the proper use of derivatives.

However, under certain circumstances, hedging strategies can lead to large losses. Long-Term Capital Management (LTCM) is a case in point.[16] LTCM was a hedge fund founded by Nobel laureates Merton Miller and

Myron Scholes, former Federal Reserve Vice Chairman David Mullins Jr, and former Solomon Inc. trader John Meriwether. In spite of their collective wisdom, insights, and sophisticated theories and models, they did not foresee the impact of the global market turmoil on financial markets. Their large bets on credit spreads and equity derivatives resulted in huge losses – $4.6 billion in 1998. The lesson to be learned here is that sometimes trading/hedging strategies and models don't work the way you think they should.

In 2006, 3rd quarter, the notional value of derivative products reported by US commercial banks was about $126 trillion.[17] The notional amount is the dollar amount used to calculate payments made on derivative product. Holdings of off-balance-sheet derivatives are concentrated in five large banks, out of 917 that participate in derivatives activities. The five large banks account for 97 per cent of the total notional value, 84 per cent of the revenues, and 88 per cent of the credit exposure.

Technology

Electronic banking/internet   Brick and mortar banks are being supplemented by electronic banking. It is changing how, when and where banks provide selected services such as payments, checking balances, making investments, and so on. Today, many banking services that used to be done in person at a banking office can be accomplished anywhere a customer has access to a computer or a cell phone. The new technologies are changing how and where the banks operate, their effective market areas, the way they communicate with new and existing customers, and they also raise new security issues.

Payments systems   Banks' role in the payments system is gradually being eroded by alternative methods of payment, such as PayPal. In addition, some cell phone companies are experimenting with wireless payments systems.

Competitors

Traditional competitors, such as other banks and credit unions, are obvious. Less obvious are non-traditional competitors, such as General Electric, Kroger, and Wal-Mart. And some foreign banks, such as the Royal Bank of Scotland and Macquarie Bank also provide non-traditional forms of competition.

GE Money provides financial services to more than 130 million customers in more than 50 countries.[18] It serves consumers, retailers, auto dealers, and mortgage lenders. Its financial services include credit cards, home equity loans, and other products. GE Commercial Finance focuses on commercial financial products in more than 35 countries. It provides asset financing, leases, lines of credit, and so on.

Kroger, one of the largest retail food companies in the US, is expanding its supermarkets to include credit cards, mortgages and home equity loans, and insurance products.[19] The financial services are provided by Citizens Financial Group, a bank holding company that is owned by the Royal Bank of Scotland Group (RBS).[20] Citizens Financial Group has over $159 billion in assets and is the eleventh largest bank holding company in the US.[21] Citizens Bank motto is "Not your typical bank." In addition to their operations in Kroger, Citizens Financial Group owns RBS Lynk Incorporated which is their US payment processing unit.[22] It is the third-largest transaction acquirer in the world. It meets the payment needs of retail outlets, restaurants, gas stations, grocery stores and other outlets.

Wal-Mart, the world's largest retailer, in cooperation with Woodforest Financial Group, operates branches of the Woodforest National Bank in selected Wal-Mart stores in Illinois, Indiana, Maryland, North Carolina, Ohio, Pennsylvania, Texas, Virginia, and West Virginia.[23] In contrast to the traditional model of banking, Woodforest bank branches are open 24 hours per day/seven days a week, except for Christmas. The bank offers immediate availability of deposits, free checking, free online banking with bill payment, and other services for consumers, as well as financial services for merchants.

Australian Macquarie Bank[24] provides investment banking, commercial banking and selected retail financial services markets both in Australia and overseas. In the United States, for example, Macquarie has a 99-year lease to operate the Chicago Skyway, and a lease to operate the Indiana toll road. Macquarie operates airports, container terminals, parking lots, ports, and other infrastructure assets throughout the world. Macquarie Infrastructure Partners bought Puget Energy in Washington State and Duquesne Light Holdings in Pennsylvania in 2007.[25]

Activist hedge funds

Where does shareholder activism end and intrusion on management begin? Do hedge funds that are shareholders of a company know how to run that company better than its management? Consider the following examples of shareholder activism by hedge funds.

United States   Sovereign Bancorp Inc., a $64 billion financial institution headquartered in Philadelphia, PA, experienced considerable growth under the leadership of Chairman and Chief Executive Officer Jay S. Sidhu.[26] Sovereign Bancorp was ranked at number 34 in a listing of the top 100 corporate citizens in 2006.[27] The listing was compiled before the bank's encounter with Rational Investors LLC.

Rational Investors LLC is a San Diego, CA based hedge fund. It was Sovereign's largest shareholder, holding about 7.3 per cent of its shares. Rational Investors was critical of Mr Sidhu. It questioned the bank's loans to officers and directors, which increased from $6.4 million to $94.1 million in a six-year period. In addition, they were not satisfied with Sovereign's stock returns. Rational Investors wanted to oust the entire board of directors. Later they modified their position and wanted two seats on the board of directors. Moreover, Rational Investors disagreed with Sovereign's decision to sell 24.99 per cent of its shares to Banco Santander Central Hispano SA in Spain for $2.4 billion in cash, and then use those funds and others to buy Independence Community Bank in Brooklyn NY for $3.6 billion. One important effect of these transactions was to dilute Rational Investor's shareholdings. A federal judge in New York ruled that Sovereign shareholders can remove directors without cause. Sovereign was expected to appeal the decision. This is consistent with the theory that shareholders have the right to elect and fire directors.

On 10 February 2006, Edward Rendell, the Governor of Pennsylvania, signed into law Senate Bill 595 "to enact the corporate governance changes that Sovereign proposed . . . for purposes of applying the definition of 'controlling person or group'."[28]

Mr Sidhu resigned as Chairman and CEO of Sovereign Bancorp in October 2006. According to the SEC Form 8-K (13 October 2006), "The resignation and retirement came in the face of threatened termination by the Company without cause." He will receive more than $40 million in payments stemming from his departure.

United Kingdom   TCI (the Children's Investment Fund Management), a $3 billion British hedge fund, demanded the break-up or sale of ABN Amro, a Dutch bank, on the grounds that it believed that ABN's management was doing a terrible job.[29] TCI, which owns about 1 per cent of ABN Amro's shares, thought that ABN Amro would be worth more if it were sold in parts, as with the sale of LaSalle Bank in Chicago. Other hedge funds also voiced their opinions. TCI stated that it would take legal action against ABN Amro to force them to consider all offers before merging with Barclays.[30] It did consider other offers, and the deal was sealed between ABN Amro and RBS (Scotland), Fortis NV (Belgium-Dutch), and Banco Santander SA (Spain) for $101 billion. This makes it Europe's largest cross-border merger,[31] with ABN Amro's assets split between the three banks.

Table 2.1   Selected US population statistics

	1967	2006
US population (millions)	200	300
Foreign-born (millions)	9.7	34.3
People 65 and older (millions)	19.1	38.8
Life expectancy (years)	70.5	77.8
Children per household	1.41	0.94

Sources: US Census Bureau, Bureau of Labor Statistics.

Japan   Shareholder activism is not limited to the US, or to banks. In Japan, for example, Ichigo Asset Management Ltd wanted shareholders of Tokyo Kohetsu Co., a steel company, to block a merger with a rival steel company. Ichigo argued that the deal shortchanged Tokyo Kohetsu shareholders, and they were successful in blocking the merger.[32]

In summary, shareholder activism is not new, nor is it limited to hedge funds. A study of shareholder activism by Gillian and Stark (2007) found little evidence that it improved long-term operating or stock market performance of the targeted companies.[33] However, the recent entrance of hedge funds into corporate governance has produced some gains.

Demographics
As shown in Table 2.1, the population in the US increased from 200 million in 1967 to over 300 million in 2006. There was a significant growth in the foreign-born population and Hispanics account for a large part of the increased population. Bank of America views the growth of the Hispanic population as a marketing opportunity. In its *Investor Fact Book, Full Year 2006* the bank points out that the Hispanic population is growing four times faster than the non-Hispanic population – and that the growth rate is particularly high in the population under age 30. It estimates that Hispanics will spend $1 out of every $10 spent in the US. The bank also describes strategies that can be used to acquire Hispanic customers, for example, offering free remittance products, opening stores in Hispanic neighborhoods and having bilingual associates, and advertising in Hispanic media.

The data reveal that the population is living longer, and the birthrate is declining. These statistics suggest that there are marketing opportunities in the aging population. A growth in wealth/asset management services, home equity loans, and increased demand for health care and insurance products are examples. The statistics also suggest that the aging population and rising costs of medical care will have important implications for the federal funding of Medicare and Medicaid.

Changing business models

According to Dr Nout Wellink, President of the Netherlands Bank and the Chairman of the Basel Committee on Banking Supervision:

> As a result of significant financial product innovation and advances in technology, the role of banks as the ultimate holders of credit assets has become less important. At the same time, however, the global banking institutions, together with a handful of securities firms, are now at the centre of the credit intermediation process. These institutions originate and underwrite the majority of credit assets. They tend to distribute them to various classes of investors through syndication, securitisation, and credit derivative technologies. Using similar technologies, they also actively manage their residual exposures. In many cases, financial institutions may retain and manage the more complex and potentially less liquid risks, for which they are ultimately rewarded.
>
> We are therefore witnessing a fundamental change in the business of banking from buy-and-hold strategies to so-called 'originate-to-distribute' models. While this change presents opportunities and challenges for risk managers and supervisors, it also serves as a useful framework for thinking about the changing risks at banks and other financial institutions.

Wellink goes on to say that:

> The originate-to-distribute business models depend on several key characteristics:
>
> - First, a growing reliance on liquid markets;
> - Second, a healthy risk appetite among various types of investors, in particular those taking on the more risky portions of structured credit assets;
> - Third, a diverse investor base to whom risk is being distributed.
>
> Ultimately, what we are concerned about is the ability to transfer or actively manage the various risks that core intermediaries face, not just under favorable market conditions, but also during periods when financial market, credit and liquidity conditions are less benign.
>
> When seen through this prism, there are a number of new risks that are not captured through traditional measures. In particular, I would highlight the following:
>
> - First, a rapid growth of trading book assets relative to traditional banking book assets and a fundamental shift in the types of risks retained in the trading book, in particular those arising from structured credit products. This is a natural consequence of the improvement in financial technology we are seeing, which enables more and more assets to be priced and traded.
> - Second, the growth of the trading book is, in turn, producing a rapid growth in counterparty credit exposures relative to traditional credit exposures. As with market risk exposures, these counterparty exposures are becoming increasingly complex and difficult to measure.

- Third, the valuation of increasingly complex products presents yet another challenge. Many of these products have not been tested under periods of stressed liquidity, which could have a significant impact on valuations.
- Fourth, the use of traditional approaches by many firms to assess their vulnerability to funding liquidity risk. These approaches may not take into account the growing reliance on active markets to manage the firm's liquidity in an environment that is increasingly capital-markets driven. Both the Basel Committee and the industry are currently exploring issues relating to the management and supervision of funding liquidity.
- Finally, the degree of risk transfer that is actually achieved through credit risk mitigation and securitisation techniques requires greater scrutiny. In particular, how well do these risk transfers hold up under stress? To what extent will risk be put back to firms if counterparties were to default, if investors were to demand compensation for losses, or if investor risk appetites were to shift abruptly?" [34]

Risk management

There is increasing emphasis on enterprise risk management (ERM). The Committee on Sponsoring Organizations (COSO) defines ERM as a process applied across an enterprise that is used to identify, assess, and manage risks within its risk appetite, and to provide reasonable assurance of achieving its objectives. [35] The Basel Committee on Banking Supervision is encouraging banks to use ERM to determine their "economic capital." Economic capital is a statistical concept – not capital held or regulatory capital. Economic capital is the bank's estimate of the amount needed to support all of its risk-taking activities, while regulatory capital only considers credit, operational, and market risks. Economic capital is sometimes referred to as the unexpected loss at the 99.97 per cent confidence level. That means a three in 10 000 probability of the bank becoming insolvent during the next 12 months.

A 2007 survey of chief executive officers, chief financial officers and directors revealed what they consider to be the top ten risks (Table 2.2). However, these do not include global risks, such as terrorism, pandemics, breakdown of critical infrastructure, and other factors. The point here is that ERM takes such factors into account. It is a forward looking concept – in contrast to regulatory capital.

Table 2.2   2007 CEO/CFO survey results – top ten risks

1. Competition	6. Reputation and financial markets
2. Customer satisfaction	7. Legal environment
3. Regulatory environment	8. Technology innovation
4. Information technology security	9. Legal
5. Market evolution	10. Human resources

Source: Protiviti (2007). "Risk Barometer Report," *Wall Street Journal*, 5 June, A16.

The impact of change on community banks

The forces of change affect banks of all sizes. The Federal Reserve Bank of Kansas City held a workshop in November 2007 that focused on the changing role of community banks.[36] According to the Federal Reserve Bank of Kansas City:

> Changes in technology, financial regulation, and the structure of the economy over the past two decades have combined to reduce the share of economic activity financed by community banks. According to some observers, the traditional advantages of community banks in relationship finance have been eroded by such factors as the increased use of credit scoring in small business lending and the greater capacity of large banks to monitor activities at widely dispersed branches. At the same time, the shift from a largely paper-based to an increasingly electronic payments system has reduced the importance of bank location for both households and businesses, allowing large banks and securities firms to compete away local deposits from community banks. Finally, the growth in the size of firms has reduced the demand for small business loans in some industries previously served by community banks, such as retailing and food processing. In response, some community banks have shifted their loan portfolios into sectors, such as commercial real estate development, that may involve greater risk.
>
> These changes obviously affect the market share, risk, and profitability of community banks, but the changes may also have implications for the strength of the local economies in which community banks have traditionally been the dominant financial providers.

Notes

1. Robert E. Grady (2007), "The Sarbox monster", *Wall Street Journal*, 26 April, A19.
2. Doug Campbell (2005), "Lights out," *Region Focus*, Federal Reserve Bank of Richmond, December, pp. 15–18.
3. US Securities and Exchange Commission, http://www.sec.gov/answers/gopriv.htm.
4. FDIC Quarterly Banking Profile (2007), Fourth Quarter 2006, "No insured institutions fail for second year in a row," http://www2.fdic.gov/qbp/2006dec/qbpall.html.
5. For information about Synovus, see http://www.synovus.com/index.cfm?catid=4& subject=4. For information about TSYS, see http://www.tsys.com/.
6. http://www.tsys.com/ir/annual_reports/2005/PDF/2005_TSYS_AR.pdf.
7. Public Law 107-56. A short title for the USA PATRIOT Act is the "International Money Laundering Abatement and Financial Anti-Terrorism Act of 2001."
8. Section 359, USA PATRIOT Act. For information on IVTS, see "The SAR activity review: trends, tips & issues," Issue 5, FinCEN, February 2003; FinCEN Advisory (2003), Informal Value Transfer Systems, Issue 33, March.
9. Board of Governors of the Federal Reserve System, (2004), Federal Reserve Press Release, 10 May (Order of Assessment of a Civil Money Penalty against UBS).
10. Citigroup's web page, http://www.citigroup.com/citigroup/about/index.htm, accessed 7 March, 2007.
11. For additional details see Benton E. Gup (2004), *The New Basel Capital Accord*, New York: Thomson/Texere.
12. David E. Vallee (2006), "A new plateau for the US securitization market," *FDIC Outlook*, fall. www.fdic.gov.
13. Wenying Jiangli, Matt G. Pritsker and Peter Raupach (2007), "Banking and Securitization," available at SSRN, http://ssrn.com/abstract=967895, 15 March.
14. Chris Isadore (2007), "Subprime woes: how far, how wide", CNNMoney.com, 5 March.

15. Ben Bernanke (2007), remarks by Chairman Ben S. Bernanke at the Federal Reserve Bank of Kansas City's economic symposium, Jackson Hole, Wyoming, "Housing, Housing Finance, and Monetary Policy," August 31.
16. For an overview of LTCMs financial problems and bailout, see Benton E. Gup and Philip F. Bartholomew, "The decision to fail banks: a global view," in Benton E. Gup (1999), *International Banking Crises: Large Scale Failures, Massive Government Interventions*, Westport CT: Quorum Books, Chapter 12.
17. "OCC's quarterly report on bank derivatives activities, third quarter 2006," Comptroller of the Currency, news release NR 2006-37, 15 December.
18. http://www.ge.com.
19. Dan Sewell (2007), "Kroger expands personal finance business," SunHerald.com, http://www.sunherald.com/307/story/143622.html, 16 September.
20. For information about Citizens Financial Group, see: http://www.citizensbank.com/au/.
21. http://www.ffiec.gov/nicpubweb/nicweb/Top 50Form.aspx, data are for 30 June 2007.
22. http://rbslynk.com/Pages/Home.aspx.
23. http://www.woodforest.com. Also see Bethany Mclean (2007), "Would you buy a bridge from this man?" *Fortune*, 1 October, 138–46.
24. http://www.macquarie.com.au/au/index.html.
25. Matt Daily and Jonathan Keehner (2007), "Macquarie Bank in $3.9bn US utility deal," News.com.au, 27 October.
26. Jesse Eisinger (2005), "Sovereign Bancorp's takeover deal looks like a dis to shareholders," *Wall Street Journal*, 2 November, C1; David Enrich (2006), "Santander enlists Giuliani firm to review deal with Sovereign," *Wall Street Journal*, 3 March, C3; Phyllis Pilch (2005), "NYSE rules divide bank, investors," *Wall Street Journal*, 21 December, B2A; Board of Governors of the Federal Reserve System, Federal Reserve Release (2006), H.2A, Notice of Formations and Mergers of, and Acquisitions by, Bank Holding Companies; Change in Control, February 10.
27. "*Business Ethics* 100 best corporate citizens, 2006" (2006), *Business Ethics*, Spring, **20**(1), 22.
28. Edward G. Rendell, Governor, Commonwealth of Pennsylvania (2006), "Governor Rendell signs senate bill 595," News Release, http://www.state.pa.us/papower/cwp/view.asp?A=11&Q=449844, 10 February.
29. Carrick Mollenkamp, Jason Singer, Alistair MacDonald, and Edward Taylor (2007), "For hedge funds, hunting in packs pays dividends," *Wall Street Journal*, A1, A18.
30. James Moore (2007), "Hedge fund TCI lobbies for break-up of bank giant ABN Amro," *Independent*, 22 February, http://www.independent.co.uk/business/news/article2293528.ece; Dennis K. Berman, Jason Singer, John R. Wilke (2007), "Takeover bids multiply as deal barriers fall," *Wall Street Journal*, 8 May, A1, A17.
31. Jason Singer and Carrick Mollenkamp (2007), "M@A milestone: $101 billion deal for ABN Amro," *Wall Street Journal*, 5 October, A1, A15.
32. Andrew Morse (2007), "Japan's shareholders find their voice, and use it," *Wall Street Journal*, 28 February, C9.
33. Stewart L. Gillian and Laura T. Starks (2007), "The evolution of shareholder activism in the United States," *Journal of Applied Corporate Finance*, Winter, 55–73.
34. Dr Nout Wellink (2007), President of the Netherlands Bank and Chairman of the Basel Committee on Banking Supervision, speech at the GARP 2007 8th Annual Risk Management Convention & Exhibition, New York, 27 February.
35. See COSO (2004), "Enterprise risk management – integrated framework," Executive Summary, Summer, http://www.coso.org/publications.htm.
36. Financial Economics Network (2007), Professional Announcements and Job Openings, Friday 4 May, Call for Papers, "The changing role of community banks in the financial system and the economy," Federal Reserve Bank of Kansas City, November 2.

References

Berman, Dennis K., Jason Singer and John R. Wilke (2007), "Takeover bids multiply as deal barriers fall," *Wall Street Journal*, 8 May, A1, A17.

Bernanke, Ben (2007), remarks by Chairman Ben S. Bernanke at the Federal Reserve Bank of Kansas City's economic symposium in Jackson Hole, WY, "Housing, Housing Finance, and Monetary Policy", 31 August.

Board of Governors of the Federal Reserve System (2004), "Order of assessment of a civil money penalty against UBS," Federal Reserve press release, 10 May.

Board of Governors of the Federal Reserve System (2006), "Notice of formations and mergers of, and acquisitions by, bank holding companies; change in control," Federal Reserve release H.2A, 10 February.

Business Ethics (2006), "*Business Ethics* 100 best corporate citizens, 2006," *Business Ethics*, **20**, (1) (Spring), 22.

Campbell, Doug (2005), "Lights out," Federal Reserve Bank of Richmond, *Region Focus*, 15–18 December.

Citigroup (2007), accessed 7 March at www.citigroup.com/citigroup/about/index.htm.

COSO (2004), " Enterprise risk management – integrated framework," Executive Summary, Summer, accessed at www.coso.org/publications.htm.

Daily, Matt and Jonathan Keehner (2007), "Macquarie Bank in $3.9bn US utility deal," News.com.au, 27 October.

Enrich, David (2006), "Santander enlists Giuliani firm to review deal with Sovereign," *Wall Street Journal*, 3 March, C3.

Eisinger, Jesse (2005), "Sovereign Bancorp's takeover deal looks like a dis to shareholders," *Wall Street Journal*, 2 November, C1.

Federal Deposit Insurance Corporation (FDIC) (2007), "No insured institutions fail for second year in a row," Quarterly Banking Profile Fourth Quarter 2006, accessed at www2.fdic.gov/qbp/2006dec/qbpall.html.

Financial Economics Network (2007), "The changing role of community banks in the financial system and the economy," Federal Reserve Bank of Kansas City, professional announcements and job openings, Friday, 4 May, call for papers, 2 November.

Gillian, Stewart L. and Laura T. Starks (2007), "The evolution of shareholder activism in the United States," *Journal of Applied Corporate Finance* (Winter), 55–73.

Grady, Robert E. (2007), "The Sarbox monster," *Wall Street Journal*, 26 April, A19.

Gup, Benton E. (ed.) (1999), *International Banking Crises: Large Scale Failures, Massive Government Interventions*, Westport CT: Quorum Books, Chapter 12.

Gup, Benton E. (2004), *The New Basel Capital Accord*, New York: Thomson/Texere.

Isadore, Chris (2007), "Subprime woes: how far, how wide," CNNMoney.com, 5 March.

Mollenkamp, Carrick, Jason Singer, Alistair MacDonald and Edward Taylor (2007), "For hedge funds, hunting in packs pays dividends," *Wall Street Journal*, A1–18.

Moore, James (2007), "Hedge fund TCI lobbies for break-up of bank giant ABN Amro," *The Independent*, 22 February, accessed at www.independent.co.uk/business/news/article2293528.ece.

Morse, Andrew (2007), "Japan's shareholders find their voice, and use it," *Wall Street Journal*, 28 February, C9.

Comptroller of the Currency (2006), "OCC's quarterly report on bank derivatives activities, third quarter 2006," news release NR 2006-37, 15 December.

Pilch, Phyllis (2005), "NYSE rules divide bank, investors," *Wall Street Journal*, 21 December, B2A.

Protiviti (2007), "Risk barometer report," *Wall Street Journal*, 5 June, A16.

Rendell, Edward G., Governor of Pennsylvania (2006), "Governor Rendell signs Senate Bill 595," news release, 10 February, accessed at www.state.pa.us/papower/cwp/view.asp?A =11&Q=449844.

Sewell, Dan (2007), "Kroger expands personal finance business," 16 September, accessed at www.sunherald.com/307/story/143622.html.

Singer, Jason and Carrick Mollenkamp (2007), "M&A Milestone: $101 billion deal for ABN Amro," *Wall Street Journal*, 5 October, A1, A15.
TSYS (2006), "2005 annual report," accessed at www.tsys.com/ir/annual_reports/2005/PDF/2005_TSYS_AR.pdf.
Vallee, David E. (2006), "A new plateau for the US securitization market," *FDIC Outlook*, (Fall), accessed at www.fdic.gov.
Wellink, Dr Nout (2007), Speech by the president of the Netherlands Bank and chairman of the Basel Committee on Banking Supervision at the GARP 2007 8th Annual Risk Management Convention & Exhibition, New York, 27 February.
Wenying, Jiangli, Matt G. Pritsker and Peter Raupach (2007), "Banking and securitization," 15 March, accessed at http:// ssrn.com/abstract=967895.

3   Starting a new bank
Laurence Pettit

Starting a new community bank can be one of the most interesting and educational endeavors an entrepreneurial group can try. This phase is an adventure, where the outcomes of your efforts are not fully predictable as you might have expected in a regulated industry. The venture, after all, is a small business with most of the risks that come with small firms. The start-up group needs to be able to respond quickly to opportunities and problems, make decisions on the move, and most of all have the patience and energy to survive the process.

The successful bank start-up leads to the establishment of an economic force in the community. The outcome of that investment in the community bank might be viewed as a long-lived asset with consistent growth opportunities or a strategic investment with a take-out through merger. Once established, the community bank is a highly desirable small business venture.

What is different from other small business start-ups is the regulated environment of the banking industry. The banking system in the US is generally characterized as a "dual" system with charters being granted by both national and state authorities. For both historic and practical reasons, the process for chartering a new institution differs in significant ways. The initial capital required for a new bank, the methods by which that capital is raised, and the composition of the board of directors may all differ significantly when comparing state and national charter requirements.

The usual precipitating event for starting a new community bank is the perception of inadequate financial resources in a community or a part of a community. The loss of an existing bank or savings and loan through its sale to a large holding company bank might be such an event. Another reason for starting a new bank is the reluctance of existing financial institutions to expand to meet the financial needs of a growing economic segment within the community.

Whatever the reason, the opportunity to start up a new community bank usually brings a group of "risk-takers" together. Some may want an institution to support the business activities of the community, while others may want to broaden consumer services, still others resent "big bank" dominance in the community and believe a locally governed institution will be benefit the community.

These risk-takers who see the need and the opportunity for a new bank become the nucleus of the organizing group and the future bank board. This small group of founders will need to expand to assist in raising the initial capital required for the bank and to broaden the outreach to the community.

Getting started
Some initial research into the opportunities available in the target community is needed before approaching the important step of selecting a board of directors. What parts of the community are not being adequately served by existing financial institutions? What new economic opportunities now exist or will exist in the community? Can improved convenience, services, and capital attract a clientele from within the existing target market?

Occasionally this information is available from existing community resources, although the founders might need time to accumulate and assemble the data. This information will be needed when the application for the bank charter is submitted to either state or national regulators. Because of the importance of this economic information concerning conditions within the target market, it is usually advisable to have a study of the markets done to support the application sometime during the process of preparing the charter application.

Equally important to the process is that enough economic information be available for the ideas driving the formation of a new bank to provide a focus for attracting board members, staff, shareholders, and later, customers. Further, to attract capital, the potential investors must be able to see and evaluate the possible success of this new venture. Can the market support a new bank? Is the long-term potential of such a bank sufficient to provide an adequate return and growth that will appreciate the invested capital?

The regulators want to see the potential for a sustainable banking entity within the target market. In addition, they will be concerned about the impact of this new bank on the existing financial institutions in the area. Thus, a positive view of the capacity of the target market to sustain a new bank in addition to the existing financial institutions should be a consideration of the founding group as they begin the process of forming the new bank.

What follows is a suggested order of actions that can take the founders from the idea of starting a community bank through the process of opening a start-up bank. The order of this process may vary according to the assets of the founders. For example, if a founder happens to be an experienced CEO, the search for that component will have been completed at the onset of the process and will not wait until after the charter choice has been made, as suggested here.

The board of directors

The critical first step after the formation of the idea and rationale for a new bank is recruiting a new board of directors. The prominence and reputation of this board will have a major impact on attracting shareholders and customers to the bank. The board will be closely investigated by the chartering regulators. Thus, the board must be financially responsible with records of outstanding character and business success.

A bank board of directors carries all the obligations and responsibilities of any corporate board plus the additional burdens placed by regulatory authorities that are unique to banking. In addition to the duties and obligations that are noted in common law, there have been a series of specific banking laws beginning with the National Bank Act of 1863 and continuing through today with such acts as the Federal Reserve Act, the Federal Deposit Insurance Act, the Bank Security Act, and Sarbanes-Oxley, to name a few, plus numerous state laws, all of which combine into a confusing array of instructions and limitations for the board of directors of any bank. While many in the past may have seen these boards as "good old boy clubs," nothing could be further from the truth in today's litigious society. The risks that arise from today's more complex business environments carry with them large liabilities, both to the bank and to the individual board member.

Practically speaking, a board of between five and 15 members provides a manageable size for rapid decision-making, but remains large enough to provide oversight for the bank and information from the community to keep the bank focused on its target market. Some charter regulators have limits on the size of the boards. For example, the Office of the Comptroller of the Currency (OCC) limits the board to 25 members. The larger the board, the larger the loss of control of the bank to the management staff. Early in the formation of a new bank, the board would be well advised to maintain close management oversight of the bank, its administration and its processes. Getting to know the management personnel, the operating processes, and policies is the best method the board has for managing the risks during the start-up phase. A large board tends to neglect this critical oversight. A well-known state regulator in his advice to a new bank states that "your bank may have as many board members as you want, but we will only approve nine," a reminder that bank chartering rules are not always what they seem. The regulator interprets the regulations according to his own experience.

Who should be on the board? Aside from the issues of character and financial stability, what other attributes make for developing a strong board? A bank start-up is an entrepreneurial venture requiring time to give to the process and willingness to undertake the risk inherent in a new venture.

Potential board members should have a strong business background. It is helpful to have businesses related to the customer universe. If that universe has a large construction component, then a board member well known to that business can be of great help both in attracting business and evaluating services to that industry. The board of directors should be diversified across a number of industry sectors found in the target market.

The board of directors should as far as possible reflect the demographics of the target market. Business experience is a must, but diversity can be achieved within this requirement. Diversity is good business. Consider the increasing number of female-owned and minority-owned businesses that need banking services. The new bank has the added burden of finding underserved customers or attracting customers from other institutions. A more diverse board may help meet these challenges. Public policy in the US encourages and sometimes requires diversification in financial institutions. If the initial board of directors has shown an effort to achieve this diversity, the chartering regulators will see this as a positive factor in the approval process, as will the bank's future customers.

This initial board of directors will have the important responsibilities of raising capital, hiring the chief operating officer of the bank, seeing the organization through the chartering process, and establishing policies and organization for the new bank. In a start-up bank, frequent unscheduled meetings and events are the norm. The first year or so of operation requires the board's attention to many of the management and regulatory details that accompany the establishment of a new business. Therefore, consideration should be given to the time a prospective board member can give to the new bank.

If a conflict of schedule exists between the bank and its board members, the result is shorter meetings or meetings without full attendance by the board. Issues that should have been addressed by the board are delegated to management without proper oversight. This presents a risk of abuse or malfeasance in the critical early stages of the bank. Remember, the responsibility of operating the bank always rests with the board of directors. In the examination process, board attendance and participation at meetings is a major point of concern for regulators. In fact, board minutes and attendance are a standard part of any examination.

In addition to time for meeting on governance issues, the director of a start-up bank needs to be willing to meet and greet the public, both for the capital-raising process and the initial customer development activities of the start-up bank. The presence of the director in these important functions is critical in establishing the credibility of the bank in the community.

The directors of the new bank must be able to show their commitment or loyalty to the objectives of the bank, independent of their personal or business activities. Future shareholders and depositors need to be confident that their best interests and those of the bank are foremost in the actions of the bank board.

In filling out the rest of the board for the start-up bank, the founding directors should think in terms of a relatively small board, perhaps ten members, with these characteristics in addition to impeccable financial condition and outstanding personal reputation:

1.   Strong business experience.
2.   Sufficient diversity to reflect target market.
3.   Time to give to the organizing effort.
4.   Commitment to the bank independent of other activities.

Once the start-up board is assembled, the board is ready to make a decision on the type of charter, initial capital, bank location(s), a chief executive officer, and legal counsel.

The bank charter
Because of the dual system of American banking, choosing between a state and national charter is a critically important decision for the start-up bank. The choice of charter brings with it a different set of regulators and a different set of requirements in starting a new bank.

The selection of a charter is also the beginning of a relationship between the board, the bank and the regulatory environment. In addition to regulatory oversight, the bank gains a source of assistance and direction from the regulator that comes with the charter. The board must decide which charter provides the most opportunity for the new bank and the most assistance in fulfilling the long-term goals of the bank. Issues such as branching requirements, long portfolio diversification, and non-bank subsidiaries, are important to the long-term success of the bank. It is time well spent in researching the operating characteristics of the agencies that accompany the charter.

National banks are chartered by the Comptroller of the Currency in the Department of Treasury. The Comptroller also provides supervision and examination for all national banks. This office is also the source of approval for branching, acquisitions, and mergers for national banks.

State bank charters are granted by a state agency for financial institutions in most cases. The state agency provides supervision and examination for state chartered banks. If the start-up bank becomes a state member bank, the questions of branching, acquisitions, and consolidation will require approval of both state banking authorities and the Federal Reserve (Fed). The Fed will also become a source of supervision and examination.

Should the start-up bank choose a state non-member status, the Federal Deposit Insurance Corporation will provide supervision and examination, along with the state banking authorities. Approval by the FDIC of branches, acquisitions, and consolidations is also required along with the state approval process.

A current trend among start-up banks is to charter as a "bank holding company." The idea is that the holding company status provides a number of banking and non-banking options for growth and diversification as the bank expands its activities. Applying for this status at the onset of the organization might mean significant savings in legal expenses by eliminating a second approval process. Regardless of the charter, state or national, the Federal Reserve grants the bank holding company charter and provides supervision and examination.

The new bank could have as many as three different agencies supervising the bank at inception. The differences between the agencies make the choice of regulator(s) important because of the requirements for start-up. A recent example of these differences for a start-up bank in a small city involved the suggested capital requirements by the OCC of $10 million. The state banking authorities, noting the absence of a state charter bank in the target market, suggested $6 million for the start-up bank's capital requirements.

In some states, authorities require that initial capital be raised by the board of directors, believing this improves the prospect of attracting customers for the bank and promotes more community involvement. National banks, on the other hand, permit capital to be raised by investment bankers. This is an example of how operational differences and policies may work to the disadvantage of some boards, while facilitating the organizational efforts with boards having a different composition of members.

Early in the establishment of the bank, the regulators will make frequent visits and have a more intense schedule of examination. In the event the bank operations fall outside the bounds set by these regulators or even threaten to fall outside these bounds, the board can expect a visit by one or more regulators. These meetings cannot be delegated to the executives of the bank; the regulators want the board to hear their concerns directly. Occasionally, the bank's board of directors will be invited (polite term) to the regulators' office for these discussions (not a good sign).

It is important to remember that the regulators are there to help the bank prosper. It is in both parties' interest for the bank to be a success. So, in addition to the advantages versus the disadvantages that an individual charter brings to the formation of the new bank, comfort with a specific regulator and its support of the bank should be considered. Therefore, check on other community bank experiences with regulators; consider the proximity and availability of the regulator to the start-up. These and other relationship issues with regulators are also important considerations in the choice of a charter.

Regardless of charter, if the bank will be publicly traded, the Securities and Exchange Commission will also provide regulatory oversight. The passage of the Sarbanes-Oxley Act has added significant regulations, costs, and risks to the start-up bank and its board of directors.

The decision to pursue a state or national charter impacts the development and management of the start-up bank in a number of important ways. When the board selects a charter:

1.   It selects its regulator.
2.   It selects the administrative requirements for the start-up bank.
3.   It selects capital, branching and operating requirements of those regulators.
4.   It selects a long-term relationship with the regulator(s).

The question of becoming a publicly traded C-corporation or a subchapter S-corporation will determine the extent of oversight by the SEC.

The "subchapter S bank"

The passage of the Sarbanes-Oxley Act in 2002 changed the economics of all banks. Designed to combat the abuses of corporate power and reporting made famous by the Enron debacle, the law restricts the auditor's activities to the audit. Many activities formally done for the bank by its auditing firm, such as financial information systems, maintenance and design, bookkeeping, and internal auditing can no longer be done by that firm. This resulted and is resulting in large expenditures in upgrading financial systems, increases in bank personnel in the systems area, and new relationships with consultants and internal auditing firms. Large holding company banks could easily absorb these new and containing costs. Some relief for publically-traded banks under $500 million was provided for in the act, but the costs remain a significant burden to community banks. If the bank delists from its exchange and reduces its shareholders to fewer than 300, it can deregister with the SEC. The start-up bank with more than 300 shareholders must absorb these added costs; plus the act's new requirements for the bank's audit committee adds an additional burden to the start-up bank. The details of the act are discussed elsewhere in this book, but in sum, the act has driven up the costs of running a bank and increased the risks to the board of directors, especially during the early stages.

The Small Business Job Protection Act of 1996 as amended in 2004 permitted insured commercial banks with fewer than 100 shares to be taxed as an S-corporation. The obvious advantage of the S-corp over the C-corp is avoiding double taxation on dividends. S-corporations pay no taxes on income paid directly to shareholders in dividend form. Since 1997, thousands of small, closely-held or family owned banks have elected S-corporation status.

It is now possible for a start-up bank to incorporate as an S-corporation. The basic requirements to form as an S-corporation are 100 or less shareholders, no partnerships or corporations and single types of shares outstanding (common stock or preferred, but not both). This is a new approach to chartering a bank. Traditionally bank regulators have believed that having a large number of shareholders insures a larger deposit base, a larger footprint in the community and a stronger financial base for the community bank. In many states, a minimum number of shareholders were imposed to encourage the breadth of the offering in the community.

The Small Business Job Protection Act of 1996 has provided a way for the start-up bank to charter without the oversight of the SEC. If sufficient capital can be raised with 100 shareholders or less, the bank avoids the requirements of a publically-traded bank, including Sarbanes-Oxley.

This is a clear cost advantage during the early years as the bank grows. Once growth requires additional capital, the bank can easily evolve into a C-corporation for subsequent public issues.

The S-corporate form has many advantages if sufficient capital can be raised with 100 or less shareholders. In the short run, reduced tax exposures and regulatory burden are appealing reasons to consider the S-corp alternative. In the long run, the high-growth bank is likely to go public for additional capital. The bank at that stage will be more fully developed administratively and in its market and ready for the transition to C-corporate charter.

Putting it all together

In order to apply to begin operations as a bank from the respective regulator, the board of directors must put together a number of documents which collectively describe their intentions for the future bank. This includes a charter, a business plan, by-laws, and if identified and available, a chief executive officer.

The selection of a bank site has a cohesive impact on the board. Selecting a site is or should be an outgrowth of the long-term strategy of the bank. The selection identifies where the bank is to be located and how it will be financed and owned, which provides insights into the marketing strategy and the use of capital by the bank. A city center location versus a suburban location begins to identify markets and how the bank will address them. The center city location might indicate a commercial banking orientation, while the suburban location might indicate a consumer banking strategy. Leasing the location instead of a purchase might be driven by a strategy to use the firm's capital in earning assets rather than a real estate investment in a location with future capital appreciation.

The decision forces the board to think about the first location of the bank and how that fits into the development of a business plan. The decision is made in the context of the target market for the start-up bank. Frequently, a board member owns a location that can be acquired at a bargain lease or purchase. This is easy; it may be priced right, but is it the right location? The first location tells the community a lot about the intentions of the bank with respect to service and even-handed decision-making.

If the board has not already employed a banking consultant, now is the time. This location needs to be viewed in the context of the best market penetration strategy for a new bank. The outside consultant can begin training the board on bank strategies and operations while being the "outside" expert in bank site location.

A more complete business plan needs to be put together, both for communication to the regulatory agency and to get "buy in" by the board, in the future directions for the bank. The business plan might be formalized by a bank consultant, but the board must participate and internalize its content.

If the board of directors has already employed a CEO for the new bank, the CEO can play a major role in putting together the business plan and other documents required to obtain a charter together with a bank consultant. Incidentally, the regulators either formally or informally must approve this individual as CEO.

It is possible to put together the application for charter without a bank consultant or an attorney. The application typically includes everything from the business plan to credit policies for the proposed bank. It is good to have help in developing the operating policies with the board and adopting by-laws to govern this organization.

Therefore, to expedite the process of obtaining the charter and permissions to begin business, it is advisable to hire a legal firm for advice to complete the charter process as well as drawing up the corporate documents to begin operations. Pick a firm that has experience dealing with the regulators that you anticipate encountering as you pass through the chartering process. Some law firms are experienced and well known to state authorities while others have experience only in working with the OCC. In general, it is not advisable to work with an attorney without experience of regulatory agencies. Attorneys specializing in this area of the law may seem expensive, but the pay-off is that they know the process, they know the business of the agencies, and they will focus on the requirements to open the new bank. Time and frustration with the process will be reduced.

Incidentally, it is always advisable for the board of directors of the start-up bank to informally visit with the appropriate regulatory agency before moving forward with the application for the new bank. Conversations with state and Federal Reserve regulators will help identify if they have concerns about your proposed banks. It is not unusual to have more than one visit. Your attorney and/or your bank consultant can expedite these visits.

The question of capital is critical to the business plan and to the regulators. From the regulatory point of view, you can never have enough capital. From the business perspective, however, raising capital is expensive and sometimes difficult. A good rule of thumb is to acquire enough to support the first three to five years of growth. If that is $100 million in deposits, about $10 million in capital should be adequate. Capital once acquired should be put to work quickly in an orderly, profitable fashion; too much capital will depress earnings.

If the firm elects to have the capital raised by an investment banking firm rather than through the efforts of the board, it can expect to spend 5 to 7 per cent of the proceeds plus expenses. Thus, a $10 million capital raise will net about $9.3 million for supporting future business.

Banking is about leverage; use only as much capital as the regulators require and the business opportunities present. This will allow the bank to get to a break-even level quickly. This level is almost universally used by regulators to permit the addition of branches and the expansion of other banking activities.

The board of directors in the start-up bank should look for a CEO with a community bank background, if possible. Large holding company-trained executives frequently do not have a broad enough background to handle the diverse problems that will face the small staff of a community bank. If the best candidate for the job only has this work experience, make sure the future CEO possesses a strong credit background – a critical skill to the future success of the bank.

Because of Sarbanes-Oxley increasing the importance of the audit committee, the board should take an active role in hiring the chief financial officer. This officer needs to have a great deal of rapport with the board.

Upon approval by the chartering agency and the receipt of the proceeds of the capital raised, move quickly to open the bank. This allows the bank the opportunity to capitalize on the publicity developed during the capital raise.

Nowhere is "you have to start right to finish right" more true than in the heavily regulated business environment of banking. Picking the right market, with a strong board and the charter that best supports the idea behind the new bank assure a strong take off for the new bank.

Developing a strong business plan for the new CEO and CFO to implement with strong control from the board of directors creates an opportunistic environment for the new bank. "Start-up" is accomplished when the new bank opens its doors. After that, the bank is in the serious competitive climate of the "real world." The bank and its shareholders will prosper in that environment because of the carefully executed start-up.

4 Improving director oversight of compliance: a bank regulator's view
Cathy Lemieux and Steven VanBever[1]

Introduction

Ensuring compliance with banking laws and regulations is one of the most important responsibilities of bank directors. Director oversight of compliance has become increasingly challenging in recent years, in part because directors' other responsibilities have required more time and increased skill-sets, leaving less time and energy for overseeing compliance:

- Oversight of strategic planning has become more challenging because the business of banking has become more demanding and competitive;
- Corporate governance has become more challenging because expectations in this area have risen significantly in the wake of Enron and other scandals; and
- Oversight of financial risk management has become more challenging because risk management has greatly increased in sophistication.

The dramatic increase in the volume and complexity of banking laws and regulations has also made director oversight of compliance more challenging. This chapter surveys each of these trends and recommends that bank directors understand and consider enterprise-wide approaches to compliance risk management and adapt them, as appropriate, to their institutions. This would help focus directors' time and energy on the most important compliance risks facing the bank.

Ensuring compliance with banking laws and regulations is one of the most important responsibilities of bank directors

Ensuring compliance with banking laws and regulations is included among the following key responsibilities of directors as detailed in the Federal Reserve's examination manual for commercial banks:[2]

- Selecting competent executive officers (including retention, management-succession planning, performance evaluation, and compensation);

- Effectively supervising the bank's affairs (including both demonstrating reasonable business judgment and competence and devoting sufficient time to director responsibilities);
- Adopting and adhering to sound policies and objectives (including both risk management and other key areas such as profit planning, budgeting, and personnel);
- Avoiding self-serving practices and conflicts of interest;
- Maintaining awareness of the bank's financial condition and management policies;
- Maintaining reasonable capitalization;
- Ensuring compliance with banking laws and regulations; and
- Meeting the legitimate credit and other needs of the local community.

For the sake of convenience, these responsibilities[3] may be grouped into the following categories:

- *Oversight of strategic planning* This involves understanding, approving, and monitoring the bank's strategic plans and annual operating plans and budgets. It also includes advising management on significant issues facing the bank.
- *Corporate governance* This involves nominating directors and committee members and overseeing the composition, independence, structure, practices, and evaluation of the board and its committees.
- *Oversight of financial risk management* This involves identifying and understanding the bank's key risks (credit, market, liquidity, operational, legal, and reputational); reviewing and approving appropriate policies and risk-exposure limits to control them; and using adequate information systems to measure and monitor these risks.[4]
- *Oversight of compliance risk management* "Compliance risk" is becoming increasingly recognized and managed as a distinct banking risk. It has been defined as "the risk of legal or regulatory sanctions, financial loss, or damage to reputation and franchise value that arises when a banking organization fails to comply with laws, regulations, or the [applicable] standards or codes of conduct of self-regulatory organizations."[5] Similar to financial risk management, compliance risk management involves understanding the bank's key compliance risks and ensuring that they are being adequately identified, managed, monitored, and controlled.

The following sections will show how all these responsibilities have become more challenging in recent years.

Oversight of strategic planning has become more challenging

Oversight of strategic planning has become more challenging because the business of banking has become more demanding and competitive.[6] In recent years, the structure of the banking industry has evolved dramatically. New laws were passed to permit both interstate branching and combinations of banks, securities firms, and insurance companies. This deregulation of products and markets has intensified competition between banks and between banks and non-bank financial companies. This competition continues to increase and to affect banks of all sizes. Deregulation, combined with advances in information technology, has accelerated the consolidation of the banking industry through mergers and acquisitions. It has also led to the emergence of huge banking organizations of unprecedented size and complexity.

Financial innovation and technological change in banking have also evolved, at an ever-increasing pace. Financial innovations have increased the ability to price risk and to spread it efficiently throughout the financial system, thus enhancing financial stability. They have also changed the traditional roles and risk profiles of banks. For example, asset securitization (the pooling of loans and their funding by the issue of securities) has reduced banks' roles in providing funding for credit. However, banks have kept significant roles in origination, servicing, monitoring, and providing credit enhancements. In addition, advances in information technology have led to the rapid development of new products and services (such as internet banking) and new risk management techniques. However, they have also generated new risks, such as those related to information security, vendor management, and business continuity.

Corporate governance has become more challenging

Corporate governance has become more challenging because expectations in this area have risen significantly in the wake of Enron and other scandals. Corporate financial scandals, beginning with Enron, Tyco, and WorldCom in 2001 and 2002, led to the collapse of employee pension plans, stock market turbulence, and rapid responses by legislators and regulators to restore public confidence. A number of corporate practices previously tolerated during the boom years of the 1980s and 1990s were called into question. Many specific new requirements were imposed to improve corporate governance, including the Sarbanes-Oxley Act of 2002 and new listing standards for the New York Stock Exchange and NASDAQ stock market. Moreover, the corporate world in general saw a significant "raising of the bar" in corporate governance expectations.

The revised corporate governance standards issued by the Basel Committee on Banking Supervision in 2006 reflect this changed environment.[7] These principles are international in scope, meant to educate financial institutions and supervisors around the world, and update an earlier version issued in 1999. The revised document emphasizes enhancements to corporate governance appropriate to a post-Enron world. Following is a summary of the expectations for directors that are newly emphasized in the updated guidance shown in Table 4.1.

Table 4.1 Expectations for directors

Expectations	*Examples*
Establish high standards of professional conduct and a supportive corporate culture, in part by setting an appropriate "tone at the top."	Directors should avoid self-dealing, such as accepting payments from the bank to companies or not-for-profit enterprises with which they are associated.
Ensure that senior management appropriately controls potential conflicts of interest arising from a wide range of sources.	A bank may have multiple relationships with the same company (e.g., lender, adviser on M&A transactions, private equity investor) that can generate conflicts.
Foster corporate values that promote the timely and open discussion of problems.	Employees should be encouraged and able to communicate (with adequate protection from reprisals) concerns about possible illegal, unethical, or questionable practices.
Enhance the effectiveness of both internal and external auditors.	Periodic rotation of the lead external audit partner should be considered.
Ensure that compensation policies and practices promote long-term objectives and strategies.	Compensation should not be based solely on volume of new business generated or quarterly earnings growth.
Promote transparency through appropriate disclosure of key elements of the bank's governance to outside stakeholders.	Information disclosed could include the bank's ownership structure, board structure, organization chart, compensation policies and actual compensation received, and policies governing ethics and conflicts of interest.
Understand the bank's operational structure, especially where it operates in jurisdictions, or through structures, that impair transparency.	Banks may operate in offshore financial centers characterized by lack of transparency and weak enforcement mechanisms. They may also use structured finance

> transactions to obscure the true economic nature of certain transactions by concealing debt or creating fictitious earnings.

Oversight of financial risk management has become more challenging

Oversight of financial risk management has become more challenging because risk management has greatly increased in sophistication. Banks have become larger and more complex in recent years. In addition, banks now face a highly diverse set of financial and non-financial risks, so risk management has become a core function for them.[8] Banks are increasing their competence in risk management both because the market (for example, stockholders, creditors, rating agencies) demands it and because bank regulators are encouraging it. Improving risk management is especially challenging for smaller banks, given their limited staff and less ability to afford outside resources such as consultants, compared to larger banks.

The banking industry has made great progress in managing credit risk. Until the early 1990s, banks generally held most loans to maturity, and credit risk was managed solely at the level of the individual loan. Since then, financial innovations (such as loan syndications, secondary-market loan trading, securitization, credit derivatives, and credit scoring) have dramatically transformed credit risk management. Large banks are now able to actively manage their entire loan portfolios, reducing the impact of loan concentrations and of individual problem assets. This allows them to continually seek the best mix of assets based on the credit environment, market conditions, and business opportunities. For smaller banks, a key challenge in recent years has been to improve their management of credit concentrations, especially those in commercial real estate lending. Areas of concentration management where some banks need to improve include reporting systems, integrating lending concentrations into strategic and capital planning, and evaluating the effects of possible adverse scenarios ("stress-testing").[9]

A similar evolution has occurred in managing market (or interest-rate) risk. Banks have traditionally used relatively simple techniques for this purpose, such as fixed position limits and basic maturity/repricing ("gap") schedules. However, advances in information technology and financial engineering have led to increasingly sophisticated approaches. Previously cutting-edge concepts such as duration and convexity and techniques such as value-at-risk and stress-testing are becoming increasingly common at banks of all sizes. Larger banks often take the lead in developing new approaches, while smaller banks that rely on vendor products must ensure that they choose the right models and implement them effectively. Overall, these advances have made banks and the banking system more resilient in the face of a risk that has caused significant banking problems in the past.

Liquidity risk management has also evolved considerably.[10] Traditionally, banks have largely relied on core deposits to fund loan growth, and on marketable securities to meet short-term liquidity needs. Consequently, many banks, especially small banks, have been able to use relatively simple balance-sheet ratios to manage liquidity risk. However, funding strategies at banks of all sizes have evolved during the past two decades. Banks now utilize a wider variety of on-balance-sheet funding sources, such as wholesale deposits and borrowings from the Federal Home Loan Bank System. They also have access to new off-balance-sheet funding sources, such as asset securitization. As a result, traditional ways of measuring and managing liquidity are becoming increasingly inadequate. Many banks of all sizes need to adopt more complex methods that capture elements such as off-balance-sheet financing, projected cash flows, borrowing capacity, and the potential impact of contingent liabilities.

Banks are also adopting new approaches to operational risk.[11] While this is a relatively new concept in banking, the specific risks covered by the concept (such as processing errors, fraud, and business disruption) are not new at all. To control operational risks, banks have historically relied on controls embedded in business lines, audit, and insurance protection. However, the increasing complexity of bank activities, large high-profile operational losses in recent years, and the evolution of regulatory capital have changed banks' approaches. The banking industry is now moving to formalize operational risk as a distinct discipline. Some larger banks have moved beyond the business-line approach to establish centralized functions to manage portions of operational risk, such as fraud or business continuity. In addition, some of the largest banks are beginning to use enterprise-wide operational risk management functions, historical loss databases, highly structured risk assessments, statistical modeling, and other advanced techniques for managing operational risk. Smaller banks also face the need to think more holistically about operational risks. Key areas of focus for small banks include thoroughly analyzing the relevant risks before engaging in new activities, and developing a sound vendor management process for activities that are frequently outsourced, such as information technology systems and internet banking.

Finally, managing bank capital is becoming more complex. In recent years, many banks have implemented advanced modeling techniques to improve their ability to quantify and manage risks.[12] These techniques generally involve the internal allocation of so-called "economic capital" to individual business lines, portfolios, or transactions. This evolution parallels (and has been encouraged by) recent efforts on the international level to revise risk-based regulatory capital standards. However, the largest banks have initiated these efforts primarily in response to market factors. In addition, some regional banks are moving toward economic capital models. For some time, the Federal Reserve has encouraged banks (especially large banks and those with complex risk profiles) to enhance their internal capital management processes.[13]

As a result of the changes just outlined, bank director oversight of financial risk management has become more challenging. In response, banks are increasingly adopting the practice of "enterprise risk management" (ERM).[14] ERM has been defined as "the discipline by which an organization . . . assesses, controls, exploits, finances, and monitors risks from all sources for the purpose of increasing the organization's short- and long-term value to its stakeholders."[15] ERM emphasizes risk management at the firm-wide (or enterprise) level, rather than in isolated business operations (or "silos"). It prevents significant risks from being overlooked, minimizes duplication of efforts, and focuses the board's and senior management's attention on the most severe risks facing the organization. Other benefits include:[16]

- The establishment of a common "risk language" within the organization;
- Early identification of problems or opportunities;
- Support for strategic and financial decisions;
- Better crisis management (due to early identification of problems); and
- Greater organizational efficiencies.

The largest banks have taken the lead in implementing ERM approaches. This evolution has been driven mainly by market forces (such as expectations from the credit rating agencies),[17] with bank regulators playing a secondary but important role. Banks are in various stages of implementing ERM, with the largest banks generally the farthest along. According to a 2006 survey conducted by the Risk Management Association of 31 large and regional banks,[18] only 31 per cent have an ERM board committee, and most (55 per cent) do not have a separate ERM unit charged with coordinating the management of material banking risks. The banks surveyed fell along a continuum from looking at each risk independently, to aggregating some risk types without necessarily considering correlations, to measuring and correlating many major risk types simultaneously.

The volume and complexity of banking laws and regulations have increased dramatically

As we have seen, corporate governance and the oversight of strategic planning and of financial risk management have become more challenging, requiring more director time and increased skill-sets. This has made it more difficult for directors to devote sufficient time and energy to overseeing compliance. Another factor making director oversight of compliance more challenging is the dramatic increase in the volume and complexity of banking laws and regulations in recent years.

Banking has always been a heavily regulated industry. However, banking regulation increased substantially in the years following the crises of the 1980s and the early 1990s and even more sharply in the past few years (Table 4.2 highlights some recent rules[19]). This increase has a number of causes. As discussed earlier, the business of banking itself has grown more complex, with a rapid rate of technological change and product innovation. The banking industry (at least at the larger end) has also become increasingly involved in financial services that have traditionally been separated from banking, such as securities and insurance. These financial services have their own, highly-specialized, compliance requirements. In addition, banking regulation has expanded into entirely new areas, such as the privacy of customer information and the security of information technology systems. Exogenous events, like the terrorist attacks of 11 September 2001, have introduced new risks to the banking system. Finally, banks increasingly must deal (directly or indirectly) with regulators that are new to them, including the Securities and Exchange Commission, the Financial Crimes Enforcement Network (FinCEN), and the Public Company Accounting Oversight Board.

Table 4.2   Recent laws and major provisions

Law	Major provisions
Federal Deposit Insurance Corporation Improvement Act of 1991	• Mandates a least-cost resolution method and prompt resolution approach to problem and failing banks • Orders the creation of a risk-based deposit insurance assessment scheme • Restricts brokered deposits and solicitation of deposits, as well as the non-bank activities of insured state banks • Creates new supervisory and regulatory examination standards • Institutes a system of prompt corrective action, with mandatory and progressively more severe restrictions on banks failing to meet specified capital levels

	• Limits the ability of problem institutions to borrow from the Federal Reserve • Expands prohibitions against insider activities • Creates new Truth in Savings provisions
Gramm-Leach-Bliley Act of 1999	• Allows affiliations among banks, securities firms and insurance companies under a financial holding company (FHC) structure • Establishes a regulatory framework in which bank, securities, and insurance regulators supervise their respective activities within an FHC • Designates the Federal Reserve as "umbrella supervisor" over the entire FHC • Provides privacy safeguards for limiting disclosures of personal customer information • Expands the number of institutions eligible for Federal Home Loan Bank System membership and advances • Provides that an FHC cannot be formed before its insured depository institutions receive and maintain a satisfactory Community Reinvestment Act rating
International Money Laundering Abatement and Financial Anti-Terrorism Act of 2001	• Authorizes and requires additional record keeping and reporting by financial institutions • Authorizes greater scrutiny of accounts held for foreign banks and of private banking conducted for foreign persons • Requires financial institutions to establish anti-money laundering programs • Imposes various standards on money-transmitting businesses • Amends criminal anti-money laundering statutes and procedures for forfeitures in money laundering cases • Requires further cooperation between financial institutions and government agencies in fighting money laundering
Sarbanes-Oxley Act of 2002	• Establishes the Public Company Accounting Oversight Board to regulate public accounting firms that audit publicly traded companies

- Prohibits such firms from providing other services to such companies along with audit services
- Requires CEOs and CFOs of publicly traded companies to certify annual and quarterly financial reports
- Includes whistle-blower protections and new federal criminal laws, including a ban on alteration of documents

Changes to New York Stock Exchange listing standards (2003)

- Require that independent directors comprise a majority of a company's board of directors
- Require audit, compensation, and nominating committees to be independent
- Require companies to develop an internal audit function
- Require members to adopt a code of business conduct and ethics
- Require stockholders to vote on stock option plans and any material changes to these plans

Changes to NASDAQ Stock Market Inc. listing standards (2003)

- Require that the majority of corporate board members be independent
- Require expanded authority for audit committees
- Require a strengthened role for independent directors in compensation and nomination decisions
- Require shareholders to approve all stock option plans
- Require companies to develop codes of conduct
- Require companies to promptly disclose insider stock deals for transactions exceeding $100 000

Fair and Accurate Credit Transactions Act of 2003 (FACT Act)

- Contains extensive amendments to the Fair Credit Reporting Act
- Is designed to improve the accuracy and transparency of the national credit reporting system and prevent identity theft
- Requires companies that share consumer information among affiliates to provide consumers notice and the right to "opt out"

New risk-based capital rules for the largest US banks (Basel II) – not yet finalized	• Require advanced approaches for computing regulatory capital requirements, consisting of credit, market, and operational risk • Provide for additional supervisory review of capital adequacy • Encourage market discipline through a public disclosure process

New banking laws and regulations continue to emerge. As of early 2007, a wide range of new measures was being considered.[20] For example, problems in the subprime mortgage market have led policymakers to propose federal legislation on predatory lending and more effective regulation of mortgage brokers, among other remedies. Some have suggested that the concept of "suitability" (found in the securities industry) should be extended to bank lending. Doing so would imply that a lender bears some responsibility for whether customers choose products that are appropriate for their financial situation. Credit card disclosure and solicitation practices were also coming under increased scrutiny from Congress and the regulators, due to continuing concerns expressed by consumer advocates. In addition, a succession of high-profile information-security breaches involving customer data, plus concerns about identity theft, has led to much new and proposed regulation on data security. Finally, the banking industry was also intensely interested in other issues, such as proposals to reform the oversight of government-sponsored enterprises and to restrict the expansion of non-financial companies into banking through so-called "industrial loan companies."

Directors should consider enterprise-wide approaches to compliance risk management
Bank directors should understand and consider enterprise-wide approaches to compliance risk management and adapt them, as appropriate, to their institutions. This would help focus directors' time and energy on the most important compliance risks facing the bank. "Enterprise-wide" compliance risk management refers to the process used to manage and control compliance risk across the entire organization, both within and across business lines and legal entities.[21] It applies the principles of ERM outlined earlier to compliance risks. An integrated approach to compliance is especially important for larger, more complex banks. These banks typically have a broad range of activities with complex compliance requirements and corporate governance issues that cross business lines. An enterprise-wide approach is especially helpful in ensuring compliance with requirements of the Bank Secrecy Act and anti-money laundering, fair lending, information security,

privacy, and transactions with affiliates (Regulation W). It can also be effective in controlling conflicts of interest.

Reduced to its essentials, a sound enterprise-wide compliance risk management program:

- Identifies and assesses the bank's current and emerging compliance risks, including those that transcend business lines and legal entities, or that result from inherent conflicts of interest between different business lines or legal entities within the organization.
- Maintains an ongoing understanding of the applicable rules and standards, including those of foreign countries, which apply to the bank's activities, products, and services.
- Establishes, maintains, and communicates effective compliance risk policies, procedures, and internal controls. Policies should be challenging but realistic, reflecting what the bank can actually accomplish.
- Develops and implements adequate risk measurement, monitoring, and management information systems (MIS) for compliance risk management.
- Establishes the appropriate infrastructure and internal controls to manage compliance risks associated with new business activities, products, or services *prior* to implementation.
- Escalates identified compliance breaches and emerging compliance risks to an appropriate level within the bank and communicates procedures for doing so to staff throughout the bank. Procedures should include criteria for escalating significant breaches and risks to the board (or a committee of the board).
- Takes timely corrective actions to address compliance deficiencies or breaches.
- Provides compliance staff throughout the bank with the appropriate authority and independence to carry out their responsibilities, conduct investigations of possible breaches of compliance policies without interference from business-line management, and communicate findings and concerns to other relevant members of senior management and the board (or committee).
- Integrates the bank's compliance objectives into management goals and compensation structure within the relevant business lines.
- Ensures that business lines do not inappropriately influence performance reviews and decisions relating to the compensation and promotions of compliance staff.
- Provides compliance staff with the resources necessary to carry out their responsibilities effectively, including a sufficient number of qualified and well-trained staff.

Although these principles are especially appropriate for larger banks, they can be adapted to banks of all sizes and degrees of complexity.

Directors play a key role in enterprise-wide compliance. The board is responsible for establishing a strong compliance culture. This culture should make compliance an integral part of day-to-day operations and hold managers and staff at all levels responsible for complying with applicable rules and standards. A strong compliance culture also reinforces the message that failure to comply may expose the bank to significant risks. In addition, it encourages employees to honor both the letter and the spirit of applicable rules and standards. To accomplish these goals, directors and senior management reinforce the importance of compliance in their internal and external communications. Compliance should also be built into existing business processes, such as human resource procedures, new officer orientations, and the new product approval process. Finally, it is especially important that communications with regulators deliver the message that the institution is serious about compliance.

There are other things the board should do. It should ensure that the bank has a sound and effective enterprise-wide compliance program and compliance oversight function and it should review and approve key elements of these processes. In addition, the board should ensure that business-line senior management has the ability and motivation to manage the bank's compliance risks, consistent with the board's compliance expectations. The board should effectively oversee senior management by understanding the types of compliance risks facing the bank. To promote a strong compliance culture, the board should also ensure that its views about the importance of compliance are communicated by senior management across, and at all levels of the bank. Finally, the board should ensure that senior management has established appropriate incentives to integrate compliance objectives into management goals and compensation structure across the bank.

Day-to-day management of compliance risk remains the responsibility of business-line senior management. However, larger banks are increasingly establishing centralized compliance oversight functions to help the business lines with this responsibility. These functions evaluate compliance risks within and across business lines and legal entities. They also oversee the implementation of the bank's enterprise-wide compliance program. The details of such a compliance function should be consistent with the nature and level of the bank's compliance risk. However, the basic expectations for a compliance function are similar to those for an internal audit program. The compliance function should be independent of the bank's operating areas, have sufficient authority and resources to effectively carry out its responsibilities, conduct independent testing, and operate according to a comprehensive, risk-focused plan.[22] In selecting compliance staff, character (that is, the ability to take a firm stand on principles and resist "pushback" from management) is at least as important as technical expertise.

Failure to establish an effective compliance program can have severe legal, reputational, and financial consequences. Let's look at three brief examples, based on publicly available information. ABN Amro, a very large non-US bank with diverse business lines and operations in many countries, experienced a severe breakdown in compliance with anti-money-laundering laws and regulations.[23] In an enforcement action,[24] ABN's regulators cited a number of serious deficiencies, in particular that it "lacked effective systems of governance, audit, and internal control [sic] to oversee the activities of the Branches with respect to legal, compliance, and reputational risk, and failed to adhere to those systems that it did have, especially those relating to anti-money laundering policies and procedures." As a result of these compliance failures, the bank entered into a settlement with US and Dutch regulators and was assessed $80 million in fines by US authorities. It has also spent many times that amount to improve its internal risk management systems and monitor transactions more closely.

A second example of compliance failure is Commerce Bank, NA, of Philadelphia, PA.[25] Primarily because of weaknesses related to real estate-related insider transactions, the bank recently entered into an enforcement action requiring it, among other things, to:

- Comply with all applicable laws and regulations, including those related to bank ownership of real estate;
- Sever relationships with real estate entities affiliated with its former chairman;
- Form a board committee to review material real estate-related transactions between the board and the bank; and
- Hire an outside investigator to verify that the bank is complying with the enforcement action.

Our third and final example relates to recent problems in the subprime mortgage market. American International Group Inc. has entered into an enforcement action to improve the practices of three subsidiaries.[26] Its regulator charged that the thrift subsidiary failed to properly control mortgage lending activities outsourced to affiliates, from both a safety-and-soundness and a consumer-protection perspective. As a result, some borrowers were adversely affected by inadequate consideration of their creditworthiness or by large broker/lender fees. AIG agreed to establish a $128 million fund to refinance affected borrowers into affordable loans and reimburse borrowers who paid excessive fees. The company also agreed to terminate the objectionable practices and donate $15 million to financial literacy and credit counseling services. In addition, the board of the thrift is required to appoint a compliance committee, with a majority of outside directors. This committee will coordinate compliance with the enforcement action and report quarterly to the full board and to the regulator.

As is the case with ERM, enterprise-wide compliance is still a work in progress, with banks at various stages of implementation. Two Federal Reserve banks recently conducted a review of compliance programs at large and regional banks in the Midwest.[27] Based on this review, most of the banks sampled had appointed corporate compliance officers. The compliance function generally reported on a functional basis to a chief risk officer and/or an executive- or board-level risk committee. Reporting lines ranged from very centralized (with compliance staff reporting to a corporate function) to decentralized (with compliance staff primarily reporting through the business lines). Some institutions had adopted the leading practice of incorporating compliance goals in performance evaluation and compensation.

The widest range of practices was noted in risk-monitoring and MIS. About half of the banks had adopted the leading practice of comprehensively mapping laws and regulations to business units. Compliance risk assessments ranged from relatively minimal listings of applicable laws and regulations to more robust methods addressing the level of inherent risk as well as the presence of mitigating controls for each risk. None of the institutions had yet established strong centralized, corporate-wide compliance testing procedures. Finally, some of the institutions needed more formal policies for escalating compliance exceptions to higher levels of management for attention.

Resources for further information
The US banking agencies have published extensive guidance outlining the responsibilities of bank directors. Several publications provide an overview of bank directors' responsibilities.[28] One, more specialized, booklet describes information generally found in board reports, highlighting "red flags" – ratios or trends that may signal existing or potential problems.[29] Another booklet focuses on the importance of establishing and maintaining effective internal controls.[30] The agencies also have well-established director training programs offering classroom-type and (in some cases) online training. Information about these may be found on the agencies' websites. Because we believe that continuing education is an important part of directors' responsibilities, we encourage directors to take full advantage of these resources, as well as the wide range of materials offered by the private sector.

Conclusions

Clearly, this is a challenging time to be a bank director, but it can also be a highly rewarding one. Bank directors play a critical role in maintaining the safety and soundness of the banking system. To continue to play this role effectively, directors at banks of all sizes can benefit from considering the enterprise-wide approaches to compliance risk management outlined in this chapter and adapting them to fit the unique characteristics and risk profiles of their institutions.

Notes

1. The views presented in this chapter are those of the authors and do not necessarily reflect the views of the Federal Reserve Bank of Chicago or the Federal Reserve System.
2. Board of Governors of the Federal Reserve System (1995b).
3. Basic responsibilities of corporate directors are outlined in Business Roundtable (2005).
4. Board of Governors of the Federal Reserve System (1995a).
5. Olson (2006).
6. This survey of the current banking environment is based on Hanc (2004).
7. Basel Committee on Banking Supervision (2006).
8. The following discussion of credit and market risk management is based primarily on Bernanke (2006).
9. Bies (2006a)
10. Hadley and Touhey (2006).
11. Seivold et al. (2006).
12. Burns (2004).
13. Board of Governors of the Federal Reserve System (1999).
14. Various approaches to ERM have been outlined in the literature. One prominent approach is that of the Committee of Sponsoring Organizations of the Treadway Commission, or COSO. See also a number of speeches by former Federal Reserve Governor Susan Bies, for example, Bies (2006b) and Bies (2007).
15. Casualty Actuarial Society, quoted in Fitch Ratings (2006, 2).
16. Fitch Ratings (2006).
17. For example, Standard & Poor's (2006).
18. Foster (2007). The 31 banks participating in the survey were divided almost equally among four ranges of asset size (less than $25 billion, $25–75 billion, $75–150 billion, and over $150 billion). The *RMA Journal* devoted an entire issue (February 2007) to ERM.
19. Federal Deposit Insurance Corporation "Important Banking Legislation"; Spong (2000, 31–3); Basinger et al. (2005, 19).
20. Kaper (2006) and Davenport (2007).
21. See Olson (2006) and Ludwig (2007) for more information.
22. See Basel Committee on Banking Supervision (2005) for more information.
23. Simpson (2005).
24. Board of Governors of the Federal Reserve System (2005). The remedial actions required by the regulators are consistent with a number of the sound practices outlined in this chapter.
25. Hopkins (2007b) and Office of the Comptroller of the Currency (2007).
26. Hopkins (2007a) and Office of Thrift Supervision (2007).
27. Federal Reserve Bank of Chicago and Federal Reserve Bank of Cleveland (2007).
28. For example, Myers (2005), Federal Reserve Bank of Atlanta (2002), Office of the Comptroller of the Currency (1997), Federal Deposit Insurance Corporation (2003).
29. Office of the Comptroller of the Currency (2003).
30. Office of the Comptroller of the Currency (2000).

References

Basel Committee on Banking Supervision (2005), "Compliance and the compliance function in banks," Basel, Switzerland: Bank for International Settlements, April.

Basel Committee on Banking Supervision (2006), "Enhancing corporate governance for banking organizations," Basel, Switzerland: Bank for International Settlements, February.

Basinger, Robert E., Daniel F. Benton, Mary L. Garner, Lynne S. Montgomery and Nathan H. Powell (2005), "Implications of the Sarbanes-Oxley Act for public companies and the US banking industry," *FDIC Outlook*, Fall, 11–19.

Bernanke, Ben S. (2006), "Modern risk management and banking supervision," remarks at the Stonier Graduate School of Banking, Washington, DC, 12 June, accessed 28 November at www.federalreserve.gov/boarddocs/speeches/2006/200606123/default.htm.

Bies, Susan S. (2006a), "Challenges of conducting effective risk management in community banks," remarks at the Western Independent Bankers Annual CFO and Risk Management Conference, Coronado, CA, 6 June, accessed 4 June 2007 at www.federalreserve.gov/boarddocs/speeches/2006/20060606/default.htm.

Bies, Susan S. (2006b), "A supervisory perspective on enterprise risk management," remarks at the American Bankers Association Annual Convention, Phoenix, Arizona, 17 October, accessed 18 May, 2007 at www.federalreserve.gov/boarddocs/speeches/2006/20061017/default.htm.

Bies, Susan S. (2007), "Enterprise risk management and mortgage lending," remarks at the National Credit Union Administration 2007 Risk Mitigation Summit, 11 January, accessed 7 February at www.federalreserve.gov/boarddocs/speeches/2007/20070111/default.htm.

Board of Governors of the Federal Reserve System (1995a), "Rating the adequacy of risk management processes and internal controls at state member banks and bank holding companies," supervisory letter SR 95-51 (SUP), 14 November.

Board of Governors of the Federal Reserve System (1995b), "Duties and responsibilities of directors," *Commercial Bank Examination Manual*, Section 5000.1.

Board of Governors of the Federal Reserve System (1999), "Assessing capital adequacy in relation to risk at large banking organizations and others with complex risk profiles," supervisory letter SR 99-18 (SUP), 1 July.

Board of Governors of the Federal Reserve System (2005), joint press release, 19 December, accessed 15 June, 2007 at www.federalreserve.gov/boarddocs/press/enforcement/2005/20051219/default.htm.

Burns, Robert L. (2004), "Economic capital and the assessment of capital adequacy," *FDIC: Supervisory Insights*, Winter accessed 9 February, 2007 at www.fdic.gov/regulations/examinations/supervisory/insights/siwin04/economic_capital.html.

Business Roundtable (2005), '*Principles of corporate governance 2005*,' November, accessed 3 July, 2007 at http://64.203.97.43/pdf/CorporateGovPrinciples.pdf.

Davenport, Todd (2007), "Review 2006/preview 2007: what's on tap (and on hold) in regulation," *American Banker Online*, 2 January, accessed 15 June at www.americanbanker.com/article_search.html?articlequeryid=1519621456&hitnum=1.

Federal Deposit Insurance Corporation (FDIC) (2003), *Pocket Guide for Directors*, Washington, DC: FDIC.

Federal Deposit Insurance Corporation (2007), "Important banking legislation," accessed April 8 at www.fdic.gov/regulations/laws/important/index.html.

Federal Reserve Bank of Atlanta (2002), *The Director's Primer: A Guide to Management Oversight and Bank Regulation*, Atlanta, GA: Federal Reserve Bank of Atlanta.

Federal Reserve Bank of Chicago and Federal Reserve Bank of Cleveland (2007), "Initial observations from inter-district coordinated reviews of corporate wide compliance," unpublished white paper, February.

Fitch Ratings (2006), "Enterprise risk management for insurers and prism's role", 26 September accessed at www.fitchratings.com/corporate/sectors/special_reports.cfm?sector_flag=4&marketsector=1&detail=&body_content=spl_rpt&start_row=101.

Foster, Beverly (2007), "Growth spurts in enterprise risk management," *RMA Journal*, **89** (5), accessed 20 February at http://proquest.umi.com/pqdweb?did=1212746791&sid=1&Fmt= 3&clientId=11417&RQT=309&Vname=PQD.

Hadley, Kyle L. and Alison T. Touhey (2006), "An assessment of traditional liquidity ratios," *FDIC Outlook*, (Fall), 11–16.

Hanc, George (2004), "The future of banking in America: summary and conclusions," *FDIC Banking Review*, **16** (1) 1.

Hopkins, Cheyenne (2007a), "AIG enters mortgage order," *American Banker Online*, 11 June, accessed 11 July at www.americanbanker.com/article_search.html?articlequeryid= 1044141851&hitnum=2.

Hopkins, Cheyenne (2007b), "Tough terms set this OCC order apart," *American Banker Online*, 2 July, accessed 11 July 2007 at http://www.americanbanker.com/article_ search.html?articlequeryid=2029345450&hitnum=17.

Kaper, Stacy (2006), "Review 2006/preview 2007: Capitol Hill priorities and probabilities," *American Banker Online*, 28 December, accessed 15 June 2007 at www.americanbanker. com/article_search.html?articlequeryid=518865318&hitnum=1.

Ludwig, Eugene A. (2007), "Viewpoint: building a top-tier compliance system," *American Banker Online*, 15 June, accessed 15 June at www.americanbanker.com/article.html?id =20070614BGHE597G&from=washregu.

Myers, Forest E. (2005), *Basics for Bank Directors*, Kansas City, MO: Federal Reserve Bank of Kansas City.

Office of the Comptroller of the Currency (OCC) (1997), *The Director's Book: The Role of a National Bank Director*, Washington, DC: OCC.

Office of the Comptroller of the Currency (2000), *Internal Controls: A Guide for Directors*, Washington, DC: OCC.

Office of the Comptroller of the Currency (2003), *Detecting Red Flags in Board Reports: A Guide for Directors*, Washington, DC: OCC.

Office of the Comptroller of the Currency (2007), news release NR 2007-63, 29 June, accessed 10 July at www.occ.treas.gov/ftp/release/2007-63.htm.

Office of Thrift Supervision (2007), press release OTS 07-041, 8 June, accessed 11 July at www.ots.treas.gov/docs/7/777041.html.

Olson, Mark W. (2006), "Compliance risk management in a diversified environment," remarks to the Financial Services Roundtable and the Morin Center for Banking and Financial Services, Washington, DC, 16 May, accessed 17 May at www.federalreserve.gov/ boarddocs/speeches/2006/20060516/default.htm.

Seivold, Alfred, Scott Leifer and Scott Ulman (2006), "Operational risk management: an evolving discipline," *FDIC Supervisory Insights*, Summer, accessed 29 November at www.fdic.gov/regulations/examinations/supervisory/insights/sisum06/article01_ris.

Simpson, Glenn R. (2005), "Risky territory: how top Dutch bank plunged into world of shadowy money," *Wall Street Journal*, 30 December, A1.

Spong, Kenneth (2000), *Banking Regulation: Its Purposes, Implementation, and Effects*, Kansas City, MO: Federal Reserve Bank of Kansas City.

Standard & Poor's (2006), "Criteria: assessing enterprise risk management practices of financial institutions," 22 September, accessed 6 December at www2.standardandpoors.com/ servlet/Satellite?pagename=sp/sp_article/ArticleTemplate&c=sp_article&cid=11458461927.

5 The risks of directing a financial institution

Ben S. Branch and Robin Russell

WARNING: Serving as a Director of a Financial Institution is Risky to your Economic Health: You may be sued by the FDIC, the SEC, the IRS, Shareholders, Creditors and others. Your indemnification may be worthless. Your D&O insurance coverage may be void or inadequate. Proceed at your own peril.

Introduction

The banking crisis of the 1980s and the resulting litigation against the officers and directors of the failed banks caused many qualified individuals to become reluctant to serve. This restricted the pool of qualified candidates. In December 1992 the Federal Deposit Insurance Corporation (FDIC) issued a statement "in response to concerns expressed by representatives of the banking industry and others regarding civil damage litigation risks to directors and officers of federally insured banks"[1] in which it concluded that "the FDIC will not bring civil suits against directors and officers who fulfill their responsibilities, including the duties of loyalty and care, and who make reasonable business judgments on a fully informed basis and after proper deliberation." While comforting on the surface, the FDIC's statement did little more than articulate established corporate governance principals. When the next banking crisis hits (and it will), we anticipate that directors of financial institutions will once again become litigation targets.

Because banks operate on thin margins with thin capital, income statements and balance sheets can be quickly devastated by either an economic downturn or a poorly underwritten loan portfolio or especially by a combination of both. Once the institution becomes financially distressed, the directors' opportunities to mitigate their risk are severely limited. Therefore, understanding the risks of directing a financial institution either in economic distress or in danger of becoming economically distressed is essential for anyone contemplating becoming a director of a financial institution. In this chapter we describe both the risks and the steps one needs to take in order to minimize such risks.

Understanding the financial institution

The potential director needs to understand clearly the nature of the financial institution in which she or he is contemplating becoming a director. Prior to accepting a directorship, a candidate should conduct the kind of extensive due diligence on the financial institution as a would-be acquirer would conduct on a potential acquisition candidate. The director needs to become familiar with such things as the institution's tax status, any pending and threatened litigation against it, and the experience and tenure of management, as well as the institution's capital structure, including debt terms, working capital and liquidity. Contingent obligations, particularly those arising from its derivative activities, need to be carefully evaluated. Among the myriad of issues, three due diligence issues rise to the top of the list in terms of assessing the risk of accepting the position: the capital structure, regulatory position and asset portfolio (including loans, leases and derivatives) of the financial institution.

Capital structure

Typically a financial institution is either a wholly-owned subsidiary of a holding company which is itself publicly owned or is owned directly by multiple shareholders none of whom hold a sufficient number of shares to qualify as a bank holding company. Serving as the director of a financial institution with no corporate parent or affiliates simplifies the task of understanding fiduciary duties. A director owes a duty of loyalty and care to *every* entity he or she serves. Thus, where multiple entities are served, duties are owed to each. Conflicts of interest arise where there is not a complete identity of interest among all entities within the affiliated group.

Where a financial institution is directly owned by a holding company, the parent's capital structure consists of securities issued at the parent holding company level. These may be publicly-traded stock or bonds and other obligations such as commercial paper and private placements of debt issued by the parent. The issuance of debt at the parent holding company level creates a creditor body distinctly separate from that of its subsidiary bank or banks. The holding company's assets will include its equity in its subsidiaries which may include both banks and non-banks. Typically the holding company will also have some directly owned assets which may include such things as cash, real estate, equipment, and directly owned debt and equity investments. By far the largest portion of its assets will be its investment in its subsidiary banks.

Under the terms of the United States Bankruptcy Code, a federally insured depository institution is ineligible to be a debtor. As a result, a bank that fails is not subject to the same kinds of treatment as are most corporations that become insolvent. Rather than file for protection under the Bankruptcy Code, a bank that is deemed by the regulators no longer to be economically viable is seized and placed into an FDIC receivership.[2] Its holding company, in contrast, is eligible (and is almost certain) to file as a debtor for either Chapter 7 or 11 protection. Typically a parent bank holding company files bankruptcy upon the seizure of one or more of its banking subsidiaries. Once its banks are put into receivership, the holding company's remaining assets are hardly ever adequate to support its capital structure. Prior to the loss of its subsidiary banks, the holding company will have relied upon dividend payments from its bank subsidiaries to fund most or all of its debt service. Once the banks are no longer in place to upstream the funds needed to service the parent's debt, and once the value of the equity in these banks is lost to the holding company, it becomes insolvent on both a balance sheet and ability to pay its bills as they come due basis. In the 1980s, this scenario occurred with some frequency. The holding companies' subsidiary banks became insolvent and were seized by the regulators. No longer able to service their debts, these holding companies had no choice but to declare bankruptcy.

A Chapter 11 filing, known as the path to reorganization for corporations, is rarely a viable option for a bank holding company. In 1990, special provisions of the Bankruptcy Code were enacted to restrict a debtor's ability to reject agreements with the FDIC to maintain the capital of its subsidiary depository institutions[3] and to make the FDIC's claim for capital support a priority claim against the debtor's bankruptcy estate. Long before the FDIC seizes the financial institutions, bank regulators will have required the institution's holding company to enter into such a capital support agreement.

A bank holding company is expected to act as a source of managerial and financial strength to its subsidiary banks.[4] This so-called "source-of-strength doctrine" is viewed by the Federal Reserve as allowing it to use cease and desist orders to force a parent bank holding company to provide financial support to its distressed banking subsidiary.[5] In the 1990s, the source-of-strength doctrine was tested and limited in litigation involving the failure of the Bank of New England Corporation. A bank holding company forced to downstream capital to a distressed bank (or which contractually obligates itself under a capital maintenance agreement) when the holding company is itself in financial distress may be found to have made a fraudulent transfer of its assets to the detriment of its creditors (and to the benefit of the FDIC).[6] Such action may also become the basis of a breach of fiduciary duty claim against the holding company directors.

Regulatory oversight
All federally insured financial institutions and their bank holding companies are subject to regulatory oversight.[7] Regulatory oversight has clear advantages coupled with clear disadvantages for a director. A regulated financial institution must have articulated policies and procedures consistent with safe

and sound banking practices for all aspects of its business, from loan under-writing to employment. Such institutions are examined by their regulators in order to insure compliance. However, directors can take little comfort from this process as negligent regulatory supervision does not give rise to a viable cause of action. Furthermore, as a practical matter most routine examinations are limited in scope and by necessity involve only a sampling of loans in an effort to determine if the underwriting process has led to a sound portfolio of loans and leases. Historically, comprehensive examinations do not occur until problems are clearly evident – at which point the results come too late to save the directors from becoming litigation targets. Nevertheless, one who is considering becoming a bank director should carefully read and discuss with management the financial institution's most recent Reports of Supervisory Activity (ROSAs).

Regulatory oversight also means extensive government involvement, which is all too frequently susceptible to political agendas. The regulators are, however, subject to the same judicial oversight as are corporations and individuals. Indeed, courts have often found political agendas rather than sound analysis of culpability to be the motivating factor behind the FDIC's litigation against directors of failed institutions. Never was this more apparent than in *FDIC v Hurwitz*,[8] where the FDIC was sanctioned for trying to use "their agency's authority to compel an illegal result wholly unconnected with their legitimate responsibilities." The FDIC had, in connection with the failure of United Savings, sought to hold Hurwitz, chairman of the institution's holding company, liable for losses at the institution. The FDIC could never clearly articulate its claims against Hurwitz but appeared to need to hold someone (with personal wealth) accountable. The FDIC also failed to disclose its records to Hurwitz's counsel, which were believed to provide evidence of the FDIC's "corrupt" motives. The FDIC's lawsuit against Hurwitz was ultimately dismissed and Hurwitz recovered his costs of defending the suit – a cautionary tale for regulators.

Investment portfolio
Probably the single most important task of an actual or potential director is understanding the financial institutions' allowance for loan and lease losses (ALLL). The bank's ALLL reflects its evaluation of the collection risk embedded in the institutions' portfolio of loans, leases and derivatives. The ALLL is ultimately a judgment call and thus most susceptible to manipulation by management. But note that their discretion is somewhat constrained by both their auditors and the regulators. Still, the bank's managers have substantial discretion in how much they allocate to this account. And various forces may push them toward a lower provision for losses than is realistic under the circumstances. Note that the greater the amount provided

to this account in a given reporting period, the lower will be the profits reported in that same accounting period.

Organizational psychologists who have studied the banking industry have identified a "bad loan psychology" in connection with the escalation hypothesis which shows a tendency by banks to remain confident that a borrower will turn around (thus making the loan good).[9] All too often banks subject to this kind of thinking fail to recognize weaknesses in their loan portfolios in a timely fashion and as a result set their ALLL at an unrealistically low level until events force them to do otherwise. In many instances the banks continue to "throw good money after bad" which leads them to suffer greater losses eventually.

This study of bank executives' unreasonably delayed recognition and write-off of problem loans highlights the need for directors to stay in close contact with this process. Furthermore, since the ALLL falls straight to the bottom of the balance sheet, a mis-stated ALLL will lead to misleading financial statements. For public companies, such mis-statements are all too likely to result in Securities Exchange Commission (SEC) investigations, enforcement actions and securities class-action litigation directed at both the banks and their officers and directors.

On the other hand, the Internal Revenue Service (IRS) is vigilant in limiting how far a bank can go in estimating potential future losses, as such recognitions have the effect of reducing the amount of income on which their corporate income tax is based. So on the one hand banks need to be careful not to underestimate their ALLL. But on the other hand another group in the government is looking to see that they do not overestimate it. The directors walk a fine line.

Banks, particularly large banks, are becoming increasingly involved in the use of derivatives. They may use derivatives both to hedge their own credit risks and to market risk-reducing products to their corporate customers.[10] The notional value of these derivatives can be enormous. Used properly, derivatives are a very effective tool for both risk reduction and as a source of revenue. Nonetheless, such contracts can involve a substantial amount of risk. Moreover, by no means do all banks understand just how risky such contracts can be and how great is their exposure. All too often they only discover the risk that they have taken when the losses start to mount up. Even the regulators are somewhat at a loss to evaluate the risks of bank derivatives activity. This is particularly the case because of the rapid development of new and different types of derivatives. If one is considering becoming a director for a bank that is active in the derivatives area, the potential director should carefully explore what the bank is doing with its derivatives program and get comfortable with the exposure thereby produced. Unless the potential director is well versed in the nature of derivatives, he or she should enlist the support of a knowledgeable expert from a respected investment bank to evaluate the resultant risks.[11]

Sources of liability
A director who commits an intentional tort such as fraud or embezzlement should clearly understand the risk he or she is taking. The unintentional failure to act or prevent the acts of others frequently makes a bank director the target of litigation. This personal liability results primarily from breach of a director's duty of care or loyalty, improper declaration of dividends or violation of regulatory enforcement actions.

Enforcement actions[12]
Most actions by government agencies such as the Federal Reserve Board (FRB) and SEC can be classified as either formal or informal. Formal actions against banking organizations include cease and desist orders, written agreements or formal agreements, and civil money penalties. Formal action against individuals includes removal actions, civil money penalties, cease and desist orders, and restitution orders. Informal actions consist of memoranda of understanding and board resolutions or commitment.

Capital adequacy is the most critical factor in terms of how and when the regulators commence enforcement action. In 1991, the Government Accounting Office (GAO) report on the failure of the Bank of New England Corporation subsidiary banks criticized federal supervision and enforcement practices and recommended that the process be more predictable, more credible and less discretionary. The GAO envisioned an approach where the regulators would be required to take specific, increasingly severe actions against an institution as its financial condition deteriorated. Following the GAO report and related calls for reform, Congress passed the Federal Deposit Insurance Corp. Improvement Act (FDICIA) of 1991. FDICIA incorporated a "tripwire" approach to supervision and enforcement. The legislation was designed to restrict the regulators' discretion by requiring them to pursue prompt corrective action against institutions based primarily on five levels of capital adequacy. Since the passage of FDICIA the SEC and the Federal Trade Commission's involvement in bank affairs has increased.[13]

Risk-focused examinations were introduced by the regulators in the late 1990s. Such examinations are designed to determine whether a banking organization's risk level is rising to an unacceptable height and, if so, make sure that appropriate action is being taken to reduce the risk to an acceptable level. Thus risk-focused examinations which reveal an unacceptable risk level are likely to lead to a number of remedial actions: opening the door for regulators to issue enforcement actions based on risk management trends and concerns, placing banks under enforcement actions even before such banking organizations experience actual financial difficulties – before financial condition ratios indicate that a problem is present.

Because of highly publicized insider lapses, the regulators are more and more frequently focusing accountability on directors, particularly outside directors. Each director, before entering into any enforcement action with the regulators, needs to understand fully the nature of the provisions, the ramifications of agreeing to abide by certain provisions, and the ramifications of failing to comply with executed enforcement actions. Enforcement actions, as originally drafted and presented by the regulators, are broadly worded, leaving the regulator with maximum discretion and rights of interpretation. Thus, regulatory enforcement actions need to be evaluated very carefully by directors prior to agreeing to their provisions.

Breach of duty
The FDIC has described the bank director's duty of loyalty as requiring the director "to administer the affairs of the bank in candor, personal honesty and integrity." This prohibits a director from "advancing [his or her] own personal or business interests, or those of others, at the expense of the bank". The duty of care has been described as requiring a director "to act as prudent and diligent business persons in conducting the affairs of the bank". This duty makes a director "responsible for selecting, monitoring, and evaluating competent management; establishing business strategies and policies; monitoring and assessing the progress of business operations; establishing and monitoring adherence to policies and procedures required by statute, regulation, and principles of safety and soundness; and for making business decisions on the basis of fully informed and meaningful deliberation."[14]

Breach of duty cases are, by their nature, fact specific. Legal scholars who have studied the case law in the area of bank director negligence have identified a number of factors which have led to successful FDIC litigation against directors:

- Excessive absence from meetings;
- Failure to give even a cursory reading of financial records;
- Failure to respond appropriately to negative information received from regulatory authorities, examiners, auditors, and other reliable sources;
- Failure to require adherence to a bank's loan policy; and
- Permitting the extension of credit on a speculative or reckless basis, without adequate security or underwriting.[15]

The existence of one or more of these factors frequently exposes a director to a liability. Accordingly, directors should carefully avoid all of the above noted behaviors. Put in the affirmative, a careful conscientious director will attend meetings regularly, read financial reports fully and carefully. In addition such a director will seek to have the bank respond to any negative information from regulators, auditors or the like with appropriate remedial measures, ensure that the bank adheres to its own loan policy, and avoid the extension of credit on a speculative and/or reckless basis. Of course an individual director cannot force the bank to do or not to do the things noted above. But the director can stand up and be counted for or against such actions and create a record of his or her stands. In extreme cases, the director may need to threaten to resign, and if necessary actually resign, if the bank takes actions which he or she deems to be improper and refuses to remedy the situation when called upon to do so.

Improper dividends
Most states have statutes which provide that a board of directors cannot declare a distribution that would cause its corporation to become insolvent or unable to pay its debt. These statutes are modeled on the Model Business Corporation Act (MBCA).[16] The determination of solvency is based upon an equity test which requires, "that decisions be based on cash flow analysis that is itself based on a business forecast and budget for a sufficient period of time to permit a conclusion that known obligations of the corporation can reasonably be expected to be satisfied over the period of time that they will mature."[17] The statutes also require a company to have a positive net worth reflected on the balance sheet. Moreover, a bank that is on the regulators' radar screen will only be allowed to upstream the money needed to fund a dividend distribution if the bank's capital will not be impaired by the distribution. In essence that means that a dividend paid by a bank cannot cause the bank's regulatory capital to fall below the percentage deemed necessary for the bank to be viewed as sound.

The MBCA suggests that the validity of the determining factors depends on the circumstances and must be reasonable within those circumstances.[18] Specifically, the statute provides that directors who vote for or concur in "the declaration of any dividend or other distribution of assets to the shareholders contrary to the provisions of this act or contrary to any restrictions in this certificate incorporation" will be liable to the corporation, which acts on behalf of its creditors or shareholders.[19] To the extent recovery is sought against the directors, the directors are allowed to be subrogated to the rights of the corporation but only "against shareholders who received such dividend or distribution with knowledge of facts indicating that it was not authorized by this act," and only "in proportion to the amounts received by them respectively."

Business judgment rule
The business judgment rule provides a defense for directors charged with personal liability for things they did or did not do in their director's capacity. The business judgment rule protects actions by members of a board of directors if the actions were made in good faith, and comport to the standard that a prudent person in the same or similar position as the director would apply. However, if the board of directors acts beyond the corporation's by-laws, the business judgment rule does not apply. Directors act prudently and therefore (in the absence of bad faith) will not be liable if they relied upon "the opinion of counsel for the corporation; upon written reports setting forth financial data concerning the corporation and prepared by an independent public accountant or certified public accountant or firm of such accountants; upon financial statements, books of account or reports of the corporation represented to them to be correct by the president, the officer of the corporation having charge of its books of account, or the person presiding at a meeting of the board; or upon written reports of committees of the board."[20] Directors who act recklessly do not act in good faith.

Potential plaintiffs
A financial institution director becomes a potential target of a plethora of plaintiffs when the institution becomes financially distressed. The plaintiffs include government agencies such as the FDIC, FRB, OCC, SEC, and IRS as well as private plaintiffs such as the institution's shareholders, creditors and borrowers. The more complex an institution's corporate structure, the greater will be the number and diversity of potential plaintiffs. Thus a director who serves both a bank holding company and its bank subsidiary could be the target of litigation by the FDIC as well as the holding company's bankruptcy trustee, shareholders and creditors, to name a few.

Derivative claims
When a financial institution fails, derivative claims against its directors are owned by either the FDIC or, if the bank was part of a holding company structure, the bankruptcy estate. A derivative claim is defined as "a wrong to an incorporated group as a whole that depletes or destroys corporate assets and, as a consequence, reduces the value of the corporation's stock."[21]

FDIC
Under the Financial Institutions Reform Recovery and Enforcement Act (FIRREA), the FDIC, as receiver of a subsidiary bank, succeeds to all

rights of the bank and the derivative claims of its stockholders.[22] FIRREA provides that, as receiver, the FDIC succeeds to "all rights, titles, powers and privileges of the insured depository institution, and of any stockholder, member, accountholder, depositor, officer or director of such institution with respect to the institution and the assets of the institution"; and "title to the books, records and assets of any previous conservator or other legal custodian of such institution." Thus, upon regulatory closure the FDIC is allowed to bring suit against former directors of the failed banks for allegedly misrepresenting the financial condition of the banks and/or failing to disclose acts of mismanagement, where the claimed injury is diminution in the value of the banks' assets.[23] Additionally, when a federally insured depository institution fails, the FDIC pays covered depositors and becomes subrogated to their claims against the bank. This typically places the FDIC as the failed bank's largest single creditor.

Holding company
Upon bankruptcy of the holding company, the fiduciary obligations of corporate directors, normally enforced by the corporation or through a shareholder's derivative action, can only be enforced by the representative of the bankruptcy estate.[24] Courts have consistently found that property of the bankruptcy estate includes actions for fiduciary misconduct, mismanagement or neglect of duty which are brought for the benefit of creditors in general.[25] Several policies underlie this principle. Allowing any one of the creditors to prosecute the claim individually would undermine the fundamental bankruptcy policy of equitable distribution among creditors.[26] It would also open the door to a multi-jurisdictional rush to judgment by the various creditors, a practice clearly contrary to a fundamental policy of the Bankruptcy Code.[27]

Fiduciary duties are owed not only to shareholders but when the holding company becomes insolvent or is "in the vicinity of insolvency" to its creditors as well.[28] Thus, when the holding company is in or near insolvency, in addition to their other duties, the directors become legally obligated to take into consideration, and to act in the reasonable interests of the corporation's creditors. Until the institution enters the zone of insolvency, the director's sole fiduciary duties had been owed to the holding company and its shareholders.

The majority of cases hold that a director's duty to the company's creditors is breached the moment the director acts in a way that causes the corporation to lack fairly-valued net worth or liquidity, and this result was inevitable, likely, or reasonably foreseeable. One of the leading cases in this area, *Geyer v. Ingersoll Publications Co.*,[29] explains the reasons for imposing liability at the point when the decision leading to insolvency is made.

The existence of the fiduciary duties at the moment of insolvency may cause directors to choose a course of action that best serves the entire corporate enterprise rather than any single group interested in the corporation at a point in time when shareholders' wishes should not be the directors' only concern. Furthermore, the existence of the duties at the moment of insolvency rather than the institution of statutory proceedings prevents creditors from having to prophesy when directors are entering into transactions that would render the entity insolvent and improperly prejudice creditors' interests.

In *Brandt v. Hicks, Muse & Co. (In re Healthco Int'l, Inc.)*,[30] the court, drawing on this reasoning, held that the director's duty to the creditors existed the moment he or she acted in a way that likely caused the corporation to lack fairly-valued net worth or liquidity. The court noted, "When a transaction renders a corporation insolvent, or brings it to the brink of insolvency, the rights of creditors become paramount. In those circumstances, notwithstanding shareholder consent, a representative of the corporation may recover damage from the defaulting directors."

Direct actions by shareholders and creditors
The FDIC does not own – and thus has no power to litigate, settle or otherwise pursue – a shareholder's direct, non-derivative claims.[31] A direct claim "arising from breaches of duties owed to the Shareholder [or creditor] as opposed to the entity." Likewise, a holding company's bankruptcy trustee does not have standing to assert claims of those shareholders and creditors who have suffered individualized injuries not in common with other shareholders and creditors.[32] The primary basis of direct actions by creditors and shareholders is sourced in 10b-5 of the Securities and Exchange Act of 1934[33] and Section 11 of the Securities Act of 1933.[34] Class actions are prevalent where a director has issued materially misleading financial information to buyers and sellers of securities.

SEC
The SEC is authorized to pursue enforcement actions against directors which can result in civil money penalties, the issuance of permanent injunctions against directors enjoining them from future violations of security laws, and imprisonment.[35] Actions have been brought against directors for, among other things, participating in decisions to withhold a company's SEC filings, and backdating options. When the financial institution becomes the subject of an SEC inquiry or investigation, directors are often the ultimate targets of litigation.

IRS
A financial institution experiencing financial distress typically has a cash flow shortage and often begins to "slow pay" its creditors. As a practical matter payments that cannot be delayed, such as payroll, will be kept current.

A financial institution in distress will, however, be inclined to postpone payment of less pressing items. Management may, for example, be tempted to delay the payment of employee withholding taxes. All too often the institution reaches the day when it simply does not have sufficient cash to pay the withheld taxes to the IRS.[36] This very dark day for directors should be avoided at all costs. Civil and criminal penalties are severe. Personal financial liability for 100 per cent of the trust fund taxes can be imposed on "responsible persons" whose failure to collect or pay over the accrued taxes was reckless.[37] A responsible person is a person who knew or had reason to know of the unpaid taxes, had the means and failed to ensure the taxes were paid. A director who has in his or her possession financial statements or other board materials showing the overdue, unpaid, taxes is at grave risk.

Pension plans
If the financial institution is the sponsor of a pension plan, a director of the plan sponsor is subject to liability as a plan fiduciary to both the Department of Labor as well as the plan beneficiaries. A director is a plan fiduciary "to the extent he or she (i) exercises any discretionary authority or control over the management of the plan or any authority or control over management or disposition of its assets; (ii) renders investment advice for a fee or other compensation; or (iii) has discretionary authority or control in the administration of the plan."[38]

Similar to employment tax liabilities, directors who fail to forward employee contributions to 401(K) or other pension plans or who know that such amounts have not been forwarded and do not seek to have them forwarded are liable. Additionally, actions taken by the corporation that negatively affect plan assets can subject directors to personal liability. To the extent available, directors should be insured in their capacity as Employee Retirement Income Security Act (ERISA) plan fiduciaries which are not part of standard directors and officers (D&O) insurance. Additionally, to the extent an institution has a defined benefit plan, liability may exist to the extent the Pension Benefit Guaranty Corporation (PBGC) must make up the shortfall in benefits due to an underfunded plan.

Disgruntled borrowers
Lender liability litigation brought by borrowers against financial institutions was popular in the 1980s. However, where individual officers and directors were named as defendants, motions to dismiss the claims against them individually were often granted. Because directors are typically far removed from the day-to-day administration of loans, a borrower will have great difficulty establishing the necessary causal link between a director's conduct and the borrower's damage.

Sources of protection

When financial institution directors become litigation targets, they look to protection from both the indemnity provided by the corporation, the firm's D&O insurance and their own personal liability insurance. When these supposed protections are unavailable or inadequate, the director's personal assets are placed at risk.[39] Because the indemnification provided by an entity in financial distress is likely impaired and the director does not want to put his or her personal assets at risk, careful review of insurance coverage is critical.

Corporate indemnity

Corporations typically indemnify their officers and directors in the Articles of Incorporation.[40] The D&O claims of indemnity for prepetition acts or omissions are normally classified as unsecured, non-priority claims against the FDIC receiver or bankrupt holding company. As such they may be worth pennies on the dollar at distribution time. In other words, if a director is assessed damages of a million dollars, the one million dollar indemnity claim against the failed corporation may only give rise to a payment of $50 000 if the estate pays a five cent distribution. Additionally, where the director is owed money by the receiver or debtor, the threat of litigation against the director may be viewed as a bargaining chip to settle an affirmative claim of the director against the failed institution.[41] The bankruptcy trustee also has the weapon of equitable subordination in his or her arsenal of defenses to the D&O claims for indemnity.

Insurance[42]

Directors must closely review the details of the financial institution's insurance policies in order to determine whether the D&O coverage provides adequate protection. Additionally, because D&O insurance forms are continually evolving, directors should regularly consult with an insurance broker and counsel experienced with D&O insurance to ascertain whether new standard terms or possibilities provide enhanced coverages which should be included in their insurance. Certain key provisions warrant further mention:

1. *Insured versus insured exclusion*   D&O insurance policies often disallow coverage when one insured party (for example, the corporation) brings an action against another insured party (for example, the directors). In receivership or bankruptcy the insurer may argue that a claim brought by the trustee in bankruptcy against the directors is not covered by the policy because the trustee stands in the shoes of the corporation. A director will want to ensure that the D&O policy does not allow the FDIC or

trustee in bankruptcy to be deemed the corporation for this purpose or otherwise expand this exclusion.

2. *Regulatory exclusion* Standard D&O insurance policies exclude coverage for actions brought by a federal or state regulatory body such as the FDIC or SEC. This "regulatory exclusion" purports to preclude any government agency from recovering under the policy, even if the losses arising from the directors' wrongful acts would have been recoverable by other claimants such as a derivative action by shareholders of the financial institution prior to its closure by the FDIC.[43] In the 1980s government agencies were able to defeat regulatory exclusions "by arguing that they were vague, unenforceable and contrary to public policy." However, more recently courts have "largely upheld regulatory exclusions" as contractual provisions negotiated between the financial institution and the insurer.[44] This is a special concern to a financial institution's director who can thereby be left without coverage on what could turn out to be the largest claim against him or her.

3. *Shared limits* D&O insurance policies generally provide coverage for both the directors and officers and the corporation itself. This "entity coverage" could adversely affect directors to the extent that a policy's per-claim and aggregate limits are reached or reduced by claims in respect of the corporation's own liability and related defense costs. This risk may be mitigated in three ways.

One option is to create different sub-limits for the corporation on the one hand, and the directors and officers collectively on the other hand. However, even with separate sub-limits, if the insured entity is subject to FDIC receivership or a bankruptcy proceeding, the individual directors and officers can be adversely affected by substantial delays if the trustee or creditors contend that the policy or its proceeds are property of the FDIC or the parent bank holding company's estate. Understandably, insurance companies now regularly seek bankruptcy approval for payments to directors and officers if they perceive any risk that the D&O policy or its proceeds will be considered property of the debtor's estate. These delays can greatly complicate resolution of potential individual liability.

A second alternative is to amend the policy so as to provide that directors' and officers' coverage is paid before the corporation's. However, these amendments may come under attack by the FDIC or bankruptcy trustee.

The best alternative is to have completely separate primary or excess policies for individuals with limits that cannot be affected by claims against the corporation. A D&O policy that insures only individuals will not be treated as property of the FDIC or the parent bankruptcy estate.

4.   *Extended reporting periods or "tails"*   D&O coverage is written on a "claims made" basis, which requires notice of claims, or notice of circumstances which could lead to claims, to be submitted to the insurer during the policy term. These policies typically include a "retroactive date" which defines the earliest date for which the policy provides coverage for wrongful acts.

Under most state laws, a plaintiff has two years to sue a director for breach of duty or other negligent acts. This period typically does not begin to run until the plaintiff "discovers" the negligence. Where a corporation is "adversely dominated" by a board made up of potential defendants, this period may not begin to run on the corporation's derivative claims until the corporation is no longer adversely dominated. When a financial institution is placed in receivership or bankruptcy, the statute of limitations is further extended or "tolled" under federal law[45] during which period D&O insurance may expire. Extended reporting periods or "tail" coverage becomes critical for directors dealing with a financial institution in distress as does prompt notice of potential claims to the carrier. A director or group of directors should consider funding the purchase of the tail if the financial institution can or will no longer do so.

Additionally, when a bank or holding company changes D&O insurers, the new insurer may be unwilling to retain the retroactive date used in the previous policy. Under these circumstances, the directors should consider whether to purchase extended reporting under the previous policy, which would preserve the old retroactive date in order to allow a year or more to report claims under the old policy. Similarly, exercise of any extended reporting option should be considered whenever a new policy provides narrower coverage than an existing policy that is about to expire. For example, when the new policy excludes claims based on circumstances of which the insureds are aware, or acts that occurred prior to the inception of the new policy, an extended reporting period should be considered.

Some insurers are limiting the availability of extended reporting options and pricing those offered at historic highs. Options for one, two and three years are desirable in order to cover claims arising from acts prior to the policy's expiration even if made thereafter. For transactional matters, a six-year period may be desired and the insurer should be asked at inception to commit to offer it.

5.   *Misrepresentation in the application*   An insurance company may refuse to pay a claim for all insured parties where the person who signed the insurance application committed a misrepresentation. The policy should make clear that the misrepresentation by the signing officer does not affect

otherwise innocent directors (that is, that the misrepresentation is severable from the coverage available to the other insureds).

6.   *Fraud*   D&O policies typically excluded claims arising out of fraud. The exclusion should only apply if fraud is found by the court in a final judgment. Moreover, the fraud of one officer or director should not be allowed to be imputed to anyone else.

D&O policies typically include exclusions for claims that arise from a director's wrongful act done for personal benefit or through his or her intentional misconduct. Final judicial determination of personal benefit, fraud and intentional misconduct should be required for these exclusions to apply. Many insurers remove the "final adjudication" limitation on the applicability of these exclusions from standard policies, which makes coverage easier for the insurer to dispute.

7.   *Preferred counsel*   A director should make sure that the insurer does not restrict his or her choice of defense counsel. Often a panel list of approved counsels mandated by the insurer does not include the desired counsel. A director should make sure his or her desired counsel is on any such list when placing or renewing coverage.

8.   *Claims v. investigations*   A director should make sure that SEC inquiries and investigations constitute a "claim" under the policy. A financial institution can spend millions of dollars responding to an SEC inquiry or investigation prior to a lawsuit being filed, even if one is not ultimately filed. Coverage should be sought for these "defense" costs. The best approach is to obtain a policy that covers both SEC investigations and criminal charges against directors which arise out of those investigations.[46]

9.   *Other exclusions*   Directors and officers should seek to understand *all* of the exclusions included in the policy. Other exclusions typically included in D&O policies deny coverage for, among other things, criminal acts, punitive damages, claims resulting from ERISA violations, and terrorist acts. Obviously, the policy should not contain a "securities law" exclusion.

10.   *Excess coverage*   Directors should also consider seeking to have the financial institution obtain non-rescindable excess executive liability insurance. This type of insurance policy covers the independent directors when the underlying policy is rescinded or commuted, has its limits exhausted, or excludes the claim due to a restatement exclusion. This policy is not cancelable (except for non-payment of premiums), defines "securities claim" to

include claims brought by a bankruptcy trustee, and does not exclude coverage due to a financial reporting restatement or insider wrongdoing.

Directors may want to seek to negotiate a provision that requires the insurer to respond if the insured corporation itself does not honor its indemnification obligations, particularly for defense costs, within a defined period of time (30–90 days) after they have made a written demand on the financial institution (or FDIC or bankruptcy trustee). This provision limits out-of-pocket advances of costs by the directors.

11. *Adequacy of coverage*   The cost of D&O insurance for financial institutions and their affiliates continues to rise. Coverage is costly. As a practical matter, often by the time regulatory seizure or holding company bankruptcy occurs policies are inadequate to cover the exposure. In such circumstances the director's personal exposure becomes increasingly likely.

12. *Financial health of the insurer*   Finally, the potential director needs to be satisfied that the insurance company which provides the D&O policy is itself financially secure. A. M. Best rates insurers in terms of their financial soundness. A. M. Best's Financial Strength Rating (FSR) is an opinion of an insurer's ability to meet its obligations to policyholders. Those who would become directors should insist that their financial institution only do business with insurers that are FSR rated as either excellent (A, A−) or superior (A++, A+) if they are to become directors.

Personal exposure
A director's personal assets are at risk if insurance coverage is inadequate or unavailable because it is either voided or it excludes coverage for the actions complained of. As a result of aggressive legislative efforts by the FDIC and SEC, declaring personal bankruptcy in order to discharge many of these types of judgments is not an option.[47] Such debt is not dischargeable if it arises as a result of the director being "reckless" in his or her failure to fulfill any obligation to the FDIC to maintain the capital of the bank; for violating any securities laws or for certain taxes and penalties. In this event, the director faces claims against his or her personal assets.

A director should consider purchasing a personal umbrella policy which should, at a minimum, cover legal defense costs. Directors' fees can be set at a level to allow the director to recoup this cost.

Conclusion
We live in a litigious society. When government regulated institutions fail, blame must be assessed for both political and psychological reasons. Directors are often caught in the crossfire. Understanding the risks and

taking steps to avoid liability or, at a minimum, personal exposure, should be the primary goal for anyone considering a position as a bank director.

Notes

1. The full text of the statement is as follows:

   Duties of directors and officers
   Service as a director or officer of a federally insured bank represents an important business assignment that carries with it commensurate duties and responsibilities.

   Banks need to be able to attract and to retain experienced and conscientious directors and officers. When an institution becomes troubled, it is especially important that it have the benefit of the advice and direction of people whose experience and talents enable them to exercise sound and prudent judgment.

   Directors and officers of banks have obligations to discharge duties owed to their institution and to the shareholders and creditors of their institutions, and to comply with federal and state statutes, rules and regulations. Similar to the responsibilities owed by directors and officers of all business corporations, these duties include the duties of loyalty and care.

   The duty of loyalty requires directors and officers to administer the affairs of the bank with candor, personal honesty and integrity. They are prohibited from advancing their own personal or business interests, or those of others, at the expense of the bank.

   The duty of care requires directors and officers to act as prudent and diligent business persons in conducting the affairs of the bank.

   This means that directors are responsible for selecting, monitoring and evaluating competent management; establishing business strategies and policies; monitoring and assessing the progress of business operations; establishing and monitoring adherence to policies and procedures required by statute, regulation and principles of safety and soundness; and for making business decisions on the basis of fully informed and meaningful deliberation.

   Officers are responsible for running the day to day operations of the institution in compliance with applicable laws, rules, regulations and the principles of safety and soundness. This responsibility includes implementing appropriate policies and business objectives.

   Directors must require and management must provide the directors with timely and ample information to discharge board responsibilities. Directors also are responsible for requiring management to respond promptly to supervisory criticism. Open and honest communication between the board and management of the bank and the regulators is extremely important.

2. Frequently a combination of poor lending practices and operating in an industry or region that has become economically depressed triggers a rash of bank failures. For example the dramatic decline in the price of oil in the 1980s had a cascading effect in the Southwest as not only loans to oil companies but also loans collateralized by real estate that depended on the health of the regional economy became troubled and in many cases went into default. As these loan losses mounted up, the banks' balance sheets saw their equity erode and eventually become negative.

3. Section 365(o) of the Bankruptcy Code provides:

   In a case under chapter 11 of this title, the trustee shall be deemed to have assumed (consistent with the debtor's other obligations under section 507), and shall immediately cure any deficit under, any commitment by the debtor to a Federal depository institution's regulatory agency (or predecessor to such agency) to maintain the capital of an insured depository institution, and any claim for a subsequent breach of the obligations thereunder shall be entitled to priority under Section 507. This subsection shall not extend any commitment that would otherwise be terminated by any act of such an agency.

See also *In re Overland Park Fin. Corp.*, 236 F.3d 1246 (10th Cir. 2001) (A "commitment" is not required to take the form of an enforceable contract to be binding upon a debtor. A chapter 11 debtor who signed prepetition, a stipulation acknowledging an obligation to maintain or infuse capital into a savings and loan institution, was found to have made a commitment sufficient to invoke section 365(o) and was required to assume and cure any deficit under that capital maintenance commitment).

4. Pursuant to its authority under the Bank Holding Company Act, the Federal Reserve promulgated Regulation Y (12 USC 225.4(a)(1) which is the "source of strength doctrine"; see also *Board of Governors v. First Lincolnwood Corp.*, 439 U.S. 234 (1978)).

5. See Adam B. Ashcroft, "Are bank holding companies a source of strength to their subsidiaries?" FRBNY Staff Report No. 189, June 2004.

6. *Branch v. FDIC*, 825 F.Supp. (D. Mass 1993).

7. The regulation is motivated by two important considerations. First, the insurance protection provided by the FDIC motivates the regulators to monitor and when necessary intervene in the operations of banks in order to mitigate the loss exposure to the Bank Insurance Fund (BIF) maintained by the FDIC. The FDIC does not want the insured losses from bank failures to threaten its own financial health. Additionally, the nation's banking system is a key component of our economy. A healthy financial industry is crucial to maintaining a vibrant economy. Moreover, the safety of the deposits of depositors is of paramount importance to the voters who have elected those who run the government and appoint those who do the regulating. For all of these reasons, federally insured depository institutions are heavily regulated.

8. 384 F. Supp. 1039 (S.D. Tex. 2005). The judge noted that the FDIC had been chastised for its "miscreant behavior," it's "foot-dragging," a "piecemeal approach to document production," and "persistent recalcitrance"; its "Protean mutability" and a "carapacial nature" that allowed it to disobey court orders; and a "confused, obstructionist, inept, and uncooperative litigating style," an "unjustified procrastination," a "Machiavellian ploy aimed at delaying the preparation of these cases for disposition," a "blatantly false assertion that the court was without jurisdiction," a "Falstaffian bit of trial tactics," and "dilatory tactics"; its "manifest" abuse of power. Noting that when the FDIC "failed to conduct reasonable inquiry into the law," "the only reasonable explanation" for the FDIC's suit was to "harass" the defendant, "to burden it with costs of litigation," and "to extract an unwarranted settlement payment" . . . the conduct of the FDIC and its counsel was "outrageous and that there was no possible justification for the infliction on [the defendant] or the judicial system for such unmeritorious litigation" (citations omitted).

9. Barry M. Staw, Sigal G. Barsade and Kenneth W. Koput (1997), "Escalation at the credit window: a longitudinal study of bank executives' recognition and write-off of problem loans," *Journal of Applied Psychology*, **82**(1), 130–42.

10. OCC's Quarterly Report on Bank Derivatives Activities, first Quarter, 2007; "How much do banks use credit derivatives to reduce risk," Bernadette A. Minton, René Stulz, and Rohan Williamson, working paper, http://www.cob.ohio-state.edu/fin/dice/papers/2005/2005-17.pdf.

11. Ibid.

12. The authors gratefully acknowledge permission granted by Karen L. Grandstrand to reprint in this section portions of her article "Enforcement actions: has much changed in the last decade?" accessed September 2002, at www.fredlaw.com/articles/banking.

13. The July 2002 enforcement action against the PNC Financial Services Group, Inc. was issued jointly by the Federal Reserve and SEC.

14. FDIC Financial Institutions Letter (FIL-87-92), 3 December 1992.

15. Minnino, Lender Liability and Banking Litigation § 11.03[c] (Law Journal Press, 2007).

16. § 6.40.

17. Model Business Corporation Act § 6.40 comment 2 (1984).

18. Model Business Corporation Act § 6.40 comment 4(b) (1984).
19. MBCA does not provide a specific cause of action by the corporation against the recipient of the dividend. Presumably because those states that have adopted the MBCA have fraudulent conveyance statutes.
20. Model Business Corporation Act comment (1984).
21. *In re Southeast Banking Corp.*, 827 F. Supp. 742, 745 (S.D. Fla. 1993) and 855 F. Supp 353 (S.D. Fla. 1994).
22. Title 12 U.S.C. § 1821(d)(z)(A)(i).
23. See *In re Sunrise*, 916 F.2d at 886-88; *Gaff*, 814 F.2d at 315 (dismissing claims of shareholder of insolvent bank against officers and directors because they were derivative and can only be brought by receiver); *Hymel v. Federal Home Loan Bank Board*, C.A. No. 87-2909, 1991 WL 126365, at *6 (E.D. La. Jun. 28, 1991); *In re Longhorn Sec. Litig.*, 573 F. Supp. 255, 272-73 (W.D. Okla. 1983); see also *Bennett v. Centerpoint Bank*, 761 F. Supp. 908, 913 (D.N.H.) (RICO action based on bank fraud belongs to bank, which is real party in interest), *aff'd mem.*, 953 F.2d 634 (1st Cir. 1991).
24. *Pepper v. Litton*, 308 U.S. 295, 307 (1939); *Mitchell Excavators, Inc. v. Mitchell*, 734 F.2d 129, 131 (2d Cir 1984); 4 Collier on Bankruptcy ¶541,10[8], at 541-72 (15th edn). "[T]hat standard of fiduciary obligation is designed for the protection of the entire community of interests in the corporation creditors as well as stockholders." *Pepper*, 308 U.S. at 307.
25. See *Delgado Oil Co., Inc. v. Torres*, 785 F.2d 857, 860-61 (10th Cir. 1986) (trustee of bankruptcy estate succeeds to right to bring action for corporate mismanagement against directors and officers of debtor corporation for benefit of all creditors of the estate). *S.I. Acquisition Service, Inc. v. Eastway Delivery Service, Inc. (In re S.I. Acquisition, Inc.)*, 817 F.2d 1142, 1150-54 (5th Cir. 1987) (claim against parent company of debtor corporation to pierce corporate veil, although ordinarily creditor's action, is property of the estate and belongs to the trustee under § 548(a)(1) of the Bankruptcy Code); *The American National Bank of Austin v. MortgageAmerica Corp. (In re MortgageAmerica Corp.)*, 714 F.2d 1266, 1275 (5th Cir. 1983) (action by creditor under the trust fund and the Texas Fraudulent Transfers Act properly belonged to the bankruptcy estate); *ANR Ltd. Inc. v. Chattin*, 89 B.R. 898, 901-02 (D. Utah 1988) (noting that Delgado Oil supports the proposition that certain claims of creditors can be grouped among claims for corporate mismanagement that are property of the bankruptcy estate); *Dana Molded Products, Inc. v. Brodner*, 58 B.R. 576 (N.D. Ill. 1986) (creditor lacked standing under RICO to sue for fraud which was committed against corporation in an attempt to hinder creditors generally); see also *In re STN Enterprises*, 779 F.2d at 904-05 (creditors committee can bring such a claim when Chapter 11 Trustee or debtor in possession fails to do so); *Koch Refining v. Farmers Union Cent. Exchange, Inc.*, 831 F.2d 1339, 1349 (7th Cir. 1987), *cert. denied*, 485 U.S. 906 (1988) (where liability to creditors arises without regard to personal dealings between officers and creditors, claim is general and may be maintained by Trustee as a creditors under the "strong-arm" provision of § 544 of the Bankruptcy Code).
26. *Dana Molded Products, Inc. v. Brodner*, 58 B.R. at 578–79.
27. *Koch Refining v. Farmers Union Cent. Exchange, Inc.*, 831 F.2d at 1341-46 (7th Cir. 1987); *In re MortgageAmerica Corp.*, 714 F.2d at 1277 (trust fund "denuding" claim).
28. *Credit Lyonnais Bank Nederland, N.V. v. Pathe Communications Corporation*, 1991 WL 277613 (Del. Ch.) p. 83 & n. 55; *accord Geyer v. Ingersoll Publications Company*, 621 A.2d 784, 1992 WL 455473 (Del. Ch.) at 3-5; *Clarkson So. Ltd. v. Shaheen*, 660 F.2d 506, 512 & n. 5 (2d Cir. 1981) (applying New York law), *cert. denied*, 455 U.S. 990 (1982); see *Francis v. United Jersey Bank*, 87 N.J. 15, 36, 432 A.2d 814, 824 (1981) citing *Whitfield v. Kern*, 122 N.J. Eq. 332, 341, 192 A. 48 (1937); *McGivern v. AMASA Lumber Company*, 77 Wisc. 2d 241, 252 N.W. 2d 371, 378–79 (1977); see also *Unsecured Creditors Committee of Debtor STN Enterprises, Inc. v. Noyes (In re STN Enterprises)*, 779 F.2d 901, 904–05 (2d Cir. 1985) (most states recognize such a duty).
29. 621 A.2d 784, 789 (Del. Ch. 1992). See also Andrew D. Shaffer (2000), "Corporate fiduciary-insolvent: the fiduciary relationship your corporate law professor (should have) warned you about," 8 *American Bankruptcy Institute Law Review* 479, 519.

30. 208 B.R. 288, 300 302 (Bankr. D. Mass. 1997).
31. See, for example, *Gaff v. Federal Deposit Ins. Corp.*, 919 F.2d 384,396 (6th Cir. 1990) (FDIC does not own the stockholder's non-derivative causes of action against the officers and directors of a failed bank), *modified on other grounds*, 933 F.2d 400 (5th Cir. 1991); *Howard v. Haddad*, 916 F.2d 167, 170 (4th Cir. 1990) (FDIC's claim does not deprive a shareholder of his own, non-derivative causes of action); *Harmsen v. Smith*, 693 F.2d 932, 941 & n.7 (9th Cir. 1983), *Cert. denied*, 464 U.S. 822 (1983) (although "a derivative claim could only have been brought . . . by the FDIC," shareholders nevertheless had standing to pursue individual causes of action).
32. See for example, *Cumberland Oil Corp. v. Thropp*, 791 F.2d 1037, 1042 (2d Cir. 1986), *cert. denied*, 479 U.S. 950 (1986) (fraud claim of contract creditor against the president of oil drilling company belonged to creditor personally and was not properly a part of estate in bankruptcy). Cases hold that shareholders have a direct action where they have been specifically misled by officers and directors to purchase bank or holding company stock. See *Hurley v. FDIC*, 719 F. Supp. 27, 30 (D. Mass. 1989) (shareholders who specifically relied on statements by bank's officers and directors could maintain Rule 10b-5 action); *Howard v. Haddad*, 916 F.2d 167, 170 (4th Cir. 1990) (plaintiff shareholder of failed bank alleged injury distinct from other shareholder when he alleged that two directors directly and specifically solicited him to purchase bank stock while misrepresenting the poor financial condition of the institution).
33. Rule 10b-5 under the Securities Exchange act of 1934 makes illegal in connection with the purchase or sale of any security the use of any means of interstate commerce, the mail system or any national securities exchange to (i) employ any device, scheme or artifice to defraud (ii) make any untrue statement of a material fact or to omit to state a material fact necessary in order to make the statements, in the light of the circumstances under which they were made, not misleading or (iii) engage in any act, practice, or course of business which operates or would operate as a fraud or deceit upon any person.
34. Section 11(a) of the Securities Act of 1933 provides that a person who purchased a security covered by a registration statement may recover damages from, among others, the directors who sign the registration statement, if any part of the registration statement, when it became effective, (i) contained a mis-statement of a material fact or (ii) omitted to state a material fact that was either required to be stated in the registration statement or was necessary to make the statements in the registration statement not misleading. A majority of the board of directors are required to sign the registration statement. Although only a majority of the directors of the issuer are required to sign the registration statement, each director has potential Section 11 liability, including those persons who consent to act as a director. Stephen E. Older and Jack R.T. Jordan (1999), "Staying out of trouble: officer and director liability in connection with registration statements; how to draft documents to limit liability," Andrews Corporate Risk Spectrum, November.
35. Devin M. LaCroix (2006), "Outside director liability: recent SEC enforcement actions," the D&O Diary, 29 November.
36. Henderson, Gordon D. and Stuart J. Goldring (2007), *Tax Planning for Troubled Companies*, accessed at CCH.com.
37. Internal Revenue Code § 6672.
38. C. Frederick Reich and Joseph C. Faucher (1998), "What's in a name? – Director and officer liability under ERISA," *WP & BC News* (Summer), citing ERISA § 3(21)(A).
39. BNEC had $25 million coverage prior to the public disclosure of its financial woes. Thereafter, it struggled to obtain a $5 million policy at a premium cost of approximately $1.6 million. Following the bankruptcy filing, the carrier threatened to deny coverage based upon allegations that the questionnaires completed in connection with BNEC's application for renewal did not adequately disclose the *magnitude* of BNEC's financial woes. The joint holding company/bank directors faced litigation by FDIC, the holding company bankruptcy trustees and shareholders.
40. See generally, Delaware Corporation Laws.

41. Claims can include such things as deferred compensation, director's fees and expense reimbursements.
42. The authors gratefully acknowledge permission granted by Valerie Ford Jacob on behalf of herself and her colleagues at Fried, Frank, Shriver & Jacobson LLP, Richard A. Brown, Stuart Gelfond, Robert Juceam, Michael Levitt, Paul H. Falon, Timothy E. Peterson and Daniel J. Bursky to reprint in this section portions of their client memoranda "D&O insurance: what directors and officers should be thinking about in the Sarbanes-Oxley world" (11 March 2003).
43. "Managing the crisis: the FDIC and RTC experience" (FDIC 1997).
44. *Ibid.*
45. 11 USCA § 108(a) (bank holding companies in bankruptcy); FIRREA 12 USC § 1821(d)(14)(A) (for insured depository institutions).
46. Stephen J. Weiss and Thomas H. Bentz, Jr (2005), "Ways to improve your D&O insurance coverage," The Metropolitan Corporate Counsel, November.
47. Section 523 of the Bankruptcy Code provides:

> § 523. Exceptions to discharge.
> (a) A discharge under section 727, 1141, 1228(a), 1228(b), or 1328(b) of this title does not discharge an individual debtor from any debt –
> (4) for fraud or defalcation while acting in a fiduciary capacity, embezzlement, or larceny;
> (11) provided in any final judgment, unreviewable order, or consent order or decree entered in any court of the United States or of any State, issued by a Federal depository institutions regulatory agency, or contained in any settlement agreement entered into by the debtor, arising from any act of fraud or defalcation while acting in a fiduciary capacity committed with respect to any depository institution or insured credit union;
> (12) for malicious or reckless failure to fulfill any commitment by the debtor to a Federal depository institutions regulatory agency to maintain the capital of an insured depository institution, except that this paragraph shall not extend any such commitment which would otherwise be terminated due to any act of such agency;
> (19) that –
> (A) is for –
> (i) the violation of any of the Federal securities laws (as that term is defined in section 3(a)(47) of the Securities Exchange Act of 1934), any of the State securities laws, or any regulation or order issued under such Federal or State securities laws; or
> (ii) common law fraud, deceit, or manipulation in connection with the purchase or sale of any security; and
> (c)(1) Except as provided in subsection (a)(3)(B) of this section, the debtor shall be discharged from a debt of a kind specified in paragraph (2), (4) or (6) of subsection (a) of this section unless, on request of the creditor to whom such debt is owed, and after notice and a hearing, the court determines such debt to be excepted from discharge under paragraph (2), (4) or (6), as the case may be, of subsection (a) of this section.
> (2) Paragraph (1) shall not apply in the case of a Federal depository institutions regulatory agency seeking, in its capacity as conservator, receiver, or liquidating agent for an insured depository institution, to recover a debt described in subsection (a)(2), (a)(4), (a)(6), or (a)(11) owed to such institution by an institution-affiliated party [as defined in section 3(U) of the Federal Deposit Insurance Act] unless the receiver, conservator, or liquidating agent was appointed in time to reasonably comply, or for a Federal depository institutions regulatory agency acting in its corporate capacity as a successor to such receiver, conservator, or liquidating agent to reasonably comply, with subsection (a)(3)(B) as a creditor of such institution-affiliated party with respect to such debt.
> (e) Any institution-affiliated party of an insured depository institution shall be considered to be acting in a fiduciary capacity with respect to the purposes of subsection (a)(4) or (11).

6 Corporate social responsibility: renegotiating corporate citizenship
Barbara Parker

Corporate social responsibility (CSR) is not a new concept, but as this chapter shows, reasons for corporations to pursue social responsibility initiatives as well as the extent and range of CSR practices are new to many if not most organizations. In the US almost all business leaders traditionally viewed their social responsibilities as those generally put forward by economist Milton Friedman: the social responsibility of business is to use its resources and engage in activities designed to increase its profits so long as it stays within the rules of the game. Countless business leaders still share Friedman's view of corporate social responsibility, believing that successful businesses produce social goods in the form of jobs, tax revenues, desired goods and services and profits. The point is that social responsibility of the passive, jobs- and profit-generating sort is nothing new.

Nor is there anything particularly new about corporate philanthropic giving which in the US was exemplified by early business leaders such as Andrew Carnegie, John D. Rockefeller, and J.P. Morgan. Using personal wealth and corporate foundations, these and other business leaders helped establish libraries, universities, art galleries, and health care, and they pursued other initiatives whose benefits continue to pay social dividends. Corporate foundations in the US now number somewhere around 2600 and this is without counting more than 36 000 independent foundations that families or donors establish; the Bill and Melinda Gates Foundation is an example of the latter. Thus, it is not new for corporations or their leaders to use profits to generate social goods. What is new is that the number, size and range of issues supported by corporations have increased in recent years.

Also new in recent years is that businesses of every size increasingly play active roles to further define corporate citizenship or corporate social responsibility. In this active phase, CSR increasingly is defined as a voluntary commitment to exceed explicit and implicit social obligations (Falck and Heblich, 2007). Large, global businesses from industrialized economies are especially likely to engage in voluntary CSR activities. In doing so, corporate leaders increasingly view corporate social responsibility initiatives as a way to negotiate and even renegotiate their roles as corporate citizens.

The next section examines why businesses adopt increasingly sophisticated CSR roles. The third section presents a continuum for CSR activities, and the fourth provides examples illustrative of the wide range of CSR practices in which businesses today engage.

Reasons for CSR initiatives

Beginning in the 1990s, social expectations encouraged businesses to integrate self-interest with community interest. Due to globalization, by which I mean growing worldwide interconnections in almost every sphere of activity, communities are increasingly international and even global (Waddock and Boyle, 1995). This expands business communities well beyond those of companies' founding nations. An expanding and more global sense of community and growing worldwide interconnections are factors that generate corporate interest in and engagement with civil society. Additionally, rather than act autonomously in each community in which they operate, global businesses increasingly find it more efficient to integrate among community interests on a worldwide basis. This they do by creating integrative social responsibility initiatives applicable to and appropriate for all or most of the communities where they operate. Worldwide integration in this and other activities may help global organizations adapt to and anticipate external shifts, but it also alters organizational autonomy. Further, managerial complexity increases when managers begin to interact with multiple constituencies simultaneously and to integrate among them.

On the demand side, the rapid, discontinuous changes that are part of recent globalization generate many uncertainties that individuals increasingly manage by connecting with and working to influence activities of large and powerful organizations. Global businesses that dominate Western society often are the target of citizen action because the former operate in a wide variety of domains and activities and are believed to have considerable clout within the capitalist system (Lawrence and Hardy, 1999). This perception of business clout and fears of it are encouraged by titles such as *When Corporations Rule the World* (Korten, 1995) and *The Corporation: The Pathological Pursuit of Profit and Power* (Bakan, 2004) and by studies that unfavorably compare annual revenues for global businesses and national GDPs (Anderson and Cavanagh, 2005). The latter report that among the top 100 annual revenue earners, 52 are businesses; Wal-Mart appears in position 16. These and many documentaries unfavorable to business interests generate public fear of and low trust in businesses. For example, public trust in businesses 'to do what is right' stands at 49 per cent in the US compared to 42 per cent in Europe and a high of 62 per cent in Brazil (Edelman, 2006).

Demonstrations accompanying WTO, IMF, World Bank, and G8 meetings, as well as institutional and individual pressure at corporate meetings and product or company boycotts provide further evidence of citizen concerns about "big business" activities. Some citizens advance their own efforts to interconnect with and influence business activities through direct action such as email campaigns or lobbying boards of directors, but they also achieve collective power via membership and support for global non-governmental organizations (NGOs) such as Greenpeace, the WWF, and similar entities. Interestingly, public trust in NGOs has increased in recent years (Edelman, 2006), perhaps explaining why citizens increasingly connect with NGOs to effect business change.

Many global businesses respond to citizen and NGO initiatives by involving external or secondary stakeholders in their decision-making processes. Broadly defined, stakeholders are individuals and groups who are affected by or can affect company decisions. Traditionally, primary stakeholders were believed to be stockholders, but increasingly other immediate stakeholders, such as employees, labor unions, customers, and suppliers (Clarkson, 1995) have gained corporate attention. Secondary stakeholders include non-governmental organizations, social activists, community groups, and governmental organizations (Waddock et al., 2002). Other external stakeholders can be those who live in communities near global company sites or where the company's products are sold. Many of these stakeholders take an active interest in CSR activities – particularly environmental sustainability – and some businesses actively work with NGO stakeholders to reach business decisions. For example, insurance companies work with Human Rights Watch to track and report the effects of changes in weather patterns or consumption of global commons like air and water. Wal-Mart worked with a former Sierra Club leader to develop a voluntary Personal Sustainability Project for its employees wherein each is encouraged to take one step that will benefit the planet and improve his or her life; examples of life improvements include quitting smoking, altering dietary habits, and exercising more. Other businesses are less inclined to involve NGOs or their leaders in business decisions or activities, but many now seek citizen input prior to making important decisions.

CSR initiatives clearly are important to a global public. For example, a study of 25 000 consumers in 23 nations showed that two-thirds of those surveyed want companies to go beyond fiscal responsibility and to take on social roles (DiPiazza, 2002). In a 2002 study of British adults, half said that a company should give equal attention to society, the environment, and financial performance (The public's view, 2002). Although public concern about the natural environment is long-standing in Europe, the US public has only recently demonstrated heightened interest in the environment.

According to a 2007 environmental survey, 93 per cent of US citizens now believe companies have a responsibility to help preserve the environment (Cone current happenings, 2007). Research also shows that public opinion about a company is based in part on CSR activities, suggesting that corporate social responsibility contributes to an organization's reputational capital. For companies that rely on brands, reputation is especially important.

Three situations that reportedly erode corporate reputation are weak internal coordination, non-alignment between reputation and reality, and when people reject what has worked successfully for the company in the past (Eccles et al., 2007). An example of the latter is tobacco companies that no longer enjoy public support for smoking. Weak internal coordination occurs when reputation-building efforts are not well integrated with other organizational activities. For example, information from offices of corporate affairs that monitor pending laws and regulations or corporate communications offices that monitor the media and marketing surveys of customers is often not shared beyond those offices. Thus one group may create expectations that another group cannot fulfill. While CSR activities may improve a company's image when consumers perceive sincere motives, they are ineffective when motives are ambiguous, and can damage a company's image when motives are perceived to be insincere (Yoon et al., 2006).

Due to globalization of information, people located everywhere and any-where can be well informed – and misinformed – about business activities. Evidence shows that monthly media volume on CSR issues has almost quadrupled between 2000 and 2003 in Europe, the US, China, Australia, and South Africa (Echo Research, 2003). Additionally, social responsibility measures are recent additions to business rating systems, for example, *Fortune*'s annual list of "Global Most Admired" companies. Some believe that increases in public ratings or ranking schemes have generated "a major source of pressure on companies' stakeholder-related performance (or social responsibility)" (Waddock et al., 2002, p. 137).

However, corporate misinformation abounds, often found on anti-corporate websites targeting corporations in general or specific businesses. Companies monitor these sites, often with searches of "Ihate[company-name].com" and "[companyname]sucks.com." Many documentaries and films critiquing organizational practices are also available. These many sources of information help individuals monitor and respond to corporations in a very direct fashion. To no one's great surprise, corporations often find they must play a more affirmative and active information management role; doing so further interconnects them in active, and often un-accustomed, ways with social networks.

Globalization has also fostered a shift from primary reliance on bricks and mortar to a more knowledge-based work world. One result is enhanced competition for intellectual talent in most industries. Unlike the tangible assets of manufacturing that businesses traditionally own, intangible assets, such as creativity, innovation, and knowledge-generation, depend on human intellect that individuals own. Many firms find that CSR initiatives help them hire and retain the people they want, thus providing an edge in the competition for intellectual talent. Business decision-makers believe CSR initiatives help them attract, retain, and motivate employees (Echo Research, 2003). A US study showed that employee morale is higher in organizations that are involved in their communities (Lewin and Sabater, 1996). An example is freight firm TNT which when measuring employee satisfaction found that 94 per cent of employees approve TNT's responsible attitude toward the community.

CSR initiatives are increasingly viewed as having a direct relationship with business performance (Lewin and Sabater, 1996). For example, firms that pursued a triple bottom line of economic, environmental, and social sustainability outperformed the global index (Green is good, 1999). Businesses leaders with CSR processes in place believe that rather than being a substitute for profitability, social responsibility is a means of achieving profitability. For example, the Millennium Poll of over 1000 CEOs in 33 nations in Europe, Asia, and the Americas indicates that most CEOs think responsible behavior toward employees, shareholders, and communities is a core concern for firm profitability (DiPiazza, 2002).

Corporate social responsibility initiatives
The focus of CSR initiatives varies widely by company, industry, and nation or region of the world. For example, environmental sustainability has long been an important CSR concern in Western Europe. A common CSR approach is for companies to align citizenship objectives with company business models that fit the industry, firm, issues, and communities served (Post, 2000). For example, companies like Levi Strauss focus CSR energies on child labor because their suppliers operate in countries where child labor occurs. IKEA focuses CSR activities on child labor issues for the same reason, but its reliance on forestry products also results in CSR initiatives around responsible forestry. These and other firms in a variety of industries often create operating guidelines for suppliers that lay out company stances toward child labor. IKEA similarly creates these guidelines for wood suppliers. British Petroleum's CSR initiatives rotate around energy use. At the same time, these and many other firms also participate in alliances that encourage and approve social responsibility. An example is the Global Compact to which over 3000 global firms subscribe, agreeing to support and protect human and worker rights, such as collective bargaining, to eliminate employment discrimination, and initiate environmentally

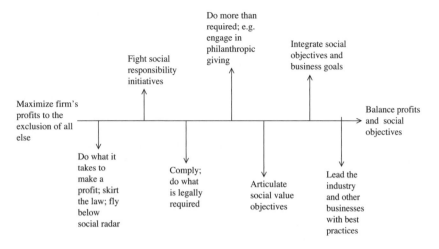

Figure 6.1   A corporate social responsibility continuum

sustainable practices. These companies also agree to voluntarily report progress on these and other social and environmental initiatives. Many firms undertake major environmental CSR projects because environmental preservation and sustainability are core concerns for consumers.

Figure 6.1 provides general categories of activities to locate companies on a CSR continuum. These categories illustrate selected CSR positions; they are by no means exhaustive but provide useful illustrations for the wide range of CSR practices found today.

Firms that adopt no to minimum CSR initiatives occupy the three positions on the left of the continuum. For example on the far left is the firm that puts profit motives ahead of all social objectives. This firm ignores CSR initiatives, will put profits ahead of social goods, and may be willing to engage in illegal or unethical behaviors to achieve its goals. An example of this firm is the painting subcontractor to Chinese toy manufacturer Early Light that circumvented Mattel's safety checks to acquire leaded paint from an unapproved supplier. Firms that use illegal or unethical practices are unlikely to survive in the long run, but in the short run they may earn profits and be a competitive challenge for firms that do conform to legal or ethical guidelines. Firms that take this position are found in developing and developed economies alike, but they tend to operate in low profile industries that attract limited public interest, and they find it easiest to operate in nations where rules of law are vague, transparency is opaque, and corruption is frequent. These conditions combine to make China a dumping ground for electronic waste from advanced economies; the companies exporting e-waste are not breaking laws, but their leaders cannot be unaware that e-waste generates toxic run-off and threatens worker health.

At the second point on the continuum is the firm that fights CSR initiatives, often by denying, avoiding, defying or manipulating evidence in support of CSR. This company usually conforms to laws because active opposition to social initiatives puts it above the public's radar screen. An example of "fight" behavior emerged from Exxon which reportedly spent nearly $16 million between 1998 and 2004 to amplify reports from climate contrarians and delay government action that would require corporations to reduce their heat-trapping emissions (Shulman, 2007, p. 5). According to Shulman and the Union of Concerned Scientists who sponsored his 2007 report, tobacco companies also tended to fight pending legislative change affecting the industry, having engaged in a 40-year "disinformation campaign" that "misled the public about the incontrovertible scientific evidence linking smoking to lung cancer and heart disease" (p. 3).

Environmental concerns expressed by the first Earth Day in 1970 similarly elicited negative business responses; some businesses ignored or fought environmental regulations. Major concerns were three: that environmental activities were not the responsibility of businesses; that environmental efforts would make businesses less competitive worldwide; and that applying stricter developed world environmental standards in developing economies would bring charges of business extraterritoriality (imposition of one nation's standards on another). Other businesses ignore stakeholders. For example, both Ahold and the Dutch building industry were observed to avoid and neglect stakeholder power and pressures (Kolk and Pinkse, 2006). As a group, these examples illustrate ways in which firms fight, manipulate and deny or ignore public thinking about social responsibility initiatives. Firms that fight CSR at one point in time sometimes move further along the CSR continuum at a later point. For example, DuPont initially resisted CFC regulations but later became a champion for environmental sustainability.

In the third position on the CSR continuum is a firm that complies with rather than fights CSR laws. This company reflects Friedman's dictate on social responsibility, using its resources exclusively to engage in activities that increase its profits. A firm in this position differs from that found in position two because rather than bear costs associated with fighting pending legislation, it watches and waits. When conforming to new legislation or social norms, it is likely to be a follower rather than a leader. In this category, firms may be positioned to make a transition from a basic law-abiding stance further to engage with broader definitions of corporate citizenship and social responsibility (Mirvis and Googins, 2006).

Firms that exceed CSR minimums cluster at the middle and on the right-hand side of the continuum. These firms engage in a wide range of CSR activities, but a common theme is that all are at an 'engagement' or active stage of corporate citizenship that represents a different view of the company's role in society (Mirvis and Googins, 2006). Sometimes an engaged stage of social responsibility results in episodic or one-time CSR efforts such as sponsorship of a community event or one-time philanthropic giving. An example of the latter is McDonald's 2007 partnership with the International Olympic Committee and China Central Television to produce a reality show competition to send Chinese children to the Beijing Olympics. Other times leaders integrate CSR with other organizational practices. In general, movement to the right of the continuum is accompanied by increasing levels of integration between CSR initiatives and an organization's existing processes, people and structures. Below are examples of how this occurs.

Example of contemporary CSR practices

Philanthropic giving
Philanthropic giving is a traditional way for companies to demonstrate good citizenship and social responsiveness. It is a form of CSR available to small firms as well as large ones. Corporate philanthropic giving today ranges in amount and impact from youth team sponsorships to substantial donations to charitable organizations. Estimates for this type of CSR activity vary. For example, the Giving USA Foundation reports that total corporate giving increased in 2005 to $13.77 billion. Corporate giving in the US coming only from its 2600 corporate foundations totaled $4.2 billion in 2006 (Giving by corporate foundations, 2007) including pharmaceutical operating foundations that provide mostly in-kind support. Various reports indicate that charitable giving on the part of corporations has increased steadily (Charity holds, 2003). The Foundation Center indicates that corporate giving doubled from 1987 to 2004 (Charitable giving, 2006), and that corporate foundation giving reached a record $4.2 billion in 2006 (Key facts, 2006). About half of corporate foundation giving goes to education and public affairs or social benefits such as community development or civil rights (Giving by, 2007), but the range of issues companies fund also has increased in recent years. For example, the Ford Fund recently pledged $250 000 to construction of a lesbian and gay community center in Michigan.

An integrative form of charitable giving is called strategic philanthropy wherein a corporation gives to a cause aligned with one or more of its core businesses. For example, Avon Products Inc. "the company for women" donates funds to breast cancer research. Many believe this form of philanthropy is in the best long-term interests of shareholders (Benioff and Southwick, 2004).

Some companies donate gifts such as volunteer time or goods. For example, pharmaceutical giant Johnson & Johnson donates medical supplies to Operation Smile – a charitable organization that repairs cleft lips and palates for children worldwide. Deloitte Touche, as another example, pays for employees to volunteer time, and major corporations such as Boeing provide executive release time to head charitable campaigns for organizations like the United Way. According to the Center for Corporate Citizenship, some 90 per cent of companies offer opportunities for their employees to volunteer; only some pay regular wages for volunteer time.

On the face of it, it might seem that corporate giving of funds, in-kind goods, or employee time always enhances a corporation's public reputation. But findings from the Reputation Institute (Alsop, 2002a) indicate that philanthropy will not enhance corporate reputation if a company (a) fails to live up to its philanthropic image or (b) if consumers perceive philanthropy to be manipulative. For example, some members of the public take a cynical view of Philip Morris's charitable giving because the company's products generate social costs due to heart diseases and lung cancer (Alsop, 2002b).

Alsop (2004a) suggests it is sometimes difficult to balance image and action. For example, both Procter & Gamble and Honda Motor Company donated supplies in the aftermath of New York terrorist attacks in 2001. Both companies decided not to publicize their involvement, but this provided room for criticism from those who thought the companies had done nothing.

Cause-related marketing
Other companies initiate 'cause-related' marketing initiatives. According to Paul Carringer (n.d.) the first recorded efforts of a business and a charity to raise awareness and funds for an issue was undertaken by a New York City candy company in 1902. This method of 'selling with a conscience' was later revived by American Express, which in 1983 raised over $1.7 million for the Statue of Liberty and Ellis Island Foundation. More recently, many more firms have pursued this approach to social responsibility. In one variation, the company donates a portion of sales on selected products to the charitable organization. For example, IKEA donates a portion on sales of its Brum soft toy to UNICEF efforts that help children recover from armed conflicts in Angola and Uganda; Welch Foods Inc. and Johnson & Johnson donate a portion of sales on particular products to WWF. Worldwide initiatives like these increased revenues for causes from $75 million in 1988 to $535 million by 1997 (Kadlec and Van Voorst, 1997). Another approach is for groups to raise money by clipping box tops that are later redeemed by the company; an example is the 'Box Tops for Education' program through which schools earn 10 cents for every box top clipped from participating

company products. Several companies participate in the box top program, but Campbell's has its own program that similarly donates money to schools for each Campbell's label submitted.

Cause-related marketing is usually an integral part of the company's marketing efforts, and many of these campaigns enhance the public's view of the organization. For example, a study of US households revealed that 83 per cent of people have a more positive image of a product or company when the company supports a cause they care about. Sixty-six per cent viewed cause-related marketing as a good way to help solve social problems, and 61 per cent thought it should be a standard company activity (Companies and causes, 2000). In the same study, two-thirds of consumers say that if price and quality are equal, they are likely to switch to a brand or retailer backing a good cause. In a British study, cause-related marketing was shown to have a significant increase on brand affinity, with 48 per cent of consumers actually changing buying behavior to companies involved in cause-related marketing (Brand benefits, 2003).

Sometimes stated preferences for cause-related products are not followed up in practice. The resulting gap between what consumers say and do may discourage businesses. For example, Philips Electronics initially found few buyers for their eco-friendly, energy-saving fluorescent bulbs. A 2007 study similarly found that concern about the environment doesn't necessarily motivate consumers to pay more for environmentally sustainable products (Going green, 2007). Interestingly, green campaigns may be attracting more adherents in developing economies than in advanced ones. For example, in a 1999 study, Environics International found that more than half of buyers polled in Venezuela, China, India and Egypt were willing to pay a 10 per cent premium for a greener cleaning product as compared to only one-fifth of consumers in Britain, Japan, and France.

Whether devoted to environmental or other issues, the kinds of activities undertaken at this point on the CSR continuum can vary from episodic efforts to more significant, longer-term efforts. Episodic activities usually are ad hoc and often isolated from other organizational activities, providing considerable flexibility to sponsoring organizations. For example, a one-time donation from a corporate foundation typically requires few resources other than those already available from foundation resources. Although a one-time sponsorship may require hiring temporary management staff, the project nature of the sponsorship allows the corporation to put the event in its past once it is completed. These and other types of episodic engagements with social responsibility initiatives generally require no changes in organizational structure, neither are permanent staff required. In general, episodic CSR activities consume fewer organizational resources than do longer-term ones.

Some organizations undertake ongoing philanthropic, sponsorship, or cause-related marketing activities. An example is McDonald's long-standing support for Ronald McDonald houses. The ongoing nature of these activities usually requires permanent staff and other resources. However, like episodic CSR initiatives, because they are free-standing they too can be eliminated from the corporate budget.

Articulate social value objectives
Other business leaders are committed to developing an integrative approach to managing corporate social responsibility. This level of commitment is not easily disentangled from other organizational activities. Examples below illustrate only some ways in which organizations link CSR activities to other organizational activities. McDonald's incorporates values in company vision statements, making it part of an articulated belief system. In 1958, Ray Kroc set the stage for this system, declaring "The basis for our entire business is that we are ethical, truthful and dependable. We are business people with a solid, permanent, constructive ethical program that will be in style years from now even more than it is today." By 1992, the statement was:

> We believe that being a good corporate citizen means treating people with fairness and integrity, sharing our success with the communities in which we do business, and being a leader on issues that affect customers. (McDonald's Corporation, 1992)

McDonald's 2007 stated emphasis was on efforts to be ethical and fair. Employees attend training on Standards of Business Conduct and each must certify annually having read and understood these standards. Further, as noted earlier, McDonald's supports ongoing philanthropic activities.

Philips's General Business Principles serve the same purpose: they articulate a single set of principles to guide employees throughout the world, "applying equally to corporate actions and the behavior of individual employees when on company business. They incorporate the fundamental principles on which all Philips activities are or should be based: integrity, fair trade, non-discrimination and equal opportunities" (Business principles, 2007). These and similar values statements provide a specific outline of the company's expectations of the company as a corporate entity and of their employees, and they illustrate that the company is willing to go public with its values. An integrative approach by definition generates systemic organizational alterations that are less easily disentangled should company priorities change. That is, integrative and systemic approaches usually engage top management, they incorporate rewards for successful integration, they tend to be ongoing in nature, and they are embedded in the organization's structure.

Public concern about the environment is widespread and it is one reason that firms often pursue CSR initiatives that emphasize environmental sustainability. A study from as early as 1990 showed that a growing number of global firms published policy statements on environmentalism (United Nations Conference, 1993), and that number has grown significantly over time. Many businesses now play active roles in environmental development and preservation. Five common practices found among environmentally responsible firms are:

1. Corporate values that promote environmental advocacy such as a clear mission statement.
2. A framework to manage environmental initiatives and activities.
3. Introduction of process and product designs that are environmentally sensitive.
4. Stakeholder partnerships that focus on the environment.
5. Educational initiatives with internal and external stakeholders to inform on environmental concerns.

Starbucks Coffee Company found that an aspiration to improve the quality of life in coffee-producing countries involved more than a statement of commitment. According to Starbucks' Senior Vice President Dave Olsen, a desire to make such a commitment caused top managers to "explore our own values and beliefs" and examine past actions as well as to involve themselves in "a lot of soul searching to come to an understanding of how we can live up to our sense of responsibility to make a difference in the world." This exploration of values consumed six months of executive meeting time to yield a four-page document of company beliefs and plans to improve the lives of people in coffee-producing countries titled "Starbucks commitment . . . to do our part." After he'd described the Starbucks experience, Olsen's first question from the audience was "why haven't you done more?" This example illustrates two important points about CSR activities: they require considerable managerial resources, and few will believe the company has done enough.

Integrate social objectives and business goals
Integration between social objectives and business goals usually leads to changes that become organizationally embedded. For example, they are incorporated in ongoing processes that are systematic, or continuous activities used to accomplish organizational purposes. Unlike programs that can be easily added or deleted, processes tend to be long term and organizationally integrated with people, structure, and other processes. For example, an embedded process requires that employees associated with CSR initiatives be

located somewhere within the formal organizational structure. Integration of processes with people means incorporating CSR progress as a measure in rewards and promotion systems. In this way, CSR initiatives are woven into the fabric of the organization and are not easily unwound. Examples of processes through which companies integrate CSR with other activities are many; those described below include stakeholder engagement, cause-based partnerships, codes of conduct and company ethics, and adoption of external codes such as professional standards or ISO 14001. The extent to which each is integrated within the organization can vary quite widely.

Environmental activities demonstrate varied ways in which companies integrate social objectives with business ones. Some participate by reducing resource consumption. In offices, this might mean using email rather than paper. In production it might mean reduced packaging, as Lever Brothers did when it reduced container size for Wisk detergent. Sometimes these changes can improve profits. For example, a new Dow Chemical plant in Canada used 40 per cent less energy and required less maintenance to release ten gallons of waste water per minute as compared to 360 gallons/minute for older plants. This also reduced longer-term environmental costs.

Other firms go beyond reduction to recycle and reuse products. McDonald's McRecycle USA is a commitment to buy a minimum of recycled products every year. Carry-out bags are made from recycled corrugated boxes and newsprint, and take-out trays from recycled newspapers. Insulated concrete blocks made from recycled photographic film are used for building construction, roofing tiles are from used computer casings, and recycled automobile tires are used in play areas. In the photographic imaging industry, Kodak recycles 70 per cent of disposable cameras and reuses 86 per cent of materials at their Guadalajara plant. Canon, a global firm headquartered in Japan, established the 'E' Project (for environment, ecology, energy). The Clean Earth Campaign, a cartridge-collection program, is an outgrowth of this concern for the environment that keeps the environment clean by paying postage for consumers to return used toner cartridges. Portions of the returned cartridges are reused and Canon USA also makes a contribution to the National Wildlife Federation and The Nature Conservancy.

In general, companies that intend to integrate CSR initiatives will link them to other activities such as training; they will develop mechanisms for auditing and evaluating behaviors; they will create disciplinary processes for use when expectations are not met; they will create formal departments and officers whose jobs include oversight and code compliance; and they will provide ways for employees to report code violations, for example, telephone lines (Weaver et al., 1999). An important mechanism for integrating codified behaviors and ideals throughout the organization is to link them to rewards for all employees, but especially leaders and managers.

Engage with stakeholders

Pressure from stakeholder groups to improve or change conduct ranked second most important among company challenges in 2000 (Most respected, 2000), and top leaders worldwide report that responsible treatment of stakeholders is an important element of CSR initiatives (Corporate social responsibility gaining, 2002). Further, a study of stakeholder relationships showed they have a direct impact on financial performance (Berman et al., 1999). This suggests that positive connections with key stakeholders can improve or sustain firm profitability.

Corporations engage with stakeholders in different ways. In some cases, stakeholders are invited to the corporate boardroom only so the company can convey their aspirations – this is not a highly integrative approach and may backfire on the company if stakeholders perceive they are being placated, patronized, or manipulated. In other cases, stakeholder engagement becomes a two-way street where corporate leaders listen to and interactively communicate with stakeholders. Moving from one to two-way communication naturally involves trust on both sides, and it may require practice. Staff members may be overwhelmed by new experiences (Mirvis and Googins, 2006) and existing animosity between NGOs and businesses can impede trust development.

In the case of Royal Dutch Shell, stakeholder engagement followed an evolutionary process painful to all concerned. In brief, at the time of the 1995 Brent Spar incident, the company had little use for Greenpeace; Shell leaders adamantly refused even to meet with environmentalists from Greenpeace and other organizations. Following Shell's forceful ejection of environmentalists from the Brent Spar oil platform, an informal boycott spread from Germany to the Netherlands and Denmark to cause a 20 per cent drop in Shell's European retail sales; that attracted company attention to external stakeholders. Later that year, Shell Nigeria was implicated in the hanging of eight pro-democracy political prisoners in Nigeria. Shell representative Gerry Matthews believes these incidents forced Shell to rethink their stance toward external stakeholders. As a result Shell began to collaborate with NGOs and pursued dialogue with organizations such as Greenpeace better to understand society's expectations. They developed a "Tell Shell" website (www.shell.com/tellshell) to solicit comments and routinely involve stakeholders in business decisions that may affect them.

The Royal Dutch Shell example illustrates that negative stakeholder action can profoundly affect firm performance. This is one reason to engage with stakeholders. Another reason for stakeholder engagement is the innovation that results with diverse perspectives from stakeholders. By 2007, a Shell website incorporated this thinking with a banner repeat of "where ideas come from the most unlikely places."

As a beginning point, the Clarkson Principles of Stakeholder Management (The Clarkson Centre, 1999, p. 4) outline company activities that tend to enhance stakeholder interactions (Box 6.1).

BOX 6.1   CLARKSON PRINCIPLES OF STAKEHOLDER MANAGEMENT

Principle 1: Managers should acknowledge and actively monitor the concerns of all legitimate stakeholders, and should take their interests appropriately into account in decision-making and operations.

Principle 2: Managers should listen to and openly communicate with stakeholders about their respective concerns and contributions, and about the risks that they assume because of their involvement with the corporation.

Principle 3: Managers should adopt processes and modes of behavior that are sensitive to the concerns and capabilities of each stakeholder constituency.

Principle 4: Managers should recognize the interdependence of efforts and rewards among stakeholders, and should attempt to achieve a fair distribution of the benefits and burdens of corporate activity among them, taking into account their respective risks and vulnerabilities.

Principle 5: Managers should work cooperatively with other entities, both public and private, to insure that risks and harm arising from corporate activities are minimized and, where they cannot be avoided, appropriately compensated.

Principle 6: Managers should avoid altogether activities that might jeopardize inalienable human rights (e.g., the right to life) or give rise to risks which, if clearly understood, would be patently unacceptable to relevant stakeholders.

Principle 7: Managers should acknowledge the potential conflicts between (a) their own role as corporate stakeholders, and (b) their legal and moral responsibilities for the interests of stakeholders, and should address such conflicts through open communication, appropriate reporting and incentive systems, and, where necessary, third party review.

Cause-based partnerships

Cause-based partnerships (CBPs) are alliances between businesses and not-for-profit organizations that simultaneously respond to the values of civil society and address organizational needs. CBPs organize in some instances to alleviate a social problem, for example, poverty, environmental degradation, or social injustices, and in others to satisfy a social need, such as the Special Olympics. The number of these relationships has grown in recent years (Berger, Cunningham and Drumwright, 1999; Crane, 2000). Major businesses and nonprofits such as General Motors, McDonald's, the World Wide Fund for Nature, and Greenpeace engage in CBPs and their numbers are expected further to grow in years ahead (Elkington and Fennell, 2000) principally because single sector organizations have proved incapable of solving intractable world problems. The recent focus of most CBPs is economic development, environmental concerns, and public issues like health and education (Waddell and Brown, 1997); projects favoring social mobilization, advocacy, or good governance are less often pursued (Ashman, 2000). Environmental CBPs are particularly active (for examples see Bendell, 2000; Lober, 1997; Murphy and Bendell, 1997).

Austin (2000) notes that some CSR activities are transactional in nature or conducted at arm's length. For example, affinity charge cards produce revenue for a social need, but they require little company/NGO interaction. CBPs involve continual interactions between partners' managers and are usually more integrative than transactional. An example is Starbucks/Conservation International efforts to promote fair- trade coffee. Another is the CARE/Glaxo/Bangladeshi government partnership to eradicate parasites in Bangladeshi communities. The Marco Polo partnership between MCI/Worldcom, National Geographic, the Kennedy Center ArtLinks, and US teachers worked to reduce the digital divide for low-income children. All these require ongoing interaction between managers from different sectors who do not necessarily "speak the same language" in term of vision, values, or operational activities.

CBPs can involve many partners or two, combine organizations of different sizes and scope, are initiated by outside influences, organizational leaders, grassroots efforts among employees, or they can be forced. Whether they come about by chance, coercion or design, these kinds of partnerships create managerial linkages that connect businesses to social goals. The inherent complexity of managing CBPs lies in differing values and visions of partners, issues of cross-sector trust and power, and operational challenges of management and structure (Selsky and Parker, 2005).

Codes of conduct and ethics

In the absence of global governance mechanisms to regulate and discipline companies, businesses face a disorganized and fragmented operating framework. Some business managers "search for principles for action that transcend national borders and cultural values, and modes of operation that will achieve the broad purposes of the corporation on a long-term and sustainable basis" (Clarkson Centre, 1999). This search is meant to help them create synergies from integration. Although companies realize that they cannot easily adopt one or more sets of business principles for overseas markets and others for their domestic market, in practice many find it difficult to create a single, integrated code of ethics or conduct. Motivations to create common company codes often differ, including some or all of the following:

- voluntary guidelines may be viewed as less problematic than those created by governments;
- guidelines may stimulate all firms to operate according to the same principles and thus create a "level playing field" for all organizations;
- ethical conduct is needed in an increasingly interdependent world;
- norms of ethics reduce operating uncertainties;
- it is simply the "right" thing to do.

According to Business for Social Responsibility (2002), the business case for ethics is that ethical behaviors enhance corporate reputation and brand image; improve risk and crisis management; create a cohesive corporate culture; and avoid fines, sanctions, and litigation. One business person turned social activist notes that businesses can either develop appropriate company policies or be forced to do so by public opinion (Chandler, 1999). Many prefer to do the former, better to shape policies that affect them.

While some undoubtedly view initiatives such as codes as public relations tools, others worldwide are acting to move social responsibility initiatives away from manipulation and influence of the public and toward serious dialogue and debate (Steinmann and Lohr, 1992). Many large multinationals introduced formal codes of ethics beginning in the early 1990s (Center for Business Ethics, 1992; Webley, 1992). A 1999 Conference Board study found 78 per cent were setting up ethics standards, an increase of 41 per cent from 1991. Joanne Ciulla (1991) observed that most companies develop internal ethics codes by looking at codes collected by centers like the Ethics Resource Center in Washington, DC or London's Institute of Business Ethics. Most are modeled along similar lines to include (1) contracts (such as conflict of interest, bribery, security of proprietary information, and receiving gifts) and (2) legally or generally accepted standards (such as relating to sexual harassment, workplace safety, or political activities).

According to Business for Social Responsibility (2002), codes of ethics have expanded beyond these two major issues to additionally focus on the natural environment, child labor, human rights, and other concerns. As a result, many codes of ethics now include statements on conflict of interest, supplier relationships, pricing and other concerns.[1] More recently, ethics codes incorporate treatments of internet and e-commerce activities. In their written "Standards of Business Conduct," Sun Microsystems specifically describes what constitutes "reasonable personal use of Sun's information resources" (Sun Microsystems, Inc., 2001, p. 8). Other companies might outline the ethics of information-acquisition or activities such as data-mining.

Ethical codes may not ensure success, but even when flawed they may prevent failures. Their existence makes it less likely that leaders or managers will unwittingly guide the firm into an ethical morass, or that individuals will rely on personal ethics that conflict with company ones when acting on behalf of the firm. This is particularly important at a global level because cultural differences in beliefs and values do lead to cross-cultural differences in behaviors. Among the most important variables for codes are top management commitment; rewards and sanctions, which have to be in place; and the fact that codes should be a process rather than a written product. Whatever form a code takes (and there are many), leaders of ethics programs need to connect their written commitments to ethical behaviors. This is part of the integrative process.

Enron had articulated a global vision of ethics, had a global code of ethics, and was often applauded for its socially responsible behavior. This example illustrates when a code functioned more as a public-relations tool than as a behavioral guide. Codes of ethics such as Enron's have little practical value when top managers flout them.

Other criticisms of corporate codes of ethics and conduct are that they lack specific content, they ignore the rights of key stakeholders in their dealings with the organization, or that code compliance is not well integrated into organizational procedures. Additionally, many codes fail when they provide no framework for communicating with external communities about their success or failure in achieving the code's objectives (Sethi, 1999). These challenges show why it is important to do more than simply write up a code – codes must be part of an integrated system for decision-making. Implementation includes at least four important activities:

- Communicate with employees so they understand what behaviors are expected and why. Communication also should include notice of sanctions for ethical violations.

- Monitor actual behavior which might include periodic inspections or progress reports.
- Link ethics to rewards and integrate ethics codes into everyday activities of employees.
- Audit results for feed-through to next-step processes.

Codes are only one mechanism used to integrate desired behaviors worldwide. Desai and Rittenburg (1997) suggest a committee headed by an adviser who can create awareness throughout the organization. This individual also manages and monitors knowledge transfer on CSR issues to subsidiaries and affiliates abroad. The company can also monitor and respond to measures external to the firm to demonstrate compliant conduct. For example, it might choose to do business only in nations where the transparency index is high and the corruption index low.

Another approach more typical for large firms than small ones is to push CSR values such as ethics through supply chains by asking or even demanding that suppliers understand and comply with established ethical standards. This approach is particularly important for firms like Henning & Mauritz whose goods are only produced by suppliers. The H&M Code lays out requirements that suppliers must follow covering working hours, wages, fire safety and freedom of association, and a ban on child labor (H&M Code, 2003). Following charges of sweatshop conditions among their suppliers, Nike became one of the first companies to publish a list of its suppliers. Examples of activities that might follow introduction of a formal code of ethics appear in Table 6.1.

External standards and codes
Rather than developing their own codes, companies may adopt principles and practices suggested by industry groups or coordinating organizations. A UK example is the Ethical Trading Initiative – a nine-point base code meant to ensure that goods produced for UK markets come from global suppliers who are working to improve labor conditions (Collier, 2000). ISO codes 14000 and 14001 provide another example. According to the International Chamber of Commerce, some 5000 companies worldwide certify their environmental management systems using the ISO 14001 guidelines; the latter requires organizations to develop an environmental policy. Supported by senior management, ISO outlines company environmental policies, integrates them into employee practice, and publicly reports them. ISO 14001 certification activities are many, but all are integrative in nature, including environmental performance evaluation, life-cycle assessment, and auditing. External certification programs that hold employees to ethical standards or encourage employee conformance to professional standards such as

Table 6.1   Develop, monitor, and enforce a code of ethics

Develop	Monitor	Enforce
Statement of corporate principles	Ethics audit	Link rewards to ethical behaviors and ideals
Ethics code or conduct code	Assess compliance worldwide	Punish failures
Adopt existing code	Produce a separate ethics report at periodic intervals	Provide non-punitive communication channel for whistleblowers
Train employees	Provide "hotlines"	Hold top officer to ethical standards
Create clear lines of ethics responsibility	Create ombudsman office for complaints/concerns	
An office for ethics and ethics officer	Adhere to professional and other standards	
	External audits	

Source: Adapted from Arlene Broadhurst (2000), "Corporations and the ethics of social responsibility: an emerging regime of expansion and compliance," *Business Ethics: A European Review*, **9**(2), 86–98.

accounting standards may also be adopted to pursue social responsibility initiatives. However, some organizations adopt external codes that require little internal integration. These codes are rarely reinforced and then with little more than memos, reminders, and written policies that have little relationship to performance.

Other companies observe the Caux Round Table Principles (1995), which call for responsiveness to stakeholders as well as shareholders, efforts to create justice and world community and business behaviors that conform to the spirit as well as the letter of the law. In terms of environmentalism, some firms follow the "Natural Step's" principles for sustainability. This is a systemic approach for measuring company use and anticipated use of scarce natural resources like fossil fuel, controlling use of substances like plastic, and making fair and efficient use of resources such as forest products to meet human needs. Some companies in the building industries pursue LEEDs certification (Leadership in Energy and Environmental Design) to demonstrate environmental sensitivity. These are only a few examples selected from the many that provide businesses with guidelines and tools for integrating social objectives and business objectives.

Many business leaders believe morality and profits are served when social objectives are inextricably linked with other business objectives and activities. Companies like The Body Shop and Esprit base their global reputation on this approach. From the very beginning, The Body Shop founder Anita Roddick intended that her company provide effective cosmetic products and be a CSR leader. In the 1996 Body Shop catalogue, she wrote: "we actively campaign for human rights and a ban on animal testing in the cosmetics industry. We wish to leave the world a better place, and in better shape, than we found it." Although Roddick was no longer running The Body Shop at the time of her death, her aspirational vision remains in Body Shop's 2007 homepage listing titled "Our values," which are against animal testing, and in support of fair trade, commitment to customers, defense of human rights, and the protection of the planet.

Lead with CSR best practices
Like The Body Shop, most CSR leaders undertake a limited number of social issues. But only a few can be thought of as leaders. The following example concentrates on human rights as one instance of CSR leadership activities. A similar review of another social issue, such as environmental protection, child labor, job creation, educational and digital inequities, disaster relief, worldwide safety standards, healthcare, and so on would highlight many of the same points.

Levi Strauss is one of the best-known CSR leaders on human rights. In 1991, Levi Strauss became one of the first multinational companies to develop a comprehensive code of conduct to ensure that workers making their product anywhere in the world work in safe conditions and are treated with dignity and respect (Levi Strauss, 2002). Evidence of human rights violations caused Levi Strauss to introduce new terms of association with business partners in 1993, thereby becoming one of the first multinationals to adopt guidelines covering worker treatment. These guidelines covered suppliers and subcontractors who might otherwise use child labor or force employees to work unacceptable hours. Levi hires private inspectors to monitor human rights in their manufacturing plants around the world.

Businesses that lead on CSR activities often draw criticism. For example, stockholders devoted to short-term profits may object when companies engage in CSR activities. Stakeholders may scrutinize and even criticize actions of leading socially responsible firms to spotlight additional unmet social needs. The public also finds it difficult to decide who to trust on CSR issues. For example, although McDonald's developed a biodegradable plastic burger wrapper, the product was withdrawn due to public fears. A similar furor continually follows comparisons of the environmental impact of disposable versus cloth diapers. The latter consume water and leave detergent and chlorine residue in water supplies; the former are not biodegradable like cloth. For many it is not clear which product is environmentally superior. These and other unresolved debates raise public concerns that are difficult to address. Resulting consumer uncertainty may be a deterrent to CSR leadership.

Further, CSR leaders can be held to a higher standard than other firms, which may lead to scrutiny by the public or in the press; and the relative newness of many CSR initiatives can mean mis-steps for organizations that pilot them. These and other challenges may depress instances of true CSR leadership.

Organizations on the far right of the CSR continuum presented earlier typically consciously address challenges and weigh opportunities associated with CSR activities before they undertake them. Further, they are very likely to integrate CSR and other organizational activities. But many if not most organizations today operate somewhere in the middle of the CSR continuum, managing social responsibility much as Friedman recommended. Simon Zadek (2002) believes that the public will increasingly reject Friedman's position as a CSR minimum. Public trust in businesses is certainly down. In the wake of business scandals at Enron, Andersen, and Ahold, 57 per cent of US respondents believed that corporate standards and values had dropped in the past 20 years (Harwood, 2002). By 2004, three-quarters of US respondents rated the image of big corporations as either 'not good' or 'terrible' (Alsop, 2004b). Further, in 2006 only 39 per cent of investors were confident that CEOs of publicly traded companies engage in ethical business behaviors; this is down from 47 per cent in the previous year (Surveying the field, 2006). These data offer compelling reasons for businesses to do more to earn and sustain public trust; CSR activities are one way to achieve that trust.

Firms located in the middle of the CSR continuum may respond to CSR demands with programs that are easily added (and just as easily subtracted) from company initiatives; some CSR programs will be associated with particular champions whose energies may not sustain them over time. The longer run result may be a hodgepodge of CSR programs whose costs may not be matched by benefits. In firms where this has occurred, it becomes important to inventory CSR initiatives. Leaders can then compare this inventory to their strategic objectives, better to achieve fit between intent and realization. Leaders considering CSR can similarly compare opportunities with strategy. The growing number of consulting and advertising agencies that build and publicize corporate responsibility programs may facilitate this and other stages of the CSR process. Leaders in every firm should decide where they wish to locate their business on the CSR continuum. This is particularly important since there are clearly challenges as well as opportunities associated with each point on the continuum. Research examining ethics (Weaver et al., 1999) and diversity initiatives (Dass and Parker, 1999) notes that top management commitment is predictive of integrative practices that reinforce stated ideals and practices. This underscores the important role of top management commitment to CSR activities.

Finally, having decided where the firm *should* be on CSR philosophy, leaders must then select CSR activities and develop organizational mechanisms consistent for the position chosen. This chapter suggests some ways in which organizations undertake this process. It illustrates that corporate social responsibility remains a choice, but also suggests that now and into the future global firms will experience growing global and local pressures not only to adopt CSR activities but also to lead other businesses in further negotiating business citizenship roles.

Note

1. Additional topics covered in ethics statement include: fundamental honesty and adherence to the law; product safety and quality; workplace health and safety precautions; conflicts of interest; employment practices; fair practices in selling and marketing products or services; financial reporting; supplier relationships; pricing, billing, and contracting; trading in securities and/or use of insider information; payments to obtain business; acquiring and using information about others; security and political activities; environmental protection; intellectual property or use of proprietary information (Business Roundtable, 1988).

References

AAFRC (2003), "Charity holds it own in tough times", aafrc.org/press_releases/trustreleases/charityholds.html.

Anderson, Sarah and John Cavanagh (2005), *Field Guide to the Global Economy*, 2nd edn, New York: New Press.

Alsop, Ronald (2002a), "Companies' reputations depend on service they give customers," *Wall Street Journal*, 16 January, B1.

Alsop, Ronald (2002b), "For a company, charitable works are best carried out discreetly," *Wall Street Journal*, 16 January, B1.

Alsop, Ronald (2004a), *The 18 Immutable Laws of Corporate Reputation*, New York: Free Press Wall Street Journal Book.

Alsop, Ronald (2004b), "Corporate scandals hit home," *Wall Street Journal*, 19 February, B1, B2.

Ashman, Darcy (2000), "Promoting corporate citizenship in the global South: towards a model of empowered civil society collaboration with business," *IDR Reports*, **16**(3), accessed at www.jsi.com/idr/IDRreports.htm

Austin, James (2000), *The Collaborative Challenge*, San Francisco, CA: Jossey-Bass.

Bakan, Joel (2004), *The Corporation: The Pathological Pursuit of Profit and Power*, New York: Free Press.

Bendell, Jem (2000), "Working with stakeholder pressure for sustainable development," in Jem Bendell (ed.), *Terms for Endearment*, Sheffield: Greenleaf, pp. 14–30.

Benioff, Marc and Karen Southwick (2004), *Compassionate Capitalism: How Corporations Can Make Doing Good an Integral Part of Doing Well*, Franklin Lakes, NJ: Career Press.

Berger, I., P. Cunningham and M. Drumwright (1999), "Social alliances: Company/nonprofit collaboration," *Social Marketing Quarterly*, **5**(3), 49–53.

Berman, Shawn L., Andrew Wicks, Suresh Kotha and Thomas M. Jones (1999), "Does stakeholder orientation matter: the relationship between stakeholder management models and firm financial performance," *Academy of Management Journal*, **42**(5), 488–506.

Brand Benefits (2003), "Brand benefits-cause-related marketing", accessed at www.bitc. org.uk/resources/research/research_publications/brand_benefits.html.

Business in the Community (2002), "The public's view of corporate responsibility," key findings 2002 for BITC website, accessed at www.bitc.org.uk/docs/MORI_article.doc.

Business Roundtable (1988), *Corporate Ethics: A Prime Business Asset*, New York: The Business Roundtable.

Business for Social Responsibility (2002), 11 March, accessed at www.bsr.org/BSRLibrary/TOdetail.cfm?DocumentID=395.

Carringer, Paul T. (n.d.), "Not just a worthy cause: cause-related marketing delivers the goods and the good," accessed at http://psaresearch.com/bib4306.html.

Caux Round Table (1995), "Principles for business," accessed at www.cauxroundtable.org/principles.html.

Center for Business Ethics (1992), "Instilling ethical values in large corporations," *Journal of Business Ethics*, 1 February, 863–7.

Chandler, Sir Geoffrey (1999), "The new corporate challenge," *Time*, 1 February, p. 68.

Ciulla, Joanne B. (1991), "Why is business talking about ethics? Reflections on foreign conversations," *California Management Review*, Fall, 67–86.

Clarkson Centre for Business Ethics (1999), *Principles of Stakeholder Management*, Toronto: The Clarkson Centre.

Clarkson, M.B.E. (1995), "A stakeholder framework for analyzing and evaluating corporate social performance," *Academy of Management Review*, **20**(1), 92–117.

Crane, Andrew (2000), "Culture clash and mediation," in Jem Bendell (ed.), *Terms for Endearment*, Sheffield: Greenleaf, pp. 163–77.

Collier, Jane (2000), "Editorial: globalization and ethical global business," *Business Ethics: A European Review*, **9**(2), 71–5.

"Companies and causes" (2000), *Business Week*, online edition, 18 December, accessed at www.businessweek.com/2000/00_51/b3712184.htm.

Cone Inc (2007), "Cone current happenings," accessed at www.coneinc.com/content69.html.

Dass, P. and Barbara Parker (1999), "Strategies for managing human resource diversity: from resistance to learning," *Academy of Management Executive*, **13**(2), 68–80.

Desai, Ashay B. and Terri Rittenburg (1997), "Global ethics: an integrative framework for MNEs," *Journal of Business Ethics*, **16**(8), 791–800.

DiPiazza, Jr, Samuel (2002), Millenium Poll survey highlights, accessed at www.pwc global.com/extweb/ncsurvres.nsf.

Eccles, Robert G., Scott C. Newquist and Roland Schatz (2007), "Reputation and its risks," *Harvard Business Review*, **85**(2), 104–14.

Echo Research (2003), "CSR & the financial community: friend or foe?" accessed at www.echoresearch.com.

The Economist (1999), "Green is good," 11 September, p. 7.

Edelman public relations firm (2006), "Edelman 2006 Annual Trust Barometer," accessed at www.edelman.com/image/insights/content/FullSupplement_final.pdf.

Elkington, John and Shelly Fennell (2000), "Partners for sustainability," in Jem Bendell (ed.), *Terms for Endearment*, Sheffield: Greenleaf, pp. 150–62.

Falck, Oliver and Stephan Heblich (2007), "Corporate social responsibility: doing well by doing good," *Business Horizons*, **50**(3), 247–54.

Foundation Center (2007), "Giving by corporate foundations rises to a record $4.2 billion, Foundation Center report shows," 15 May, accessed at http://foundationcenter.org/media/news/pr_0705a.html.

Harwood, John (2002), "Public's esteem for business falls in wake of Enron scandal," *Wall Street Journal*, 11 April, D5.

H&M Hennes & Mauritz AB (2003), "H&M Code of conduct," 28 December, accessed at www.hm.com/us/hm/social/coc.jsp.

Kadlec, Daniel and Bruce Van Voorst (1997), "The new world of giving," *Time*, 5 May, 62–5.

Kolk, Ans and Jonatan Pinkse (2006), "Stakeholder mismanagement and corporate social responsibility crises," *European Management Journal*, **24**(1), 59–72.

Korten, David C. (1995), *When Corporations Rule the World*, San Francisco, CA: Berrett-Koehler.

Lawrence, Thomas and Cynthia Hardy (1999), "Building bridges for refugees: toward a typology of bridging organizations," *Journal of Applied Behavioral Science*, **35**(1), 48–70.

Levi Strauss (2002), home page, 27 March, accessed at www.levistrauss.com.

Lewin, David and J.M. Sabater (1996), "Corporate philanthropy and business performance," in Dwight F. Burlingame and Dennis R. Young (eds), *Corporate Philanthropy at the Crossroads*, Bloomington and Indianapolis, IN: Indiana University Press, pp. 105–26.

Lober, D.J. (1997), "Explaining the formation of business-environmental collaborations: collaborative windows and the paper task force," *Policy Sciences*, **30** (February), 1–24.

Mirvis, Philip and Bradley Googins (2006), "Stages of corporate citizenship," *California Management Review*, **48**(2), 104–26.

Murphy, D.F. and J. Bendell (1997), *In the Company of Partners: Business, Environmental Groups and Sustainable Development Post-Rio*, Bristol: The Policy Press.

Post, James E. (2000), "Moving from geographic to virtual communities: global corporate citizenship in a dot.com world," *Business and Society Review*, **105**(1), 27–46.

PriceWaterhouseCoopers (2000), "Most respected companies," PriceWaterHouseCoopers survey, accessed at www.pwcglobal.com.

PricewaterhouseCoopers (2002), "Corporate social responsibility gaining higher awareness among CEOs, says PwC survey report," accessed at http://pwcglobal.com/extweb/ncinthenews.nsf.

PRNewswire News and Information (2007), "Going green bandwagon stalls among consumers," 13 August, accessed at http://sev.prnewswire.com/environmental-services/20070813/NYM07713082007-1.html.

Royal Philips (2007), *Business Principles*, accessed at www.philips.com/about/investor/businessprinciples/index.page.

Selsky, John and Barbara Parker (2005), "Cross-sector partnerships to address social issues: challenges to theory and practice," *Journal of Management*, **31**(6), 849–73.

Sethi, S. Prakash (1999), "Codes of conduct for global business: prospects and challenges of implementation," in Clarkson Centre for Business Ethics (ed.), *Principles of Stakeholder Management*, Toronto: Clarkson Centre for Business Ethics, pp. 9–20.

Shulman, Seth (2007), "Smoke, mirrors & hot air: how Exxon Mobil uses big tobacco's tactics to manufacture uncertainty on climate change," report prepared for the Union of Concerned Scientists, Spring, Cambridge, MA.

Steinmann, Horst and Albert Lohr (1992), "A survey of business ethics in Germany," *Business Ethics: A European Review*, April, 139–41.

Sun Microsystems, Inc. (2001), *Standards of Business Conduct: Our Reputation – A Shared Responsibility*, Palo Alto, CA: Sun Microsystems, Business Conduct Office.

United Nations Conference on Trade and Development (UNCTAD) (1993), "Environmental management in transnational corporations: report on the Benchmark Corporate Environmental Survey," New York: United Nations.

USA Today (2006) "Charitable giving in U.S. nears record set at end of tech boom," 19 June, http://www.usatoday.com/news/nation/2006-06-19-charitable-giving_x.htm.

Waddell, Steve and L. David Brown (1997), "Fostering intersectoral partnering: a guide to promoting cooperation among government, business, and civil society actors," *IDR Reports*, **13**(3), accesses at www.jsi.com/idr.

Waddock, Sandra and Mary-Ellen Boyle (1995), "The dynamics of change in corporate community relations," *California Management Review*, **37**(4), 125–41.

Waddock, Sandra, Charles Bodwell and Samuel B. Graves (2002), "Responsibility: the new business imperative," *Academy of Management Executive*, **16**(2), 132–48.

Wall Street Journal (2006), "Surveying the field," May 22, p. B3.

Weaver, G.R., Linda K. Trevino and Philip L. Cochran (1999), "Integrated and decoupled corporate social performance: management commitments, external pressures, and corporate ethics practices," *Academy of Management Journal*, **42**(5), 539–52.

Webley, Simon (1992), *Company Values and Codes: Current Best Practices in the United Kingdom*, London: Institute of Business Ethics.

Yoon, Yeosun, Zeynep Gurhan-Canli and Norbert Schwarz (2006), "The effect of corporate social responsibility (CSR) on companies with bad reputations," *Journal of Consumer Psychology*, **16**(4), 377–90.
Zadek, Simon (2002), *The Civil Corporation: The New Economy of Corporate Citizenship*, London: Earthscan.

7 Quiet turbulence: advice for financial officers of not-for-profit financial institutions
Ronald Dulek

Fall of 2007 marked for me a decade of service as a board member of a mid-size ($200m +) credit union. As I searched for words to describe that decade of experience, the phrase "quiet turbulence" continued to pop into my mind. No matter how diligently I sought other descriptors, "quiet turbulence" kept returning to my head. I finally decided to accept the descriptor and "give it some thought."

The financial industry as a whole has undergone radical transformation over the last decade. The credit union movement has not been immune to these changes. Electronic banking, internet banking, new kinds of ATM's, telephone banking, "pfishing" and email fraud have altered the costs and the avenues through which credit unions today reach out to their members. Additionally, Sarbanes-Oxley, which technically does not apply to credit unions but whose guidelines credit unions are encouraged to follow, and the Patriot Act, along with other rule changes, have complicated the regulatory landscape where credit unions reside.

Yet while the above-mentioned changes, along with significant industry-wide consolidation, have made headlines for banks and other for-profit financial institutions, credit unions have undergone almost exactly the same changes – along with one even more significant change – with almost no fanfare. Thus, in the midst of these traumatic changes, credit unions continue to "plug along" with their democratic one-person/one-vote annual meeting philosophy. The turbulence certainly has been silent. From the outside, almost no one has noticed.

The purpose of this chapter is to offer a few useful tips for credit union directors to consider implementing during this time of quiet turbulence. Officers at other financial institutions may find the advice applicable as well – although the turbulence they have experienced has certainly been louder and more profitable. Officers from AmSouth and South Trust – two major regional banks that have been acquired – as well as those from their acquirers, Regions and Wachovia, can certainly document that turbulence.

The issue for credit union directors is that the turbulence has been less public, although perhaps equally dramatic. Additionally, the experience

Table 7.1   *Credit union trends, 1999–2006*

	Number of credit unions	Credit union membership
2006	8 362	85.8
2005	8 695	84.8
2004	9 014	83.6
2003	9 369	82.4
2002	9 688	80.9
2001	9 984	79.4
2000	10 316	77.6
1999	10 628	75.4

for credit union directors has probably been more lonely since they are not surrounded by hordes of "change consultants" advising their every move. Perhaps this chapter will help provide credit union directors with a similar kind of advice – and a little company to keep while pondering the future.

Credit union turbulence

Table 7.1 documents the turbulence that credit unions have undergone between 1999 and 2006. The figures are astounding. The number of credit unions has declined by more than 20 per cent in that time period; yet credit union membership has increased by almost 15 per cent.

The numbers speak for themselves. Credit unions have undergone significant consolidation. Even more importantly, however, and perhaps directly under the surface, a significant figure lurks that identifies an additional threat faced by credit unions. That figure, the number of members per individual credit union, has increased significantly in the time period examined. The data show that the average number of members per credit union has gone from 7094 in 1999 to 10 260 in 2006. This is a 44.6 per cent increase in members per credit union.

This increase can certainly be handled at one level by the changes in technology that have occurred during this time. But at another, more human, level these changes bode ill for credit unions. Stated simply, an important aspect of the credit union tradition is service – particularly individualized service. Credit union executives across the country love to brag that their tellers and member service clients know the names of most if not all of their members. The obvious hidden implication is that credit unions are warm, friendly, personalized places to do one's financial transactions – not cold and impersonal like the banks.

Yet personalized service is under threat as long as these trends continue. At some point the "law of memory" kicks in. The tellers and member service representatives give up hope of knowing the names and faces of the customers. And customers lose contact with individual tellers and service representatives as credit unions add more staff to handle the influx of additional members. Thus, a distinctive feature of credit unions disappears.

Cause of consolidation: HR 1151

The causes of consolidation are numerous. Economies of scale, efficiency improvement, added product offerings, and financial stability all come to mind immediately as causes for consolidation. Interestingly, these causes relate as much to the banking industry as they do to credit unions. But credit unions have undergone one other significant source of change – a legislative one that probably altered the credit union landscape forever. That change was as large and as significant for credit unions as Sarbanes-Oxley was to public financial institutions. That change was an alteration in the way that credit unions define their field of membership.

In a nutshell, and with a little over-simplification, prior to 1998, credit unions had fields of membership that were stringently defined and generally well protected. Membership in a particular credit union was limited to a particular set of people. Other credit unions could seldom impinge on that field of membership.

The passage of HR 1151 in 1998 significantly altered the definition of fields of membership. Stated simply, HR 1151 changed the membership body that credit unions can attract. Essentially, and again at the risk of over-simplifying, this new regulation allowed overlapping fields of membership. Suddenly, members had more ways to join different kinds of credit unions. The choices and options for members increased significantly.

These increased choices and options have changed the ways that credit unions function. Equally importantly, these changes mean that the jobs of credit union directors have changed as well. The board meeting is no longer a social event at which friends exchange pleasantries and enjoy a casual lunch together. Boards now have added responsibilities to their members. Below are three key issues that board members need to keep in mind as they steer their organizations through waters that seem still on the surface but are turbulent underneath.

Strategy

Too often, especially with small to mid-size credit unions, strategy is an afterthought. Strategic initiatives are reactive rather than planned. When the CEO has a few minutes – a not too frequent occasion – he or she will spend some time "jotting down" a strategy. That is not the way to devise or implement a strategy in times of turbulence. Those who fail to plan often fail to survive.

At the outset, we need to acknowledge that strategy is the responsibility of the CEO and his or her executive team. Yet while setting and implementing strategy is within the CEO's domain, the board has oversight capacity with regard to the strategy. The changes wrought by the implementation of the field of membership rule change means that boards are well-advised to exercise their oversight power.

My own credit union board had what would prove to be the most important strategic planning session in its history in the fall of 1999. We studied and pondered the implications of the field of membership rule changes. We did so as objectively as possible and speculated about the possible consequences of these changes. Eventually, we decided that credit union consolidation was inevitable – the aforementioned figures demonstrate our prescience.

At the time of this meeting our credit union had under 20 000 members and two offices – one in our base city and another in a city 150 miles away. We also had a new CEO and two new board members. After a half day of healthy debate about the consequences of the field of membership changes, we came to the realization that we had to make a choice. We could either remain as we were and face eventual takeover. Or, we could become more aggressive, begin looking for possible acquisitions, and pursue an active growth strategy over the coming decade.

After additional debate, along with acknowledgement that both strategies contained inevitable risks, we chose the latter. Since then we have opened seven new branch offices, acquired four credit unions, more than doubled our assets, and have almost doubled our membership. These strategic changes have at times challenged our organizations; and our expenses have risen commensurate with our income; but we are vibrant, alive and a "force to be reckoned with" on the state credit union front.

Perhaps most amazingly, the vast majority of our employees and our members report that they are pleased to be part of a vibrant, active, growth-oriented organization. That's the benefit of having a strategy.

A few words of caution about a growth strategy – and these are words that my own credit union has had to remember since our CEO is extremely growth-oriented. Credit unions that choose a growth strategy must be careful – especially as they begin to grow – to distinguish strategic from opportunistic growth. Not to do so can be fatal.

Six years ago I assisted in a potential major acquisition for a private publishing company. The acquisition would have quadrupled the revenues of company, and would have added twenty-one new business lines to an existing set of ten. Financial and strategic reasons stopped the acquisition.

Six months after the deal collapsed, I had the opportunity to interview the firm's top management team about the acquisition. The leaders' insights were remarkable, but none more so than the chairman of the board and major owner of the company. This man was initially the lead force behind the acquisition; however, as events unfolded, he became less enthusiastic.

When I finally interviewed him after the deal had been declared "dead," I asked him to list the main things he learned from the experience. He was, I should add at the outset, an extremely successful entrepreneur who had grown this company into one of the three largest private publishing companies in the world.

He pondered my question about what he learned and answered as follows:

> I learned a lot, but the main thing I learned was that at some point the leaders of an entrepreneurial company have to grow strategically rather than opportunistically. When we were small, I could make acquisitions on a whim. We would adjust "on the fly." But as we've grown, and as our acquisitions have become larger, I've noticed that I'm beginning to strain the system more.
>
> Acquisitions aren't as easy to integrate as they once were. Bringing new companies into the fold is more difficult. We have a corporate culture now, and I risk that culture with each acquisition.
>
> This last acquisition would have strained our resources, pushed our systems to the limit, and possibly changed our culture dramatically. Those changes could have been fatal. When my people warned me about these threats, I began "backing off."

Credit unions pursuing an acquisition strategy, and the numbers in Table 7.1 certainly demonstrate that many are, should remain aware of this CEO's advice. Opportunistic growth through acquisition of smaller, less stable credit unions may look appealing. But at some point CEOs and boards may begin to strain the resources and threaten the cultures. If so, then boards and CEOs need to get together and outline a more specific, strategic plan for continued growth. Failure to do so may have significantly negative consequences.

Competition
Historically, the notion of competition, especially competition between existing credit unions, has been anathema to credit union boards. Credit unions have seen themselves as competitive alternatives to banks, but they have meticulously avoided competing against each other.

The old field of membership rules promoted this lack of competition. There was no need to compete since one credit union could seldom impinge on another's domain. The result of this lack of competition was the development of a strong camaraderie among credit union leaders. These leaders, as well as their board members, attended various state, regional, and national conventions together, freely intermixed, and shared best practices without fear of retribution. Competition between credit unions was simply not a part of the movement's DNA.

The change in field of membership rules drastically changed the genetic makeup of the credit union industry. Though reluctant to admit it, credit unions of the twenty-first century are in direct competition with one another. They are competing not just for loans and deposits, but also for members. Few like to admit it – but that's the way it is today.

Boards of directors and credit union CEOs need to recognize that competition is now a part of the scene. And they must respond accordingly. Specifically, boards would be well advised to "push" CEOs into identifying and designing ways for their credit unions to gain competitive advantages not just over banks, but also over other credit unions.

Years of research on competition have taught us that a "stuck in the middle strategy" can be disastrous. Hence, boards should participate in discussions about whether their credit unions want to compete on a cost-efficiency basis – that is, a strategy that involves having leading edge loan rates and higher returns on savings than every other financial institution in the area – or whether they should compete on service. This latter approach involves friendly, personalized service as well as high cost products and services that benefit members but may generate negative cash flow within their area. Bill payment and free checking come to mind as examples of these latter services.

Figure 7.1 shows these choices visually. It also shows categories that credit unions want to select as well as those to avoid. Put another way, two of the quadrants are recipes for disaster; two of the quadrants are areas of positive financial opportunity. But reality dictates that you can not do both.

One other note worth mentioning about competition. Stated simply, the decision to compete through a particular strategy should derive not just from the credit union's own desires but also from the external environment that surrounds the credit union. Credit union leaders should thus look both at the strengths of their own credit unions and at the strengths of other credit unions in the area. If all the other area credit unions are competing on service, then your own might be wise to examine some other possible ways to compete. Environment influences strategy.

Communication

Credit unions are structurally different from all other financial institutions. By definition, they are member-owned and member-driven. Hence, the owners are the customers. Equally significantly, directors are elected by democratic vote, with each credit union member having a single vote. The

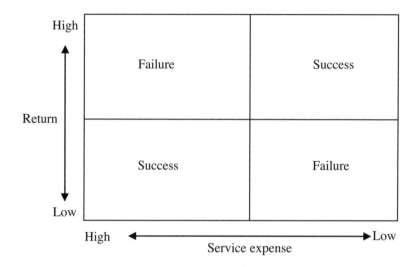

Figure 7.1   Credit union competition model

number of shares an owner holds in the credit union is irrelevant from the democratic perspective – each member has one vote.

These structural anomalies, combined with the quiet turbulence that has followed the industry for the last decade, make communication a vitally important key success factor for credit union boards to monitor. Again, as with strategy, it is important that the boards monitor rather than micro-manage the process – but monitor and support communication they must do.

Communication is a complex topic that organizations can approach from a number of different perspectives. For the purposes of this chapter, we will focus on two particular communication components that credit union boards must be certain are occurring within their organizations.

Communication topic 1: vision/mission statements   Having a direction is always important, but it is doubly important in times of turbulence. Members as well as credit union employees need to know the planned direction of the organization. The organization's planned initiatives, including the overall strategy, need to be publicized in a number of different ways, including via newsletters, podcasts, and websites. But nowhere does this vision/mission/strategy statement need to be made clearer than in the organization's annual meeting.

It is at this meeting that the one-member/one-vote underlying structure – and the need to communicate the credit union's vision and mission statement – is most apparent. Directors are elected at this meeting. It is, therefore, an important time for members to know and be able to evaluate the organization's vision and mission statement – as well as its overall strategy. Only with such knowledge can members vote intelligently about the credit union's direction as well as its leadership.

Communication topic 2: feedback   Even the most well-meaning CEO will filter information going to the board. His or her job is, after all, to determine what is and is not worthy of board attention. Inevitably, this job will lead to some accidental and perhaps some intentional bias with regard to the information that the board receives.

Additionally, the most well-meaning CEO will frame some if not most of the information that goes to the board members. Specifically, the CEO will "spin" or guide the interpretation of the board's analysis with regard to organizational challenges, pitfalls, and financial outcomes. Again, human nature and natural instincts influence the way information is presented to the board. Leaders are seldom, if ever, intentionally deceptive. But they are human and they want to "put their best foot forward." Sometimes this "foot forward" steps over "potholes" that the board members may not notice unless they are perceptive.

Board members must be aware of these "informational potholes" and seek to identify and find ways to repair them. Specifically, board members must insist that leaders conduct frequent checks with members and employees with regard to the day-to-day operation of the organization. These checks might come in the form of questionnaires to members and employees, web surveys, or the hiring of an outside firm to monitor member and employee satisfaction. The more information the board has about the organization's performance, and the more objective that information is, the better the board is able to fulfill its governance and its monitoring roles. And again, to repeat the oft mentioned point, the board's job is to monitor not micro-manage the daily operation of the credit union. But it is impossible to monitor performance without information. So boards must devise strategies to gain the most objective information possible. Only in that way can they fulfill their obligations as elected representatives – and help credit unions survive into the foreseeable future.

Credit unions have a unique place in twenty-first century society. In a society driven by for-profit enterprises and profit maximization run amuck, especially within the financial community, credit unions lope along as not-for-profit ventures that share resources with all of their members. Antiquated? Perhaps. Out of date? Definitely not!

The unique aspect of the credit union business is that everyone benefits when credit unions work well. Member savers get higher rates of return on their accounts; member borrowers get competitive rates on their loans; and volunteer board members get the satisfaction of knowing that their efforts have helped others benefit financially through their efforts. That is a good feeling to have when an otherwise turbulent day draws to a now quiet close. Ideally, this brief chapter will help board members do that important job just a little bit better. If so, the chapter and the board members will both have served a noble purpose.

8 Advice for new directors
Benton E. Gup, David L. Bickelhaupt, and Irv Burling

This chapter consists of three parts. Part 1, by Benton Gup, provides an overview of the composition of boards of directors. It also contains the results of a survey of directors and officers that asked for their advice for new directors. Part 2, by David L. Bickelhaupt, presents ten things that he learned while serving on various boards. In Part 3, Irv Burling discusses how to create a sustainable future in the financial services business.

Part 1   An overview of boards of directors, and the results of a survey
Benton E. Gup

Board size and insiders
The size and composition of boards of directors has changed over time. A study by Lehn et al. (2003) examined the boards of 81 publicly traded non-financial US firms that survived over the period 1935 to 2000.[1] As shown in Table 8.1, they found that both the average board size and the percentage of insiders has declined over time.

ExxonMobil further illustrates the point that board size and composition within a firm can vary over time. ExxonMobil's "Board size will be within the limits prescribed by ExxonMobil's By-Laws, which currently provide that the Board may have no fewer than 10 and no more than 19 members. Normally, the Board intends to have approximately 11 to 13 members with two to three employee directors and nine to ten non-employee directors."[2] In 2007, the board had 12 members including two employee directors (16.7 per cent) – very close to the data shown in Table 8.1.

However, the size and composition of boards can vary widely from the averages shown in Table 8.1. Synovus, a diversified financial services holding company, has 33 directors of whom 30 per cent are insiders.[3] A study by Belkhir (2004) found that increasing the board size of banks and savings and loans tended to improve their financial performance.[4] The reasons for the improvement may have more to do with who was on the board rather than the number of people on the board.

Finally, in the United States, the United Kingdom, Australia, and at least 37 other countries there is a *sole-board* system – one board of directors.[5] In some other countries, there is separation between management

Table 8.1   Selected average statistics about boards

Year	Board size	Percentage of insiders
1935	12	44
1960	14	40
1980	14	33
1990	13	26
2000	11	16

Note: Figures are rounded.

Source: Lehn et al. (2003).

and a supervisory board. Germany, China, and Spain are examples of such countries. In addition to the supervisory board, companies also may have a management board. For example, "The Management Board of Deutsche Bank AG has as its prime responsibility the strategic management, resource allocation, financial accounting and disclosure, risk management and control of the Group."[6] Companies in France, Switzerland, Finland, and Bulgaria have a mixed board structure, which means that firms can choose between sole and supervisory boards.

The bottom line is that there is no magic formula for the best number of directors, or the composition of the boards. Each firm has to figure out what is best for them.

Who are the directors of the top 50 bank holding companies?[7]
The top 50 bank holding companies in the US range in asset size from Citigroup Inc. (New York), with $1.9 trillion in assets as of December 2006, to Fulton Financial Corporation (Lancaster, PA), with $14.9 billion in assets. As noted in Chapter 1, a small number of large banks hold the majority of the assets of US banks.

About 90 per cent of the directors of the top 50 bank holding companies are men. The majority of the directors are current or retired chief executive officers, presidents, or chairmen of non-bank corporations (for example, health care, oil/gas), or other financial institutions. About half of the boards include an attorney and an academic.

Survey of directors and officers
A survey was sent to a sample of directors and officers of firms listed in the *Standard & Poor's Register of Corporations, Directors & Executives* (2006).[8] The stated purpose of the survey was research for this book. The survey asked "what three pieces of advice would you give to a new

director?" The following are selected responses. Because most of the respondents wanted to remain anonymous, the decision was made not to list any names.

Serving on a board

"Do research on the company that you are considering joining. Reach out to current directors and management and don't be afraid of asking penetrating questions about the company and its personnel."

"Understand clearly the specific objectives of the organization. The more quantifiable and exact, the better. Ask for specifics."

"Develop a good understanding of what the company does – how it makes money."

"Try to determine how suitable the resources – human, financial and technical – of the institution are to accomplish the goals."

"Try to determine how realistic the objectives are and how well the organization is doing in relation to the industry and peers."

"Obtain and read board minutes for the past two years in order to obtain a sense of history, continuity, and recurring issues."

"Obtain and read all corporate governance documents including bylaws and committee descriptions."

"Seek an understanding of the difference in roles between *governance* and *management*."

"Fully understand your *obligations and duties* of being a board member and director."

"Are you on a board for money or prestige?"

"If you decide to join the company, be prepared to devote the time necessary to do your job."

"Spend a day every month or every quarter on-site at the company to walk the halls and pick up the feel for operations."

Board meetings

"Prepare for the meeting in advance. Too many board members show up for the meetings without having read the material."

"Review board packet materials before the meeting."

"Do your own fact checking, when possible, vote responsibly and ethically, and annually re-visit policy limits on your D&O insurance."

"Prepare for meeting by putting in the necessary time to 1) read the material prepared by management; and 2) do independent reading" . . . of outside sources.

"Look for 'spots' to interject your best expertise and experience in helping the board and institution meet its objectives."

"Attend meetings."

"Exercise fiduciary responsibility. Stay on top of what is going on and attend meetings and read materials."

"Be skeptical of almost everything, but not cynical."

"Always be skeptical. Probe deeply on key issues and demand details. But be sensitive to the need for confidentiality of the information provided."

"Question items other than those listed for discussion by chairman or others."

"Think strategically, and avoid conflicts of interest with the company. And don't be reluctant to ask questions."

"Work diligently to maintain true independence. Maintain friendly but arm's-length relationships with senior management."

"Don't allow the current emphasis on board independence blind you to the importance of nurturing and supporting management, particularly the CEO."

"Support the CEO though one-on-one meetings. If the CEO is not performing, change CEOs."

"Before voting on any action, ask yourself 'If this were my family company, with the welfare of my children and grandchildren dependent on my decisions, how would I vote?'"

"Insist on high ethical standards in all instances. Push for total transparency and consistent adherence to generally accepted accounting practices. Don't push the envelope."

"Contribute your time, money, and wisdom."

Part 2   Ten things that I learned while serving on a board of directors
David L. Bickelhaupt

It's said that you learn from your experiences, and that's true. It also may be true that sometimes you learn more from your bad experiences than from good ones. However, I found it much better to learn from good experiences, and fortunately most all of my experiences during service on three different boards of directors have been good. The learning was very worthwhile – not necessarily easy but challenging and even fun at times!

Here are ten things I think I learned. Perhaps you can learn something, too, in reading this list of "do's and don'ts" that I experienced on these boards.

1.   *Whatever time you think it will take each week being a director, it will take at a minimum of at least twice as long*   That "one quarterly or monthly

meeting" is misleading. I was surprised to be elected to the Board of the State Teachers Retirement System (Ohio), because there hadn't been any college teacher elected for more than 20 years. I was more surprised to find out how much time the unpaid job took. What I thought would be one or two days per quarter rapidly escalated to include one or two days a week. There were many reports and related articles to read, numerous phone calls from board and other members, extra committee assignments and travel and time for out-of-town educational meetings. I did receive many plaudits from Ohio State University colleagues and administrators, but no reduction from a regular teaching load of classes.

2. *In another time dimension, you will be on that job as director a lot longer than you think you will be there* Probably you were thinking about "maybe a couple of years," but it often becomes many years. It is not easy to stop. My STRS board position lasted eight years. For the State Automobile Insurance Companies, I was a director for 11 years, and that only stopped because I couldn't be re-elected after age 65. The worst example of this phenomenon was my unpaid "extra" job as a "trustee" on the "Board of Trustees" of the Griffith Foundation for Insurance Education. (Don't let that "trustee" title fool you, because it involves equal or more responsibility than the title of "director.") I became a GF trustee when I started teaching in 1959 at OSU, and 47 years later I'm still an Emeritus trustee.

3. *Don't be surprised if politics enters into your job as director* I didn't realize – until my first meeting on the Board of STRS – that politics had anything to do with being a director. Three of the four elected directors were public school teachers. I was the only college professor. The first vote concerned the number of days of work after retirement that disqualified a member from receiving retirement benefits. The specified number of days made it impossible for a college teacher to work even a semester without losing retirement benefits, while public school teachers with a more flexible schedule could do so. There were three other board members (those appointed by the State of Ohio), and I used my "political" position as a "swing vote" to make the rules fair for all retirees. That position also made it possible for me to be sure popular proposals for increased benefits were carefully scrutinized as to their costs. On any board. Politics should help rather than prevent the best decisions. Too much politics is not good, but it is naive to expect that there will be none!

4. *There will always be an element of "management" versus the board of directors* The board's job is to oversee the decisions of management.

For some institutions there is little conflict because the board merely "rubber stamps" the decisions of management; in other companies there is so much conflict that it is difficult to get anything accomplished. Happily, none of the boards I served on were of these extreme types. Occasional conflicts did occur, but not so frequently as to hamper progress for the institutions. The ideal board sets "policy" as the basis for many management decisions, but leaves the day-to-day decisions for management to make without interference, and with freedom to do their job.

5. *Good communication is absolutely essential between the Board and management* Management must understand the policy framework within which they are expected to operate. Directors don't intercede on unimportant decisions that belong to management. However, every board member has an obligation to participate in discussions – enough but not too much! Finding the middle ground on participation is a continuous challenge. I also learned on all my boards that some members asked very few questions, and questions are important to good communication. Rather than make statements in too adamant a manner, I found that asking relevant questions that got others to think about the best answers was most effective.

6. *Don't get carried away with your own importance as a board member by accepting too many positions as director* If you're good at being a director, undoubtedly you will be asked to serve on other boards. Experience on several boards is beneficial. I found that especially true as I served on the boards of both profit and non-profit institutions. Their goals and methods are very different. However, to try to serve on too many boards simultaneously will lead you to become mediocre (or worse) on all of them. When you have the opportunity to be on multiple boards choose carefully in order to end up with the ones for which you can do the best job. Too many boards become a detriment to your regular job. When teaching, I declined several other directorships that would cause me to miss or rearrange too many classes.

7. *Try to look at everything impartially* A completely unbiased director is hard to find, but a good one tries to achieve this position as often as possible. That's why most boards want more than just directors who are present or past managers of their company. They purposefully elect "outside" directors to achieve a balance of ideas and viewpoints. As a teacher, that was probably a prime reason I was asked to be on all three boards on which I served. Some bias is natural, based on position, experience, attitude and

many other factors. Staying impartial and avoiding unwise bias is the desired objective for all directors.

8. *Flexibility in your voting decisions is important, too*   Recognizing that politics is often involved in many proposals is only the first step to the best voting decisions. Adjusting your actions to achieve maximum value is the secret of success in making your vote count. I tried to do this by expressing myself emphatically when it was needed, raising questions (as earlier noted), compromising when it was the best and most expedient way to getting things done, and trading my vote for someone else's proposal in order to obtain support for mine. All these things may help develop the "team spirit" so essential to success, very much like coaches do to create winning sports teams. The enthusiastic president at State Auto Insurance had a wonderful knack for flexibility, coupled with a positive attitude for progress.

9. *A corollary to flexibility is to expect and support change*   Many boards become too fixed in their decisions. Change is always more difficult than just accepting the status quo. Today's environment is moving too fast in too many ways for you to remain in a fixed position very long. (Obviously, the old saying "If it ain't broke, don't fix it" may apply occasionally, too.) A good director must be willing to accept and encourage change, rather than being an obstacle to progress. I recall realizing this as I resigned from the Griffith Foundation Board in order to make way for an overdue and much needed full-time executive director with an adequate salary. The change would not have been made if I had continued as an unpaid, part-time director. On the State Auto Board, I also gave full support for a major change for the formation of a new stock company subsidiary. This change was an unusual action at that time for a well-established mutual insurance company, but it proved to be the basis for much success during the following years.

10. *Don't stop learning when you become a director*   It's too easy to be complacent, especially if the organization is receiving recognition and praise for doing well. Being a director gives you an opportunity, at every meeting and activity in which you participate, to learn something that will make your decisions better. The need for studying reports and issues is obvious, and extra research is often advisable. Learn about your fellow directors, too. You'll know and understand their positions on various subjects better. For example, I found many of the public school teachers on the STRS board had much less business experience than I, because I was teaching business subjects and doing business consulting. Sharing my ideas with

them by doing a little low-key teaching was usually appreciated, and very important to our working together. Again, on the State Auto Board, I found that I could learn, too, from the other directors who had current legal and other experience that I did not have. The final word (from a biased teacher?) is "Keep on learning"!

Part 3   Creating a sustainable future in the financial services business[9]
Irv Burling

The twentieth century had been for the most part calm and stable in the life insurance business. That changed as the millennium approached. In the twenty-first century the line between insurance companies, banks and brokers, became blurred because they were permitted to compete in what had been each other's business. Because competition was becoming more intense, life insurance companies would have to become more product-driven instead of process-driven.

Interest-sensitive products were in vogue, which meant increased expense administrative and smaller margins to support the distribution system. Furthermore, in a product-driven environment, the distribution system was instinctively more loyal to the customer than the company since the customer demanded the best interest in the near future.

Thus the twenty-first century for insurance companies is going to be more challenging than has been the past 100 years, because of increased competition, volatile interest rates, increased expenses, and less loyalty from the distribution system. To create a sustainable future, companies have to increase their productivity by administering a greater volume of business through mergers and thus reducing administrative expense per unit, and in the long term, increase the amount of distribution at a reduced unit expense rate in a niche market.

The following pages give a general description of the process used to accomplish these objectives and to create a sustainable future.

Initial step in transformation: creating a permanent affiliation
Individuals involved in the business of mergers estimate that 70 per cent of them fail to produce the results intended. There are a number of reasons why this happens. The first reason is probably the result of putting "structure" ahead of "strategy." It is much harder to retain focus on a key strategy than to combine two similar functions.

In one particular case, we decided to combine two functions, investment and legal, and pick the leader for the function by a process defined later in this chapter, and move that function to a larger city to facilitate recruiting. The rest of the 3,000 staff of the larger company serviced over 90 per cent of all the property-casualty needs of the financial institutions in their niche market. The smaller company's staff of 300 sold a simplified portfolio of life insurance and annuities. The two companies started working together by creating a permanent affiliation which 15 years later resulted in a merger.

The key strategy, which was the linchpin for the future of both companies, was transferring and growing the distribution system in existing financial centers around the country. This protected a niche market for the larger company and provided a future niche for the smaller company with a reduction in the distribution cost.

To make certain that neither company could simply walk away from the affiliation, two of the professional units were integrated, with each company assuming the leadership of one of them. The leader was chosen through intense competition and located in the larger city where it would be easier to recruit in the future.

All business of an individual nature was sent to the smaller company since processing was their particular strength. This reduced their unit costs, which was one of their key objectives.

The two CEOs shared leadership by each assuming the role of deputy CEO in the other company. Specifically, the CEO of the larger company concentrated his strength in the marketplace and the other concentrated on the administration in each home office.

Our primary effort was focused on the key strategy or linchpin. We created a binding agreement between the two companies with professional oversight. Normally what we created would be called a strategic alliance. However, if we found that we continually referred to the legal document, then we weren't working hard enough on the intent of the alliance. The initial moves made in the affiliation were scrambled to the extent that it would have been impossible to separate.

Fifteen years after the affiliation was undertaken, the two companies were legally merged. The key linchpin was permanently established and rather than being a dramatic event, the merger represented a means of achieving further cost savings.

Servant leadership established with the help of a life coach
One of the most significant weaknesses in CEOs is an attitude that they have or are expected to have all the answers. A clear message from the tragedy of Enron was that corporate America needs more humble servant leadership. The following paragraphs give some examples of how a "life coach" was used to shape a servant-led management style.

The basic idea behind the hiring of a life coach is the recognition that the CEO is fallible. The transformation needed was so critical to the success of the company that a life coach was important to make certain that mistakes made by the CEO in striving to reach a vision were minimized.

The coach sat in on performance appraisals. He didn't participate in the discussion, but did critique the CEO's performance in the session. This was motivating to individuals because what the company asked of an employee should also apply to the CEO.

The coach also attended scheduled meetings and helped in laying out a format that would be utilized for all meetings in order to expedite the process. In addition, he attended board meetings and offered suggestions on how to engage staff in the process.

Transforming a company is a traumatic experience. Some individuals simply can't handle drastic change. The coach had the capacity to recognize special situations where the CEO needed to exercise restraint or to deal with the problem in a constructive manner, even if meant providing a package to help the employee either survive or find another option.

The coach was available on a 24/7 basis to be a sounding board for making cultural changes with empathy. He brought an added plus to the company since he was an industrial psychologist by trade.

Using servant leadership to change the corporate culture
The smaller insurance company sold primarily two lines of business, namely, life insurance and annuities. A simplified product line should help in the transformation.

Servant leadership means de-emphasizing the typical hierarchical management style and giving more responsibility to the staff. It was useful before a transformation was required, but can be particularly effective during a period of rapid change. It requires a collaborative effort by senior management with the staff, and prompt communications throughout the organization.

You can prepare the staff for a cultural change through a series of performance measures. First, we measured the climate for productivity of the total organization every other year. In off years we did attitude surveys. We used these instruments to move the organization closer to being a product-driven organization which was more sensitive to the market place.

Second, we did a series of what we called "unit physicals." We retained the services of a recently retired executive from another company as an expert in an organization where the particular unit was twice the size of ours. We had the expert give us an opinion of what staff we needed in the future. If our staff had the innate capacity to assume broader responsibility in the future, what would be an effective development program? Finally we did lengthy individual career development programs for individuals who had the capacity to grow with the company. If an individual was not able to adapt to rapid change, we helped them through the services of an industrial psychologist to find a better job-fit in the company or with another company.

The company spent several years on this development effort before the time of transformation was required. Normally, in a merger the employees of the smaller company are "stomped on," but that didn't happen. Employees from both companies were individually assessed by an independent psychologist and put in a "pool." An organization chart for the combined companies was created and staff were selected from the pool based on not only their current ability, but also on the excess capacity that had been developed through career development. Instead of being "stomped on," 30 per cent of the employees in the smaller company assumed increased responsibility in the larger entity. This, of course, created more jobs in the smaller company. The intense effort to change the culture preserved the most important asset, human resources.

Essential characteristics of a servant-led management style
Servant-led leadership de-emphasizes the typical hierarchy of management and empowers staff in reaching for corporate and individual objectives. Communications must be thorough, crisp and timely in order to make optimum progress toward corporate objectives. The following list identifies characteristics which need special emphasis in a servant-led management style.

- *Transparency* Strive to have no hidden agendas. Be authentic, open and honest. Don't let problems simmer. Discuss conflict openly.
- *Integrity* Emphasize the importance of keeping the absolute truth on the table. The truth in small issues will encourage the truth in the larger issues.
- *Development* Work with staff to have a career development plan and work the plan constantly. Human resource is your most important asset.
- *Teamwork* Emphasize the importance of working as a team. When one wins we all win.
- *Trust* Work for a high level of trust. Failures in trust take years to restore.
- *Leadership* Most students of business can manage, that is, adapt to changes, whereas leaders can create the future.

- *Vision*   Strive for a simple vision and communicate it constantly. Make yourself available to answer questions about the future.
- *Sitting loose*   Develop a good sense of humor. Try to develop an environment of enjoying life while doing well.
- *Empathy*   Try to walk in the shoes of others. People don't mind change as much as they mind being told they have to change.
- *Humility*   This is probably the glue to all of the elements. Recognize that you are fallible and therefore solicit input from all of the stakeholders, for instance, employees, retirees, community leaders, investors, suppliers, the broader network of business leaders and so on. Use a coach.

Elements of success in times of change
The lessons learned in creating a sustainable future are grouped into five major categories: strategic, cultural, communications, transformation, and governance plus further additional issues.

Strategic issues

- Keep strategy ahead of structure
- Develop a well-thought-out strategy
- Develop a plan so that the entire organization will keep a focus on your primary strategy

Cultural issues

- Understand the difference in corporate cultures and define what type of culture you want to create
- Develop a method to work through differences in culture

Communications issues

- Plan and orchestrate communications carefully
- Do not delay passing on information
- Do not oversell the change
- Do not withhold information longer than necessary
- Do not make promises you cannot keep
- Be acutely aware of your comments

Transformation issues

- Appoint a transformation director
- Senior management should keep hands-on during the change process

- Clarify the role of any consultant
- Do not use the most extreme example of your culture as your cultural change agent
- Have a technique for counterparts in the organizations to become better acquainted
- Involve human resource staff on the high level transition team

Additional issues

- The CEO must focus on board integration early in the process
- Do not depend exclusively on economies of scale to ensure your future
- Integrate the CEO positions carefully
- Work hard at keeping your ego under control
- Strive to create a transparent organization

Governance issues

The CEO is the primary catalyst for setting governance discipline, working collaboratively with the board of directors. The objective of CEO in this instance was to establish a transparent management style in a "service above self" organization. Governance policies are to be fair and just to all the stakeholders.

Board of directors

- *Chairperson*   The chair should always be an "outside" stakeholder since he/she should have the primary control of the board agenda. A different member of the board should assume the role of the chairperson every two years to distribute authority among the members.
- *Paid employee*   The only paid employee on the board should be the CEO. Board membership should not be a perk. Staff should attend board meetings as subject matter requires.
- *Board committee membership*   Committee membership should change on a rotating basis every year with staggered terms to provide continuity.
- *Meeting expense*   Since you're setting an example for the rest of the organization no meetings should be held in a resort location unless the members pay the increased cost.
- *Executive session*   Every board meeting or board committee meeting should hold an executive session to answer questions such as

(1) Are we getting the information we need? (2) Is the organization transparent? Or (3) Is the CEO meeting our expectations?

Chief executive officer

- *Outside boards* Avoid serving on any other board for pay. In particular, avoid "exchanging" board seats with another organization in order to retain objectivity on the board.
- *Charitable organizations* Commit at least 10 per cent of your time to community and regional charitable organizations. If possible choose commitments that are completed in short periods of time instead of years (for example, fund drives instead of boards).
- *Report to stakeholders* Make at least annual "state of the company" reports to stakeholders such as community, vendors, retirees, retired directors. Make at least monthly reports to employees.
- *Internal auditor* Periodically visit with your internal auditor and make sure that if they see something you've done that doesn't look as "clean as a hound's tooth," they owe it to you to tell you immediately.
- *Golden parachutes* Avoid them! Remember "This is not about me, it's about you." Money can't buy the many thank-you notes you'll receive in the following years. They are life-giving.
- *Consulting role* Avoid a consulting role upon retirement. It is an unnecessary perk that is an additional expense to the company and can be confusing to the new management.
- *Compensation* The current rate of pay for CEOs has been reported to be over 500 times the average rate of pay for employees. This is excessive. For the company I represented I recommended ten times the average rate.

Notes

1. Kenneth Lehn, Sukesh Patro, and Mengxin Zhao (2003), "Determinants of the size and structure of corporate boards: 1935–2000," November, available at SSRN, http://ssrn.com/abstract=470675.
2. ExxonMobil, accessed 14 April 2007 at www.exxonmobil.com/Corporate/InvestorInfo/Corp_II_Guidelines.asp.
3. Synovus, accessed 14 April 2007 at www.synovus.com/index.cfm?catID=4&subject=7&page=7.
4. Mohamed Belkhir, "Board of directors' size and performance in banking", October 2004, available at SSRN, http://ssrn.com/abstract=604505.
5. Renée B. Adams and Daniel Ferreira (2005), "A Theory of Friendly Boards," European Corporate Governance Institute (ecgi), Finance Working Paper no. 100/2005, October.
6. Deutsche Bank, accessed 14 April, 2007, at www.deutsche-bank.de/ir/en/index.html?contentOverload=http://www.deutsche-bank.de/ir/en/497.shtml.
7. The author thanks Jacquelyn Hartmann for her research on this topic. Selected information about the top 50 bank holding companies can be found on the National Information Center's (NIC) website, http://www.ffiec.gov/nicpubweb/nicweb/

Top 50Form.aspx. The NIC is a repository for data and information collected by the Federal Reserve System.

8. *Standard & Poor's Register of Corporations, Directors & Executives* (2006), Vol. 2, Charlottesville, VA, 2006.

9. For additional information on this topic, see Irv Burling (2006), *Winning without Greed*, Theodore, AL: Evergreen Press.

9 Bank directors and the information problem with special regard to subprime markets

Júlia Király and Katalin Mérö

9.1 Introduction

One of the issues of banking involves asymmetric information. Bank directors face the problem of asymmetric information in two senses. First, the bank as a lender is less informed than its customers as borrowers. The board of directors has to take strategic decisions under conditions of imperfect information. Second, non-executive directors are always less informed than the executive management. An appropriate reporting system is required to fill in this information gap.

The initial problem is the classical "asymmetric information" situation first analysed by Stiglitz and Weiss (1981). Their main conclusion was that the problem may lead to credit rationing and non-market-clearing equilibrium. The basic assumption was that bank management is risk-averse and makes decisions in a neutral environment.

In this chapter a slightly different situation will be analysed. We highlight a special market with one dominant local player and several subsidiaries of foreign banks, who are eager to seize the market even at higher risk. At the same time, the clientele comprises retail customers who earlier had been strictly liquidity-constrained, while the newly available bank loans make it possible for them to smooth their consumption path and invest in real estate. The situation is a special one in that there is a less risk-averse lender aiming to increase its market share and a less risk-averse borrower who over-appreciates the availability of credit to its high cost. Directors have to find a reliable strategic path to become a "responsible lender." The situation is analysed in Section 9.2 with reference to the Hungarian retail market.

The second problem is a classical incentive problem: how to achieve the relevant information necessary for making decisions. Only one part of this issue will be analysed – the structure and content of risk reports. A risk report actually should cover all the relevant risks of the bank. Market, credit and operational risks should be analysed equally and the relevant measures should be proposed. There may be two serious problems facing the decision-makers: the information is so detailed and so abundant that it hides the "broad picture," which is necessary for efficient decision-making, or, on the other hand, details are hidden and the broad picture is not supported by elementary information. In Section 9.3 another case study will be provided from the recent past in relation to the world-wide subprime crisis.

9.2 Making strategic decisions with imperfect information in retail lending

Due to the information asymmetry between the debtor and the bank, lending decisions are always made under conditions of imperfect information. However, in the case of countries where the modern commercial banking system has had a very short history, where the relation between the bank and the customer has typically been shorter than three to five years, the shortage of data on the borrower's financial position and behavioral patterns makes this type of information asymmetry even more difficult.

Most of the present market participants entered the Hungarian banking market in the late 1990s or early part of the present decade. Initially the banks entered only the retail deposit market. They started to develop their retail lending business gradually only from the mid-1990s. Accordingly, concentration on the retail lending market remained extraordinarily high. Between 1989 and 1993, the Herfindahl index of retail lending exceeded 9000, and it fell below 5000 only in 1997. In the early years of the new century it stabilized around the 2000 mark. The slow decrease and lasting high level of concentration was coupled with characteristic changes in lending volumes. In 1998 the proportion of retail lending to GDP was only about 3 per cent. From 1999, a new increasing trend emerged. First, consumer-type loans started to increase and this was followed some years later by a mortgage lending boom, which has lasted ever since (see Figure 9.1).

One of the widely analysed consequences of this type of development is the low level of retail market competition – see Móré and Nagy (2004) and Várhegyi (2003). However, there is another important, but less analysed consequence: the banks have no proper information about the credit-worthiness of their clients, partly because they are new participants on the market and partly because the clients themselves are new as borrowers. To make a good strategic decision on business development the bank directors have to have intimate knowledge of the presence and characteristics of these informational differences.

This section of the chapter deals with two typical information problems which have a serious effect on the risk profile of the Hungarian retail banking: the lack of a credit register in general and the lack of proper information in relation to the mortgage market in particular.

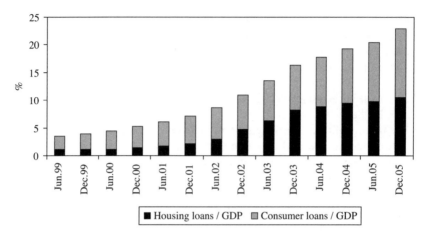

Source: National Bank of Hungary.

Figure 9.1   Composition of retail loans as a proportion of GDP (%)

9.2.1   Lack of a credit register in retail banking

According to Jappelli and Pagano (2006) the advantages of information
sharing among credit market participants are as follows: (i) it improves the
bank's knowledge about the borrower's characteristics, which reduces
adverse selection and facilitates more precise credit pricing; (ii) it reduces
banks' informational rents; (iii) it works as a disciplining device for borrowers; and (iv) it eliminates incentives to over-borrow with multiple lenders.
These advantages would be particularly acute and their absence is extremely
painful in Hungary, where all the related disadvantages can be observed.

The costs of retail lending are outstandingly high on the Hungarian
retail market. Since the dominant and less expensive market segment
involves foreign currency denominated lending (first of all in euros and in
Swiss francs, which have a highly correlated exchange rate movement), for
international comparison it seems justified to compare euro-denominated
credit prices with those of Eurozone countries. As shown in Table 9.1 there
is a significant premium on all categories of credit. Although we have no
appropriate methodology to separate the different components of this
premium, there is no doubt that it has two main factors: the low level of
competition, which allows the banks to work with high cost and profit
levels, and the lack of proper information, which counteracts proper
pricing and allows the realization of informational rent. However, if we try
to make a very rough and simple estimation regarding decomposition of
the 2.88 percentage point premium, we have to decrease it by the differences
in cost to assets ratio. As a result, it seems that about two-thirds of the

Table 9.1   *Interest rates of euro-denominated retail credits in Hungary and in the Eurozone, 2005 (average for newly granted loans)*

	Hungary	Eurozone	difference
Mortgage loans (APRC – annual percentage rate of charge)	6.37	3.92	2.45
Consumer credits (APRC)	10.24	7.79	2.45
Other retail credits (nominal interest rate)	4.67	4.06	0.61
Retail interest rate – average weighted with volumes	7.59	4.71	2.88
Cost to total assets ratio (2004)	3.43	1.46	1.97

Source: European Central Bank and National Bank of Hungary.

premium is caused by the higher cost and about one-third by the informational deficiencies.

Despite the sharp increase in retail lending volumes that can be observed in Figure 9.1, the ratio of Hungarian retail lending to GDP (and especially mortgage lending to GDP) is a number of times lower than that of the Eurozone countries or the US banking system. At the same time, due to higher interest rates and typically shorter repayment periods, the indebtedness of households is relatively close to the international level. In 2005 the debt service to disposable income ratio was about 10 per cent in Hungary, 12 per cent in the Eurozone and 14 per cent in the US. As a consequence, rapid credit growth generates the disciplinary and incentive problems arising from the lack of credit information, even at the low level of credit volumes. The average Hungarian household has very little experience with credit and a low level of financial culture, so the main point of a borrowing decision is whether or not the monthly repayments under the current conditions are manageable or not. This type of decision-making avoids calculating the risks of increasing credit burdens due to either interest rate or exchange rate changes. As in recent years newly granted credits have been almost fully denominated in foreign currencies, the exchange rate risk has become highly significant in terms of overall credit risk. In the case of materialized risk, households have very strong incentives to fly forward and become over-committed by borrowing from new banks. Since the retail lending market is a rapidly growing market segment and almost all the dominant market participants want to increase their market share, some deficiencies in responsible lending are also observable. Banks want to sell their credit products and prefer not to disclose all the related risks with due emphasis. As an excuse, they can refer to the lack of information sharing which defeats proper risk analysis.

To increase responsibility in both the lending and borrowing attitudes of banks and households the introduction of a proper credit sharing mechanism would be the most adequate tool.

In Hungary there is an existing credit sharing mechanism, but its deficiencies prevent the advantages of informational sharing from emerging. The systemic banking crisis of the early 1990s raised the need for a Hungarian Central Credit Register (HCCR). In 1993 the Hungarian Banking Act was amended, obliging all credit institutions to join the HCCR. The crisis had originated in corporate lending, but the Hungarian data protection law is very strict and collecting data on retail customers was definitely forbidden for HCCR. As the retail lending market developed and the retail repayment problems started to emerge, the need for information sharing about retail customers became increasingly articulated. At the same time, under the oligopolistic retail market structure it was (and is) not in line with the interests of the main market participants to build up a voluntarily constituted credit sharing mechanism, since they think that their contribution would be disproportionately high. With the information shared with competitors they get less than they give to their competitors. So it seemed that the only possible way to create a retail information sharing mechanism would be to create it as a part of the existing HCCR.

The 1998 amendment of the Banking Act gave a green light to the collection of retail data but at the same time, very strict constraints were built into the retail information module of HCCR. Data on private individuals could be entered into the HCCR system only in the case of repayment delay accurately defined by the law. This meant that the banks could only share data on bad debtors, not on all the debtors. Five years after the closure of a credit contract the data of the given debtors are deleted from the HCCR's files. This peculiar solution was a compromise between the more and more strongly emerging needs of lenders and the data protection requirement.

In view of the aforementioned advantages of credit sharing highlighted by Jappelli and Pagano (2006), this solution has a very limited effect. Of course, it improves a bank's knowledge about credit applicants, but only partially. The bank knows whether the applicant had repayment problems in the last five years or not, but it has no information whether the applicant has credits with other institutions or not. So the repayment capacity of the clients cannot be evaluated properly and behavioral scorings cannot be applied. As a consequence, the advantage deriving from the possibility of a more accurate calculation of repayment capacities and more precise pricing are limited, and so the informational rent can be reduced only partially. The discipline effect is limited as well, as the system only goes back five years, so after a relatively short period one can appear as a good debtor again. Naturally the incentive to become over-indebted stands unchallenged.

The shortcomings of the HCCR became evident after some years of its operation. Hence the authorities responsible for financial stability (the National Bank of Hungary and the Hungarian Financial Supervisory Authority) together with the Hungarian Banking Association made a joint proposal in 2002 to construct a new credit information sharing system which would fulfill the following requirements:

- The system is not restricted to the data of bad debtors; it should contain data on all the retail clients of the banks. (Making a distinction with the existing system which contains only negative data, this is called a "positive" credit information system.)
- All the banks are obliged to join the system and enter their clients' data.
- Providing data is obligatory by law; there is no need for the clients' formal agreement.
- It is necessary to include data on already existing credit contracts within the system as well.

Since then there has been an ongoing debate about the establishment of a positive credit information sharing system. The ombudsman responsible for data protection is against this initiative, since, according to the Hungarian constitution, it would be against the right of private persons to dispose freely of their personal data. The only reason for an exception is when the data revelation increases the common good to such the extent that it is in the public interest, and there is no other way of achieving the same result.

Up to now the debate has not been concluded. However, since Jappelli and Pagano (2002) have shown that the better and sounder a country's credit information sharing system is the higher is its credit-to-GDP ratio, this debate can be seen as another example of the contradiction between a rigid legal code and the need for a deeper financial system to promote economic growth.

9.2.2   Lack of proper information in mortgage lending

At first sight the information problems seem to be less significant in the case of mortgage lending, where real estate serves as collateral for a loan. The function of real estate as collateral involves not only covering the losses of banks in the case of a loan default, but, as all the relevant surveys show, it significantly increases households' propensity to make repayments compared with other types of loans. However, as both the earlier financial crises caused by real estate bubbles and the present US subprime crisis show, the collateral itself gives only the illusion of security in times of sharp falls in real estate prices or household income shocks (or when the two come together). Mortgage loans, like all other loans, can be considered problem-free only if the borrower is able to repay. So a decision regarding mortgage lending does not require less information about the borrower than other types of loans. Just the opposite – since valuation of the collateral is generally more difficult than in the case of financial collateral (as the markets for real estate are characteristically more opaque and less liquid, mortgage lending is an information-intensive market segment).

The above forms the basis of differentiation between prime and subprime mortgage credits. According to an extremely simplified but practical definition, loans with a high probability of repayment are the primes and those with high default probability are subprimes.

Yet how can we distinguish between prime and subprime mortgages when we have insufficient information about mortgage borrowers? Do the loans granted by banks to customers without knowledge of the borrowers' credit history and credit repayment patterns accumulate extra hidden risks that can be materialized under certain circumstances? Especially after the occurrence of the US subprime crisis, these questions are of outstanding importance in all countries where a rapid mortgage lending increase has evolved without the previous accumulation of the relevant information on borrowers by an institution such as the HCCR. Hence, to make well-founded decisions about business policy and related risk-taking policy, bank directors should raise and address such questions.

In the following we analyse recent developments on the Hungarian mortgage lending market to illustrate the above dilemmas.

On the Hungarian mortgage market, it is possible to differentiate between two market segments: loans for house purchase and consumer loans covered by mortgages (see Figure 9.2)

Despite the sharp increase in housing loans (see Figure 9.1), the rate of increase does not seem extraordinarily high, being just about in line with the financial deepening taking place in recent years in Hungary. Between 2003 and 2006 the proportion of loans for house purchases remained at about 20 per cent of total banking loans. During the same period, mortgage-covered consumer loans showed an outstanding growth rate and tripled in volume. From the supply side, this sharp increase is motivated by the illusion of an almost total risk-mitigating effect of real estate, which is based not only on the value of the collateral but also on the attitude of households towards the repayment of real estate loans. From the demand side, the main incentive is the more favorable conditions, as mortgage loans are typically cheaper and have longer maturity.

The mortgage lending expansion was not coupled with an increase in real estate prices. Prices typically remained unchanged in real terms. However,

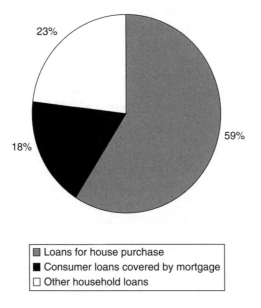

Source: Hungarian Financial Supervisory Authority.

Figure 9.2   Composition of household loans, end 2006 (%)

the loan-to-value (LTV) ratios permanently increased. Entering the mort-gage market, banks' policy towards the LTV ratio seemed conservative enough – the average ratio was about 50 per cent. As competition became stronger, the easing of credit standards came into focus, especially in the form of increasing loan-to-value. One hundred per cent or sometimes even higher LTVs became generally accepted practice in certain client segments. This means that, even if there is no real estate price bubble on the Hungarian market, the sensitivity of the mortgage portfolio to a real estate price decrease has become significantly higher.

Another characteristic of the mortgage lending is that, due to much more favorable interest rates, its denomination has strongly shifted towards foreign exchange – at the beginning of the decade predominantly to euros and from the middle of the decade to Swiss francs. This forex lending has not resulted in an increase of exchange rate risk for the banks, as they can either fund themselves in euros or cover their open position on the forex market. However, an adverse exchange rate shock could increase the repay-ment burden of borrowers who have their income in Hungarian forint (HUF). That is a typical case of risk transfer, from exchange rate to credit risk. Of course, this is a natural accompaniment of borrowing, just as is the increase of repayments due to an interest rate rise in the case of borrowing in local currency. The relevant question is whether the banks are lending responsibly and their clients have risk-awareness.

In this sense, responsible lending means that the bank is aware of all the relevant risks of lending and while determining the amount of a particular loan granted to a client takes into account not only the market value of the collateral but the repayment capacity of the client, even in the case of adverse shocks, either in relation to his/her income position or on the markets (an increase in interest rates and/or exchange rates). The other dimension of responsibility involves improving clients' risk-awareness by informing them about the related risk and the potential increase of instalments. However, since in the lending contract the bank is the professional participant, primarily it is its responsibility to consider all the potential risks.

There are many methods the banks can use to take into account the effect of potentially increased repayment burdens. They can use discount factors based on historical or hypothetical interest rate and/or exchange rate movements or decrease the LTVs applied. Nevertheless, the limitations of HCCR inhibit the banks from assessing the financial status of their clients properly. This means that all the risk assessment methods, even the most sophisticated ones, have a weak foundation as they are based on incomplete information.

According to the US definition of subprime lending, not only a weak credit history but also a limited one makes a loan subprime.[1] In this sense one can say that the entire Hungarian mortgage portfolio is subprime, since, given the lack of proper client information, the banks cannot have strongly established data on the creditworthiness of those applying for a loan. Does the quality of the mortgage lending portfolio reinforce this judgment? Up to now it seems not. The mortgage portfolio is the best quality portfolio segment of the banks, enjoying very low default rates and consequently a low provisioning-to-loan ratio. However, this good quality partly arises from the rapid increase of volumes, which automatically keeps the portfolio "young" and the need for provisioning on the average low.

Returning to our calculation of 2.45 per cent interest rate premium realized on Hungarian mortgage lending and the rough estimate that one-third of it can be considered as informational rent, we can argue that the market doesn't treat the Hungarian mortgage market as subprime, since this rent is lower than the average subprime premium, even on markets with an existing credit information sharing mechanism.[2] Of course, as the reference rate is the Eurozone mortgage rate, we should refine our statement: the market doesn't consider that the Hungarian mortgage market has a significantly higher proportion of subprime lending than the Eurozone countries' market.

Taken as a whole, it is difficult to evaluate the situation from the perspective of riskiness and determine the entire Hungarian retail market as predominantly prime or as by definition subprime. The default rates, the provisioning and the prices are characteristic for primes, while in contrast the available information is typical for subprimes. Given that since the housing loan expansion evolved, there have not been extreme adverse shocks which could cause the deterioration of the loan portfolio of the banks, there is no evidence for either definition. The only way to make a better-based analysis is to establish the HCCR. Until that happens, the above dilemma itself is a sufficient source of risk, which strongly emphasizes the need for very cautious risk management practices and responsible lending.

9.3   Contagion effect of the subprime crisis of 2007
In the previous section we analysed a non-typical "subprime" market and described the problems directors face in identifying the real causes of increasing subprime lending.

It is now well known that the so-called subprime crisis emerged from the US retail market. Subprime lending – that is, lending to borrowers with impaired credit history or adverse demographic characteristics regarding place of living, age, and so on – began to develop in the US in the 1980s. Subprime loans are typically granted to people with a less than perfect credit history. The loans have low interest rates for the first two or three years.

As we have shown above, the general features of subprime lending are higher LTV ratios, but relatively smaller loan size, lack of credit history, inadequate scoring, higher risk reflected in higher delinquency rates, and higher interest rates.

To determine which lending institutions are subprime lenders is as difficult as defining subprime borrowers, because financial institutions operate in a complex environment and some quasi-financial institutions lending subprime loans are often out of the range of financial supervision monitoring. As time went by, more and more universal banks started to advance subprime loans and, according to various estimates, before the peak 10–15 per cent of total retail loans in America could have been classified as subprime, with more than 30 per cent originating from commercial banks.

As interest rates increased and real estate prices stagnated, the delinquency rate on subprime loans increased, and at the end of 2006, nearly 20 per cent of subprime mortgages issued between 2005 and 2006 were projected to fail (Centre for Responsible Lending, 2007). Several subprime lenders went bankrupt and in the summer of 2007, some major players, such as American Home Mortgage and Countrywide Financial also failed.

Of course, this was not the end, but only the beginning of the story. For a long time it has seemed to be a "local problem" of the US market. Even in the spring of 2007, European analysts stated that the European banking sector was not threatened by the American developments. Then in the late summer of 2007 there was more and more bad news about the European banks: an increasing number of market players, among them the biggest ones, such as BNP or UBS, turned out to be facing serious problems. The interbank market dried up from one day to another – banks no longer trusted each other, nobody knew the real exposure to the subprime problem of its counterparty. Even the European Central Bank had to intervene with a significant dose of liquidity.

As the story slowly unfolded, the US "market efficiency" caused the European banks to panic (Peston, 2007). Subprime loans, like any other mortgage loans, have been securitized by efficient Wall Street players. First, the loans were bundled and appeared on the market as plain mortgage-backed securities (MBS). Of course, since the high delinquency rate was well known to the originator, there were different tranches of MBS, from AAA to the equity class. However, the rating of the AAA paper was based on historical default rates, which proved to be highly erroneous, as it turned out. Later, these first generation papers were re-bundled and resold as special collateralized debt obligations (CDOs), that is, these CDOs had been backed by other securities whose rating was based on a low default past. Triple A rating has increasingly lost its significance on the market. First, funds investing in these highly leveraged, highly risky instruments realized that model pricing fails in turbulent times. Several commercial banks relied on cheap funding promising high return investment: these were the asset-backed commercial papers (CPs) issued by several European banks. The liquidity mismatch became apparent when lenders declined to repurchase the maturing CPs and banks were not able to convert to cash their high return CDOs backing the CPs.

However, for a bank in central Europe all these events were quite distant. Or were they? Let us imagine an average central European bank, which is the subsidiary of some European big player. The bank has deeply engaged in the retail credit boom summarized above. Since retail deposits have not matched retail loan growth, the bank has financed its credit growth partly from its mother bank and partly from the European money market. The bank has a subsidiary, an investment bank with significant market share.

At the first directors' meeting after the crisis, the directors get an overview prepared by the strategic department and the treasury of the bank about the possible consequences of the crisis. The report gives an overview about the American market, the contagion mechanism in Europe, the MBS/CDO failures, the liquidity squeeze and the CP-funding problem. The study carefully analyses the "flight to quality" problem, that is, the significant fall of equity prices throughout the world, including the local stock exchange index. It is pointed out that the flight to quality phenomenon is responsible for the diminishing carry trade positions, and, as a consequence, despite the strong macroeconomic figures, this is the reason for the devaluation of the local currency. According to the report, the currency was devalued by more than 5 per cent and its volatility has again significantly increased.

Nevertheless, the head of the strategic department and the head of the Asset Liability Committee (ALCO) declare that in the bank "business is as usual," there is no contagion effect; they have no direct or indirect US subprime exposure and their FX positions are covered.

The directors could have been satisfied with the broad picture. However, they have read controversial evaluations of the events in the local media – some analysts try to mitigate the significance of the whole issue, declaring that a 10 per cent drop in equity is far from being the Asian crisis or the 1998 crisis and the banking sector is much more healthy than it used to be, while other investment analysts paint a much more obscure picture about credit crunch, liquidity squeeze, significant second-hand effects and a partly collapsing banking market.

The directors decide to have a much more detailed picture about the bank. First, they would like to check the retail portfolio – whether the "quasi-subprime" character of the retail market may result in delinquency rates as high as on the US subprime market.

The retail risk report (see Table 9.2) includes the total amount of different retail loan amounts, the recently originated loans, the loan loss provision of the previous quarters and the loan loss reserve. According to these figures, the portfolio of the bank is evolving in parallel with that of the sector and no special features emerge. However, reporting in conformity with new Basel II recommendations does reveal some interesting phenomena:

Estimated probabilities of defaults (PDs) are based on a longer-term model of the bank, while measured PD is the actual delinquency rate of the previous quarter. In the particular case of free utilization mortgage-backed loans, the measured PD is significantly higher than the estimated one. Since loss given default (LGD) figures suggest the same, the directors request

Table 9.2   Risk report on the retail mortgage portfolio, 31 August, 2007

	Estimated PD (%)	Measured PD (%)	Estimated LGD (%)	Measured LGD (%)
Retail mortgage loan	1.47	1.75	13.2	12.5
Retail mortgage backed free util loans	4.8	6.2	8.7	12.2

some more detailed analysis. It turns out that the bank started to build up a sales agent network some three years ago and in the past two quarters, the amount of loans sold by the agents has exceeded the amount sold by the branch network. The directors, who have read about the "liars' loans" problem in the US market (Peston, 2007; Caputo, 2006) will require strict monitoring of the agent network and a monthly risk report. However, the directors do not consider the problem acute, since the 6.2 per cent default rate is far from those characteristic for the present US subprime market.

The retail risk manager, who has recently gained his international financial risk manager (FRM) degree, distributes another paper for the board, in which, according to the new Basel II suggestion, he had run a stress test based on an adverse macroeconomic development with special regard to devaluing local currency and high volatility. The test is based on Monte Carlo simulations and calculates the expected shortfall of the retail portfolio. The results do not contradict the supposed strong capital position of the bank: in the worst case at 99.9 per cent probability the portfolio loses 23.3 per cent of its value, though it does not eat up the excess regulatory capital of the bank. The board members feel safe, though one of them, a former professor of mathematics (actually, the CEO of the largest local IT developer) questions some detail about the modeling exercise, but the precise answers convince him, as well.

Then the directors examine the funding problem of the bank. The first question concerns whether the parent bank is involved directly or indirectly in the subprime crisis, and, consequently, does the liquidity squeeze of the European markets have any effect on the funding of the bank. The reports from the parent bank are not easily available, since the information flow is generally a one-way traffic – the subsidiary provides the parent bank with information, but not vice versa. However, the risk manager of the bank has developed a good informal relationship with his counterparty at the parent bank and soon the report is in front of the management. The reported subprime exposure of the parent is less than €200 million and it is not involved in any form of CP funding. However, due to increased ambiguity and decreased risk appetite the risk spreads have increased on the banking market as well, and, since the parent bank has an AA rating, its cost of funding has increased by 15 basis points, which will have an effect on the funding cost of the local bank.

One of the directors remembers that in the usual "risk-table set," the funding gap of the bank is always demonstrated. They ask for the chart and most of them are struck by the threatening tendency revealed by the picture (see Figure 9.3).

It seems that the bank really is losing its stable funds and that in fact more than 25 per cent of loans cannot be financed from deposits but only from the

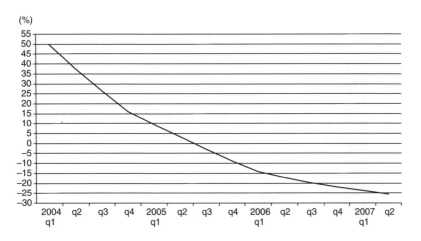

Figure 9.3   Funding gap

money market. The directors immediately call an exceptional ALCO meeting to check the funding cost sensitivity of the bank. They look at the mismatch, that is, they carefully analyse the maturity ladder of the bank, and agree with the head of the ALCO that for the relevant time interval, that is, from one week up to three months, the bank is not exposed to serious liquidity risk.

At the ALCO meeting the usual table-set ("Quarterly Risk Assessment Report") is presented to the board. Usually, they do not pay too much attention to this, since for most of them, the different charts do not actually "tell the story." They rather rely on the presentation of the ALCO secretary. At this meeting they decide to analyse one by one all the tables and charts. Besides the funding gap and maturity mismatch, the interest rate gap analysis and the attached interest stress test are scrutinized. They realize that the economic value of bank equity would change within limits due to unexpected movements (+/− 200 basis points) of interest rates – the maximum loss is less then 2.5 per cent. However, they are less pleased with the net income simulation, since the best interest income of the bank is highly sensitive to high interest rate volatility. The ALCO secretary explains that the simulation is an old style one, that the sensitivity of the net interest income is not well reflected in the tables and promises to produce new simulation results for the next meeting.

The board spends more than an hour in a detailed examination of the trading book analysis. Questions are asked about the value at risk (VAR) figures and the trading limits (the bank has been applying VAR limits for five years now). They gain some comfort from seeing that the bank's positions are in line with the accepted strategy and that no sudden shock due

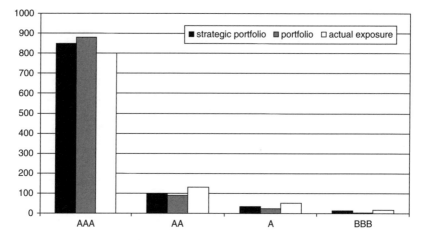

Figure 9.4   Structure of the bond portfolio according to credit risk buckets

to the consequences of the subprime mortgage crisis is expected. The meeting is almost over when one of the members puts a question about one of the less interesting charts, which presents the structure of the bond portfolio according to credit risk buckets (see Figure 9.4).

The directors do not usually pay attention to this chart, since there has never been any problem with debt papers. However, this time, the board is more sensitive to credit risk problems and they start to put questions about the detailed explanation of the individual columns. The head of the treasury explains that the board accepted the strategic portfolio – which serves as a benchmark – at the beginning of the year, and they have the right to exceed the individual exposures in the strategic portfolio by 50 per cent in each credit notch. This means, for example, that in the strategic portfolio the share of the AA papers is 3.5 per cent, and the treasury is authorized to invest 5.2 per cent. The board is surprised, but the risk manager presents the relevant document and they have to admit that in this sense, they have been quite careless.

Another member asks "what is the difference between the 'portfolio' and the 'actual exposure'?" The head of the treasury explains that the bank has different agent contracts on security lending and a part of these contracts lets the agent reinvest the cash collateral in different papers. The directors slowly understand that their triple-A liquid papers are converted into less liquid papers, which represent higher risk but promise higher profitability. From the detailed analysis of the "actual exposure," they learn that in the form of security lending they have invested 8 per cent of the assumed triple-A portfolio into less liquid and more risky asset backed securities/collateralized debt obligations (ABS/CDO) papers, and a part of it has been directly affected by the subprime crisis, that is, they have suffered non-accrued losses in the recent past. The head of the treasury admits that the actual loss is unknown, since the agent is compelled to evaluate the reinvested portfolio only once a month and the actual evaluation is expected in a week's time.

The final conclusion of the ALCO meeting is that the ABS/CDO portfolio should be marked to market on a daily basis and daily losses should be reported to the board. The directors drew the lesson: they should pay much more attention to the accepted portfolio strategy, the limit structure and the actual portfolio of the bank, since until than a tricky security lending business was being run according to the accepted risk strategy, though neither the treasury nor the risk unit could be blamed.

9.4 Conclusion

Lack of information is one of the main problems facing the boards of directors of most banks. In turbulent financial market conditions, proper and timely information is of an even higher value than usual. In this chapter we have analyzed the type of information problem that can lead to misinterpretation of the risks related to Hungarian retail lending, as well as to problems in connection with exposure to contagion from financial markets. The present US subprime crisis is making bank directors re-evaluate their earlier strategies and pay more attention to relevant information, even the smaller details.

In this chapter, two different information-related aspects of the subprime problem have been presented.

We have argued that the general need for a proper credit information sharing system is especially important for less mature retail lending markets such as the Hungarian one, where even the largest market players have no proper credit history data about their clients. In view of the present US subprime crisis, it has become even more evident that the lack of reliable customer information may contribute to quasi-subprime lending phenomena involving not correctly measurable and, as a consequence, not fairly priceable risk.

In the form of a case study of an average bank in central Europe, we have also demonstrated that in an atypical risk environment routine risk analysis offers little help in understanding the real risk profile of the bank. One of our final conclusions is that the regular revision of risk strategy and the detailed analysis of the standard risk reports, especially those which have been prepared in line with Basel II principles, may help directors to have a clear picture of their bank. However, they have to be careful with Basel II reports as well, as these build heavily on rating information which has proved to be less relevant in the present crisis, primarily, as we also demonstrated, because they use historical default rates, which can rapidly change during a crisis. This contributes to the fact that the contagion of the crisis has not yet fully unfolded. In other words, at the most unexpected moments directors may discover new skeletons in their cupboard.

Notes

1. "The term 'subprime' refers to the characteristics of individual borrowers. Subprime borrowers typically have weakened credit histories that include payment delinquencies and possibly more severe problems such as charge-offs, judgments, and bankruptcies. They also may display reduced repayment capacity as measured by credit scores, debt-to-income ratios, or other criteria that may encompass borrowers with incomplete credit histories" (see the 2001 interagency Expanded Guidance for Subprime Lending Programs).
2. According to Comsisengphet and Pennington-Cross (2006) the premium charged to subprime borrowers is about two percentage point on the US market.

References

Caputo, Stephanie (2006), "A review of the OCC's recent residential mortgage lending standards," accessed at www.occ.gov/cdd/newsletters/summer 05/cd/areviewofocc.htm.

Centre for Responsible Lending (CRL) (2007), "Subprime lending: net drain on homeownership," CRL issue paper No. 14, 27 March.

Comsisenghpet, Souphala and Anthony Pennington-Cross (2006), "The evolution of the subprime mortgage market," *Federal Reserve Bank of St Louis Review*, **88**(1), January/February, 31–56.

Jappelli, Tullio and Pagano, Marco (2006), "Role and effects of information sharing in credit markets," in Bertola Giuseppe, Richard Disney and Charles Grant (eds), *The Economics of Consumer Credit*, Cambridge, MA: MIT Press, pp. 347–71.

Jappelli, Tullio and Marco Pagano (2002), "Information sharing, lending and defaults: cross-country evidence," *Journal of Banking and Finance*, **26** (10), 2017–45.

Móré, Csaba and Nagy, Márton (2004), "Competition in the Hungarian Banking Market," National Bank of hungary working paper 2004/9.

Office of the Comptroller of the Currency, Board of Governors of the Federal Reserve System, Federal Deposit Insurance Corporation, and Office of Thrift Supervision (2001), "Expanded guidance for subprime lending programs," attachment to SR 01-4(GEN) letter issued 31 January, accessed at www.federalreserve.gov/boarddocs/srletters/2001/SR0104.htm.

Peston, Robert (2007), "Liars' Loans," 20 August accessed at www.bbc.co.uk/blogs/thereporters/robertpeston/2007/08/liars_loans.html.

Stiglitz, Joseph E. and Andrew Weiss (1981), "Credit rationing in markets with imperfect information," *American Economic Review*, **71** (3), 393–410.

Várhegyi, Éva (2003), "Banking competition in Hungary," *Közgazdasági Szemle* [*Hungarian Economic Review*] (December), 1027–48, in Hungarian only.

10 Bank governance: perceptions from experience

Warren Hogan and Rowan Trayler

Introduction

This chapter examines provisions about governance in Australian banking and related activities in light of past experiences. Most attention is given to the provisions for corporate governance laid down by the Australian Prudential Regulation Authority (APRA) and recommendations from the Basel Committee on Banking Supervision as well as commentaries from officers associated with those entities. The latter segments are directed to an appraisal of requirements in light of experiences of banking activities during recent decades.

Bank governance has been of major interest ever since the introduction of internationally-agreed capital requirements, referred to as Basel I, under the auspices of the Bank for International Settlements in 1988. During the past decade this focus was heightened by the failure of Barings Bank in early 1995 and Long-Term Capital Management in 1998.

Governance issues have long been a focus for all corporate activities. So much so that in recent years the implementation of measures to comply with legislative provisions and listing requirements on securities exchanges has become a major issue for boards and management of companies. The importance of these concerns has been sustained by the results of a recent survey of perceptions of risk management across corporate entities in Australia and New Zealand (Aon, 2007). The latest survey for 2006–07 shows issues related to corporate governance as the most important concern for risk management as was also the position the previous year, 2005–06.

The analyses of issues associated with governance requirements for banks and related services offered in this chapter reflect historical experiences in the banking industry including those from turbulent years associated with major structural change between 1983 and 1987 and their aftermaths. Those experiences have been treated at length in a commentary covering those years by a former chief executive of a major bank (White and Clarke, 1995). Other commentaries are drawn upon to illuminate issues from an Australian perspective (Carew, 1997; Davidson and Salsbury, 2005) However, international aspects may be drawn upon to explore contentious issues, especially those concerning the role of boards in relation to management (Hogan, 1997).

The basis for policies and practices in the financial services sector

A basis for an examination of the rules bearing upon the conduct of boards and management of major financial institutions, especially banks, may best be determined by taking up comments made by the chairman of the Australian Prudential Regulation Authority, Dr John Laker, when addressing a conference on corporate governance (Laker, 2005). On that occasion he stated that, "the prime responsibility for the prudent management and financial soundness of a regulated financial institution rests with its board and management." This definitive position should be understood in the context of quite comprehensive measures for monitoring and supervision of prudential efforts bearing upon various participants in the financial services sector.

This prime responsibility is assigned to the board of a financial entity in very clear ways. The board sets the strategic direction for the institution just as it must set all significant policies. While the precise meaning of the word "significant" is not spelled out, the meaning reflects a notion of responsibility for all policies having a material impact on performance.

This means all policies relating to risk and risk tolerance, the capital commensurate with the risk assumed by these policies and the systems to ensure the risk features are accurately measured and reported. Should steps taken by the board to achieve these outcomes lead to creation of board committees, the ultimate responsibility still lies with the board as a whole.

The role for corporate governance of banks is of greater importance than for other companies because of the crucial role of financial intermediation in the functioning of the economy (Laker, 2005, p. 2). This explains why the Australian Prudential Regulation Authority (APRA) requires all entities subject to its supervision to adhere to requirements. The difference in application is made clear in prudential guidelines issued by APRA (Prudential Standard APS 510: APRA, 2006). These reflect minimum standards to be met by regulated institutions.

As revealed in Aon (2007), individuals and groups having to work with the various authorities monitoring adherence to regulatory and statutory requirements have concerns no less important than those required of the supervising agencies. The strains brought about by efforts to meet these requirements may help explain the very recent decision to moderate the listing requirements for publicly-listed companies on the Australian Securities Exchange (ASX).[1] An important feature of these requirements allows companies to opt out of ASX requirements by way of explaining circumstances for not meeting a particular obligation.

In contrast, adherence to prudential standards across the financial services sector is obligatory. Hence, issues associated with listing requirements for the ASX are not considered here except where they may be revealing of issues linked to monitoring and supervision of prudential standards.

Practices in the Australian setting

Independence is defined for purposes of assessing board membership. Apart from a non-executive role the role of independent director excludes having a substantial shareholding, or any involvement in past management, as a supplier, customer or adviser. Any of these activities or connections which could materially interfere with the exercise of judgment breaches independence. This begs the question of what constitutes a materiality, or the perception of it.

Three years must lapse before a former chief executive officer of the regulated entity can become chairman of the board. Provisions of the same sort apply to relationships between auditors and members of boards with an audit background or connection.

The minimum size of a board must be five at all times with the chairman an independent director. The stipulation "at all times" means having more than five ordinarily. The required board audit committee must have three members, all non-executive and the majority independent, while the chairman of the board cannot be chairman of the committee. The relationships between the board audit committee and the external and internal auditors are specific about independence from management and direct access.

The board is required to have in place policies and procedures for the assessment of individual members. It must also have a formal policy on measures to renew itself to "ensure it remains open to new ideas and independent thinking, while retaining adequate expertise."

This prudential standard on governance does not cover all the possibilities advanced prior to implementation in May 2006. A major omission was dropping any mention of a requirement for a board risk committee, though this had been canvassed in the months prior to the announcement (Laker, 2005, p. 4). This change recognizes the fact that small entities would not need a comprehensive committee structure while larger entities could be expected to provide one.

International perspectives

If the prudential requirements on banking and related entities are more onerous than the flexible "if not, why not" provisions on governance for publicly-listed companies, there remain some limp provisions in Prudential Standard APS 510, such as with the notion of materiality in relation to the concept of independence where the expectation may be less than that for Caesar's wife.

Table 10.1   Basel Committee, sound corporate governance principles

---

Board members should be qualified for their positions, have a clear understanding of their role in corporate governance and be able to exercise sound judgment about the affairs of the bank.

The board of directors should approve and oversee the bank's strategic objectives and corporate values that are communicated throughout the banking organization

The board of directors should set and enforce clear lines of responsibility and accountability throughout the organization

The board should ensure that there is appropriate oversight by senior management consistent with board policy

The board and senior management should effectively utilize the work conducted by the internal audit function, external auditors, and internal control functions.

The board should ensure that compensation policies and practices are consistent with the bank's corporate culture, long-term objectives and strategy, and control environment

The bank should be governed in a transparent manner

The board and senior management should understand the bank's operational structure, including where the bank operates in jurisdictions, or through structures, that impede transparency

---

Source: BIS (2006).

The Basel Committee on Banking Supervision associated with the Bank for International Settlements (BIS) published a report on requirements for governance of banks (BIS, 2006). Eight principles were listed in this report, all of which have bearings on the Australian position. These are summarized in Table 10.1. This chapter is restricted to those aspects which cast further light on ways of interpreting or understanding Australian provisions.

Given the importance attached to the independence of board members in the Australian setting, some provisions associated with Principle 1 in this report, being about board members, should be noted. These include that board members should "avoid conflicts of interest, or the appearance of conflicts of interest, in their activities with, and commitments to, other organizations"; they should also "Commit sufficient time and energy to fulfilling their responsibilities," which include to "Develop and maintain an appropriate level of expertise as the bank grows in size and complexity." These three features bear upon board members' capacity to perform as well as their independence, though the second one is about curtailing the extent of commitments to other entities.

These features do not clarify to any great extent the independence theme for board members. What emerges in the commentaries upon Principle 1 is the importance of boards not succumbing to the influence of dominant shareholding(s) or senior management let alone political influences.

When viewing the role of boards in setting strategic objectives, the report emphasizes strongly the impact of corporate culture on establishing professional conduct conducive to a bank's best interests, more so than any written statements. The same attitudes have been advanced in Australia (Somogyi, 2005). Having established the strategies to be pursued the board should put in place effective measures to ensure clear lines of responsibility and accountability. This is most important for the effective workings of subsidiaries as well as securing transparency in the reporting of activities. This is the basis for substantiating adherence to the strategic objectives and policies laid down by the board.

This BIS report is directed predominantly to large internationally-operating banks. In its commentaries reference is made to smaller banks, especially those with a single or a few owners; but these are treated almost as exceptions to the general experience. In such circumstances the recommendations and suggestions on prudential procedures allow, in the event of shortcomings, for the direct involvement of prudential authorities in changing ownership or the exercise of changes to the board. This is mentioned here because the thrust of the general analysis advanced here is to expect boards of internationally-operating banks to match the needs for breadth of experience and understanding with the tasks assumed. Australian banks fall into this latter category by any reasonable measure. Their collective experiences in recent decades would point to the testing circumstances which arise from time to time for internationally-operating banks.

Independence
The concept of independence applying to members of boards of financial services companies, not just banks, is onerous. The essence of independence lies in the capacity to take a comprehensive view of strategies and policies in place and the prospects for new measures to optimize the earnings of the entity as measured by the return on equity. By implication the choice for an optimum outcome includes assessments of risks associated with the management of liabilities and assets.

Explanations of those features which do not reflect independence are revealing. Substantial shareholders do not necessarily have a comprehensive view of the workings of a bank. Their time horizon may reflect short-term goals of maximizing the share price in order to sell their holdings. Another potential worry is seeking preference in access to borrowings for entities linked to the substantial shareholder.

Board members drawn from management ranks may be queried as to the stance they might take on a number of issues. There is the possibility of supporting existing policies at the expense of failing to explore new opportunities. Then there is the self-interest embodied in circumstances where the former bank officer holds options reflecting previous management contracts. Expectations for exercising options could bring a focus on measures affecting short-term pricing of shares, though conditions of their issue bear upon value. No less important in circumstances where options are on issue to staff, "buy backs" by the company may be deemed to enhance the relative value of the remaining shares and the options yet to be exercised.

Suppliers would not seem to have substantial prospects of influencing the workings of a board when the great bulk of supplies by value come from individuals and households in retail funding and wholesale markets bring together a wide array of funds managers. Only on occasions of severe market disruption, as in August 2007, might a highly liquid supplier be in a position to gain influence on policy directions.

The significance of the customer as a potential source of bias in deliberations of a board might arise were the business brought to the bank by that customer of sufficient scale to be significant to the totality of earnings. But this influence would be there whether or not that customer was a board member. This is little different from the substantial shareholding being a basis for judging a lack of independence.

The role of adviser is a special case of the broad category of supplier. Those fitting this category include legal and financial entities and partnerships as well as management consultants. Other categories would include actuaries and personnel consultants of various persuasions.

The most sensitive of all these categories relate to auditing and accounting services.[2] With these two, the requirement of a three-year separation between the provision of services and the joining of a board is understandable as a discontinuity to bring a distance between the practice of professional advice in particular circumstances and a broader participation in board deliberations. However, this distinction is not anywhere near so precise as this statement would imply because other requirements associated with board membership include having some members with financial skills and capacities.

The preceding paragraphs offer a framework for understanding the concept of independence. There are the precise restraints requiring a three-year gap between ending a role as an auditor and becoming a board member in the company previously audited. A similar time lapse applies to a former chief executive officer before she or he may become chairman of the board of that company. Then there is the substantial shareholding, which may be measured as some percentage of total shares on issue; depending on circumstances and specific legislation this may be deemed to be 5 per cent or 10 per cent.

Apart from these precise requirements, the matter of independence is one of perception best illuminated by tests of the materiality or significance of the links. For suppliers of services, including advisers, the test of materiality should be the impact of the earnings from the links to the bank to the total net earnings of the participating company or practice.[3] Less than 10 per cent, and most certainly 5 per cent, would be immaterial. Specification of tests is one thing but assessment is another. Moreover, these tests cannot apply to past management owing to pension payments.

The relationship between customer and bank is also different from suppliers because ties to a bank may be essential to survival through provision of working capital. For them the links are material and costly to alter, should that even be a possibility.

Ultimately, the prudential authority must query claims about independence.

Board matters
The importance attached to the ultimate responsibility of the board for the conduct of the bank in all the significant manifestations of policies cannot be understated. In all this the chairman has a guiding role. These obligations are stipulated by the Australian Prudential Regulation Authority for its monitoring and supervision of the business conducted by banks and other financial services activities. How a bank conducts itself is no less a concern to the Reserve Bank of Australia which bears responsibility for the stability of the banking system basically through exchange settlement arrangements.

These provisions place on boards two very distinct sets of obligations. One relates to how the board informs itself about the ways in which management implements policies and procedures laid down by it, usually on the recommendation or endorsement of the chief executive officer. The other relates to the ways the board pursues measures to ensure it is not only alert to new ideas and possibilities but is in a position to test their worth.

The first of these reflects the need for mutual confidence between board and senior management as the basis to secure honest and effective transmission of all information about the workings of the bank. In important respects the culture generated within an organization determines the scope for securing the integrity of relationships. Undoubtedly, during periods of substantial structural change, such as occurred during and after the deregulation of the banking and financial system between 1983 and 1986, longstanding practices may be diminished or abandoned. For example, the experiences in Westpac Banking Corporation between 1985 and 1992 bear ample witness to the strains and dislocation which may arise (Davidson and Salsbury, 2005, Chapters 20–24). While the basic culture of a bank is a credit culture that cannot be applied without acceptance of qualities reflecting accountability, integrity and responsibility, most of these features are beyond the capacity of a prudential authority to implement let alone impose.

This brings attention to a second theme: the capacity of each member of a board to reflect on her or his performance as well as that of their colleagues and the board as a whole and to explore ways of renewal. In Australia, prudential supervision calls for boards to address these issues by having in place policies on review and appraisal of individual members as well as measures to renew itself. In all manner of ways, this reflects the age-old question of who guards the guardians or who takes custody over the custodians.[4]

Should a board seek the advice and counsel of outside consultants, then some internal control is lost. Where this relates to the recruitment of new board members much rests upon the ways these consultants go about their explorations. The only important question is whether or not the consultants canvass a wider population for potential entry into the ranks of board membership than the board itself could achieve. Either way the consultants are the gatekeepers.

Internal assessments of performance of board members may be drawn from their peers at the instigation of the chairman. But taken further, to include views of senior management, brings the risk of inhibiting the questioning of management about the implementation of policies and the surveillance of risks associated with liabilities and assets.

Themes of renewal as openness to new ideas are impressive as a declaration of purpose but less satisfactory in practice. The successful bank may have provided a firm basis for strategies and policies from which benefits have been secured. That very success may bring an alertness to innovations whenever possibilities arise.

All these prudential strictures read well reflecting worthy objectives of the *bien-pensant* of society and the banking community, but ease of implementation, other than where time lapses are required, is not at hand. The best features may well lie in a cautionary role for boards in their deliberations about performance and renewal, not to rely upon the appointment of yet another "safe pair of hands."

Prudential regulations do not allow for the influence of shareholders. Where a bank has recorded a less than satisfactory performance by comparison with peers, the likelihood is for major shareholders to bring influence to bear for changes in board membership and direction. A most revealing example of these influences came after Westpac Banking Corporation recorded a loss of AU\$ 1.667 billion in the half year to 31 March 1992. Following the announcement of this loss, reflecting provisions for doubtful debts of AU\$ 2.205 billion, the decision was taken to raise AU\$ 1.2 billion by way of a new issue. The underwritten issue was not subscribed anywhere near fully.[5] The aftermath was the resignation of half the non-executive members of the board, including the chairman and deputy chairman. Further controversies followed, to be discussed below, so that between October 1992 and February 1993 every board meeting ended with fewer board members present than were recorded at the start.

Board size and committees

Issues about the number of persons on a board and the number of board committees have attracted much attention in the past decade. The stipulations conveyed in prudential requirements point to a modest minimum size of five and the mandatory role of an audit committee. However, the reasonable expectation would be for a bank of any significant size to have a credit and market risk committee and, in light of the quest for board renewal, a nominations committee. Much less attention has been directed to the balance between non-executive directors and executive directors.[6]

At issue with board size and committee structures is how well the board is informed on the workings of the bank for which it has responsibility and the breadth of views conveyed within the board on the issues illuminating the effectiveness of those strategies. Any appraisal has to reflect the responsibility of the board as a whole for the direction and performance of the bank.

A bank, as with some other entities in the financial services sector, has a broad reach across and beyond the national economy or economies in which it is located. A small board in terms of members has some prospect of relying heavily on senior management for information on developments across a range of productive activities bearing upon the bank's business. Board members are likely to be members of other boards, though not too many, so information on activities outside the bank may be secured to inform board policies and possibly enlighten management

Nonetheless, small membership restricts the breadth of views directly available as well as diminishing the avenues of experience by which management may be tested on performance. There is a strong case for a broader membership to ensure the widest possible canvassing of ideas and experiences. This stance reflects the prudential injunctions for appraisal and renewal of ideas in a bank board.

The question of board size is most challenging when committees are to the fore. The membership of the audit committee as required by prudential regulation ensures a substantial proportion of the total board is involved when membership of the board is few, perhaps the minimum of five at all times. Other committees, such as a credit and market risk committee and nominations committee, would have substantially overlapping memberships. Thus the small board might just as well constitute the committees as well, subject only to the stipulation that the chairman of the board should not be the chairman of the audit committee. In this way, the risk with committees of the diminution of information flowing to all board members would be avoided. However, the narrowness of the information set within a small membership outweighs these possible gains.

Policies and performance

Harsh circumstances arise for a bank when directions taken bring excesses leading to misjudgments about risk and consequent mispricing of assets as well as misallocation of components in portfolios. These situations do not arise from events within the financial services sector but may be induced when macroeconomic settings reflect a laxity in monetary or fiscal disciplines or both by national authorities.

The scene in the third quarter of 2007 reflects these outcomes. Easy financial liquidity worldwide over a number of years had fostered a quest for ways to fund real activities while earning rewarding net margins. Low nominal and real interest rates had stimulated the search for new avenues and techniques for enhancing margins. Thus hedge funds and private equity capital groups flourished. Banks found the means to leverage their portfolios by selling assets into special investment conduits seemingly divorced from their control, which were made attractive to banks because so long as the funding of these entities could be done on a short-term, less than one year basis, there would be no claims on banks to set aside capital to match the lending. Regulatory arbitrage fostered the leveraged forays.

The enthusiasm with which these policies were pursued brought about a declining focus on the quality of assets being funded. Realization that something was amiss with asset quality came towards the end of the first quarter of 2007. But it was another six months before there was a general recognition of the problem in Europe despite some public examples of losses in preceding weeks. Huge cumulative losses are now commonplace among North American and European banks. As with Westpac's experiences in 1992, some board members and chief executives have lost positions.

Lessons from the past may illuminate the contemporary scene. As is so often the case in developed market economies, these strains reflect exposures to residential, commercial, and industrial buildings. The circumstances which led to the resounding AU$ 1.667 billion loss by Westpac referred to earlier were a reflection of these activities. However enthusiastic the chairman of the board and the chief executive officer claimed to be for the expansion of Westpac's business, the essential source of problems lay in the structural deficiencies of the Westpac Group whereby the bank did not exercise effective control on its subsidiaries in matters of lending policies, especially with property.[7] These features are depicted fully in the recently published history of Westpac over the past 50 years to 2000 (Davidson and Salsbury, 2005, Chapter 23).

The most revealing aspect of the relationship between bank and subsidiary is in the troubled efforts to bring the activities of the subsidiary into coherence with the lending policies of the bank. Efforts during the closing days of 1989 by a most senior credit officer to bring about control in accordance with bank policy were rejected in circumstances which suggested that the future role and purpose of the subsidiary had not been thought through, let alone that steps taken to implement a comprehensive integration (ibid., especially pp. 305–7). This was the very time when earnings by the subsidiary were starting to collapse, leading to record losses within two years.

The wider lessons from these experiences within Westpac are not those about matters of history repeating itself. Rather they concern much broader and more focused issues about the ways that commitments within one strategy can blinker the possibilities for critical appraisal and reassessment within an organization. Moreover, an organization lacking integration and revealing disparities of purpose is one grievously exposed to instability and potential loss. The lessons from these experiences should not be lost on present board members.

Board and management

Where the Australian provisions on prudential matters have little to offer directly on the relationships between board and management, those emanating from Basel are more explicit. The board is enjoined to work with senior management to ensure activities are consistent with board policy and board and management must understand the operational structure of the bank. These are onerous requirements.

The extent to which board members should pursue their inquiries on management practices cannot be specified – so much depends upon the culture of accountability and responsibility understood across the organization. Where there is uncertainty about the acceptance of these two requirements, there is every prospect for relationships to be impaired.

These issues arose during and through the tumultuous period associated with Westpac's loss of AU$ 1.667 billion. In part, this was a result of the lack of a coherent structure within the Westpac group and the worries about property lending from the finance company subsidiary which came to a head in the latter months of 1989. Another concern was the nature of the consensus management style among senior executives. These features, among others, generated tensions between board and management, as is well documented (Davidson and Salsbury, 2005, pp. 294–327).

Just how far a board or board members should delve into management practices and performance can be problematic. Reference has been made earlier to the raising of an additional AU$ 1.2 billion by a share issue. Prior to the closing date of the issue but well after due diligence verifying the prospectus for the share issue and the underwriting agreement had been completed, a query arose about the extent of tax obligations generated in the United States' operations of Westpac. The problem was not specific to Westpac, but applied to all banks working in the United States and engaging in similar transactions. Moreover, the matter was unresolved because no determination had been made by American tax authorities. Comprehensive treatment of the problems arising in this long-running issue is available (Carew, 1997, pp. 368–85).[8]

The essence of the problem was the recommendation of the American tax advisers for a provision to cover potential tax obligations; the sum involved would not have been material to the total earnings of Westpac. This recommendation was not accepted by senior officers in Sydney. They judged a much larger and material sum to be required because they wished to make full provision for any potential future obligation. This stance was taken despite there being no ruling on the problem from the American tax authorities. Once the decision was taken to make this much larger provisioning, the bank was obliged to announce the decision to the market.

The repercussions were immediate. The integrity of the share issue was questioned but not formally challenged. Subsequently, investigations were made as to whether or not the problems were recognized or addressed by the due diligence committee. Contrary to beliefs that are still held to this day, the specific issues associated with this matter had been discussed previously within Westpac. Senior officers involved in the due diligence were aware of the matter, but the size of any potential provisioning had not been deemed material to deliberations.

The investigation and determination of the best course of action to deal with the matter involved board members in many direct meetings and negotiations with senior management from Sydney and New York as well as with the American tax advisers and the bank's auditors. Acceptance of the recommendation to make the large and material provision was as misplaced as it was inevitable.[9] The position of the tax advisers from New York proved to be very near the eventual tax obligation in America.

The most telling feature of this experience is the involvement of board members in adjudicating between different management groups.

Occasions arise when delving into management practices is essential for the workings of the bank. On this occasion, the results were disappointing for the lack of cohesion across the ranks of management at a time when the heavy losses earlier in the year had brought sustained harsh public criticism. Public admission of further provisioning for this potential loss heightened and sustained these criticisms.

Transparency
So much of what is demanded of boards and management of banks comes down to issues about transparency. Thus there can be little surprise in the emphasis placed on this quality by the Basel Committee on Banking Supervision under the auspices of the Bank for International Settlements. The goal of transparency should allow all those with an interest in banking activities to judge the quality of any one bank's performance. However, should that transparency not be achievable then the board and management of a bank must be in a position to know what is taking place and how. By implication, should board and management not understand these workings then they should not be participating in these transactions.

At a time of rapid innovation in banking processes and products, the prospect of understanding the workings of new financial instruments and the markets in which they are transacted is challenging. Much of what has taken place over the past three decades stems from the development of rapid and accurate transmission of information by electronic means. Those technological developments have changed irrevocably the nature of markets in financial instruments so that physical location is no longer binding the limits on transactions. Most importantly, the scale of transactions possible has been extended greatly by the speed to completion of contracts.

Distinctions may be drawn between types of markets served in this way. Exchange-traded markets are organized entities with sets of trading rules, the success of which depends in some measure on the quality of management of those markets. That quality would encompass the provisions to ensure the safety and completion of each side of any transaction negotiated. In that setting, transparency is available to all participants even if understanding of the purposes served by the instruments may not be complete.

Over-the-counter markets are a very different species. There, each counterparty represents a potential source of credit and market risk, which should be assessed as with any conventional bank loan. Equally publicly-traded securities rest for their acceptability in markets on the assessments of risk bestowed upon them by the recommendations from ratings agencies.

What has changed in the past decade has been the availability of new techniques to shift the risks at a fee to some other entity through credit default instruments or to transfer the ownership to some other independent entity subject to some fee for continuing to manage the asset on the new owner's behalf.

Events in August and September 2007 across international financial markets have been revealing of just how far the transparency of transactions had been obscured. As we have observed, the quest for earnings leads to searching out means to secure higher margins. What was not transparent in the activities of many banks in North America and Europe (and probably elsewhere) were the ways the use of stand-alone entities established by these banks allowed greatly expanded leverage of a bank's capital and thus higher earnings. But the process was supported, if not fueled, by the questionable assessments of the quality of the securities traded through these conduits.

This blindness to the full implications of policies being pursued is familiar from past experiences. A striking example is the failure of the Barings Group early in 1995 (Hogan, 1997). The remarkable feature of that experience was the way in which the board and senior management of the parent company transferred their entire capital to support operations in Singapore with apparent disregard for the maintenance of the group as an ongoing entity. Commitments and obligations were assumed without transparency being tested until too late.

Appraisal

This chapter is offered as a basis for getting to grips with the issues at stake in the provisions for the prudential supervision of banks and related financial services in Australia. The guidelines drawn from the Basel Committee on Banking Supervision are drawn upon to bring an additional perspective to the Australian arrangements. In most respects, the prescriptions advanced provide some broad guidance as to what conduct and performance is expected of banks. Less clear are the means of implementation. Hence market participants can but await determinations by the prudential authority to gain further insights into expected practice.

Notes

This contribution reflects the personal views of the authors and not those of any organization with which they have been associated. Warren Hogan was a member of the board of Westpac Banking Corporation between 1986 and 2002 and the principal board of the Australian Mutual Provident Society between 1993 and 1995.

1. The requirements laid down in 2003 have been moderated substantially in the new measures announced in August 2007. Contrast the two series from the ASX Corporate Governance Council for those years as well as the Council's responses to submissions about revisions, all listed in the references (ASX 2003, 2007a, 2007b).

2. This does not involve the quite separate matter of ensuring auditing firms do not quote low fees in order to gain access to additional payments for professional advice other than for the audit.
3. More correctly this should be the total net earnings plus the total salary package of the executives or partners responsible for the work with the bank.
4. The Latin tag is "*Quis custodiet ipsos custodes.*"
5. This was the largest share issue ever in Australia at that time.
6. Practice amongst the major Australian banks has been for non-executive members with only the chief executive officer a board member. With Westpac there was an exceptional period in the early 1990s when Stuart Fowler as CEO was joined on the board by two other executives, Frank Conroy and Tony Walton. Today, additional executive membership of bank boards is more common.
7. The main subsidiary was a finance company, Australian Guarantee Corporation. This did not become a wholly-owned subsidiary of Westpac until 1988, by which time it had a large property portfolio and commitments to further lending in that broad area; its historical and very successful role had been in consumer finance, especially automobiles and durable goods.
8. A briefer and much less informative explanation is given in the recent history (Davidson and Salsbury, 2005, pp. 327–9).
9. The decision to accept the higher sum was inevitable, as the likelihood of the discussions about the appropriate level of provisioning not becoming public knowledge was slender in the current circumstances.

References

Aon Australia (2007), "Australasian risk management and total cost of insurable risk survey," May, accessed at www.aon.com.au/general/publications/risk_management_2nd_tcoir_2006_2007.asp.

Australian Prudential Regulation Authority (2006), "Prudential Standard APS 510 governance," May, accessed at www.apra.gov.au.

ASX Corporate Governance Council (2003), "Principles of good corporate governance and best practice recommendations," March, accessed at www.asx.com.au.

ASX Corporate Governance Council (2007a), "Corporate governance principles and recommendations," 2nd edn, August, accessed at www.asx.com.au.

ASX Corporate Governance Council (2007b), "Response to submissions on review of corporate governance principles and recommendations," August, accessed at www.asx.com.au.

Bank for International Settlements (2006), "Enhancing corporate governance for banking organizations," Basel Committee on Banking Supervision, February.

Carew, Edna (1997), *Westpac: The Bank that Broke the Bank*, Sydney: Doubleday, Transworld Publishers.

Davidson, L. Sharon and Stephen Salsbury (2005), *Australia's First Bank*, Sydney: University of New South Wales Press.

Hogan, W.P. (1997), "Corporate governance: lessons from Barings," *Abacus*, **33**(1) (March), 26–48.

Laker, John F. (2005), "Corporate governance in financial institutions," presentation to Asian Bankers Association Conference on promoting Good Corporate Governance, Melbourne, 19 October (Australian Prudential Regulation Authority).

Somogyi, S. (2005), "APRA advocates a prudent culture," 17 June (Australian Prudential Regulation Authority).

White, R.J. and Cecelia Clarke (1995), *Cheques and Balances*, Sydney: Penguin Books.

11 A simple guide to Islamic banking and finance
Mohamed Ariff

This chapter is a guide to the essential principles and practices of Islamic banking in some 70 countries. The guide is a simplified introduction to what constitutes this special form of banking; the special form arising from its profit-seeking through profit and loss sharing deposits and loan contracts and fee and mark-up based lending for purchasing real assets, both modes replacing conventional, interest-based banking practices. The chapter describes the way in which this niche banking, which began in 1963, has grown to the present size of about US$500 billion in equity capital, successfully making profits in some 50-odd legal jurisdictions. The organization, the working principles, and selected key terms used in this form of banking are explained. Also included are the philosophical basis on which this different form of banking is constructed and brief comments on other forms that are yet to be experimented with.

Introduction

This chapter provides a simple introduction – a beginner's guide – to the current practices of Islamic banking and finance, which is found in about one-third of the countries in the world.[1] Islamic financial institutions are legal entities that are licensed under banking laws of a given legal jurisdiction in a country, or economic entities that are authorized to operate in one or more of the following areas: banking, insurance, treasury, bond, equity, mutual funds and bills markets. These institutions originate and transact financial activities that are designed with special contract provisions to avoid receipt or payment of interest. They are also permitted to earn a profit via profit-and-loss sharing (PLS) terms and/or fee-based mark-up (FBMU) terms in the contracts.

Islamic banks constitute one class of such licensed institutions and they engage in all typical banking transactions. Those engaging in PLS and FBMU in insurance are classed as *Takaful* insurance, those engaging in funds management are Islamic mutual funds, and so on. Non-interest-based bonds are traded by authorized firms that engage in transacting *sukuk* bonds, which are traditional bonds but based on profit shares of the issuers. Credit cards have been issued based on pre-designated cash accounts earning a PLS income to the credit card company and card payments are made without the use of interest. Islamic banking and finance normally refers to the more restricted practices of profit-seeking by a bank using PLS and FBMU in place of interest while carrying out the same transactions as a typical conventional bank. Thus, an Islamic bank takes deposits, creates savings accounts, lends money to customers, finances mortgage purchases of property, invests a customer's fund, issues a bill of lading, and so on, but always without the use of interest in the contractual agreements.[2]

The rest of the chapter is organized into five parts to explain Islamic banking practices. The typical organizational structure of an Islamic bank is provided in Section 11.2: the key difference of this niche banking is the presence of a surveillance body, the Board of Scholars (*Shari'ah* Board), which oversees the operation of a bank to ensure that it is in line with the avoidance of interest-based financial activities. The popular press has either ridiculed this as a religious surveillance board or sees it as a good thing. Supporting the latter view is the presence of a control beyond the money-hungry or corrupt influences of bad bankers and bad central banks that are too often the reality in the current banking environment in many countries. In Section 11.3, we discuss the general principles of financial transactions that are permitted in an Islamic bank under the strict doctrine of avoiding receipt or payment of interest in financial transactions. The reader will find, in Section 11.4, a quick introduction to what the balance sheet and income statement of an Islamic bank looks like. We also explain the underlying operating principles of the items in the accounting statements. Section 11.5 provides an explanation of a selection of special terms to identify how these are defined and have special meaning in implementation. The chapter ends with some suggestions as to the direction in which Islamic banking is likely to progress in the near future.

11.2 Organization of an Islamic bank

The organization chart of an Islamic Bank based on PLS and FBMU resembles the organization chart of a typical conventional bank. A conventional bank has a board of directors with legislated fiduciary duties imposed on them by the laws of a country in which the licence for the bank is issued. These are corporation laws, trust laws, banking laws and prudential regulations, income tax laws, and laws relating to legal transfer of ownership as well as accounting and financial reporting regulations. This aspect of an Islamic bank is exactly the same as is the case for a conventional bank; all the same laws apply to an Islamic bank.

Below the board of directors is the president or CEO, who may also be a member of the board. He is required to manage the banking operations and is responsible to the board for carrying out the policies of the bank.

Increasingly, in almost all countries, there is an audit board that reports to the board to ensure that the activities of a bank are compliant with the laws and regulations. This is also found in an Islamic bank. Banks are further supervised by the central bank, and the visiting examiners constitute a supervisory board of commissioners reporting to the board of directors bypassing the president or CEO. This is also the case in Islamic banks. The only exception to this will be the case of an Islamic bank that is not by law required to be supervised by the central bank: however, this is not a desirable situation as unsupervised banks, whether Islamic or conventional, have a greater frequency of bank failures.

Unlike the conventional bank, the Islamic bank has a board of scholars – the *Shari'ah* board – whose members are trained in both conventional laws and in Islamic laws as far as they relate to financial transactions. In the current shortage of such people, more broadly-trained religious scholars are filling places on this board, with the consequence that their advice appears to be much more focused on broader ethical standards than would be the case with the strict adherence to Islamic financial transaction laws. The duty of this board, which gives independent advice to the board of directors, bypassing the CEO, is to ensure that banking transactions do not include receipt or payment of interest-based activities and that the products on offer to the customers pass the test of reasonableness in risk, in that the risk is not excessive, bordering on gambling. New banking products must pass the same tests.

Continued oversight by the board of scholars introduces a degree of conservatism – in current circumstance much more than is warranted – into business practice. Some describe it as introducing a moral compass that possibly reduces the incidence of high-risk activities that are often reported as having created serious systemic problems for banks.[3] One example is that of the Barings bank failure. A board of scholars would have not approved a financial practice based on excessive speculation – in this case excessive speculation on the Japanese Yen that produced huge profits for Baring banks and bonuses for its key directors – which would be deemed closer to gambling.

Recent discussion on the activities of the board of scholars has led to two views. Some have criticized it as an extension of religious doctrine. In the current context, where there are insufficient trained men, the few such specialists that there are charge exorbitant fees to sit on many boards – a rich source of income. Many are religious scholars, but most are secular individuals trained in the laws: a few are non-Muslims who are known to be experts in this regard. The second view is that the board's oversight is necessary to ensure that a bank does not earn income as receipts or payments of interest in its activities, and that this is an essential element of this niche bank. The customers who wish to be sure that there is an ongoing oversight

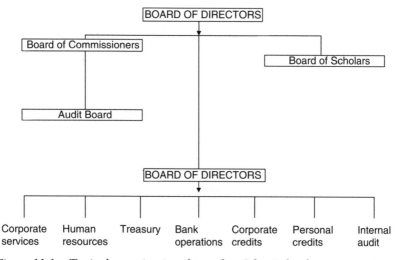

Figure 11.1   Typical organization chart of an Islamic bank

of practices and the imposition of *Sharia'ah* rules need to know that this is being done. It is a sanitizing exercise. Hence the second view is that this is a good practice. A consequence of this is that Islamic banks in general are conservatively managed, not just in order to avoid interest-based activities, but also to avoid activities based on excessive risk-taking bordering towards gambling (which is also proscribed by religious doctrine in Islamic economics literature), and to limit the damage to the community from excessive risk-taking in financial activities.

Thus, the top management levels consist of the board of directors, the board of commissioners, the audit board, and the special board of scholars, the last being an organizational unit in Islamic banking only. Below that are other levels of management reporting to the CEO. The levels reporting to the president or CEO are identical to those found in conventional banks (see Figure 11.1).

Divisions commonly found in such organizal structures include secretariat, internal audit, operations, treasury, loans (this may comprise several divisions depending on the size of the bank), international banking, branch office, and business development. All these divisions bring different expertise and professional skills to the successful operation and management of a bank. The larger the bank, the greater the number of divisions under the CEO. These divisions are very similar in Islamic banks, which compete in the same market for personnel and look for the same qualities in personnel as conventional banks. However, with the rise of training at professional levels and certifying institutions in Islamic banking practice, key trained personnel in Islamic banks are increasingly individuals who have some knowledge of the product design and operations of a PLS and FBMU in banking operations.[4] This only began in the 2000s, and it may take a while before there are sufficient numbers of people trained in the intricacies of this niche banking practices.

The upshot of this discussion is that the bank *Mualamat* – to use the more descriptive name – is a form of banking that specializes in implementing financial practices based on profit-share and fee and mark-up contracts. These banks have to comply with the same banking laws as conventional banks, while its operations are based on PLS and FBMU. The organization chart of such a bank has an additional committee of trained legal persons who ensure that the financial practices and the new products on offer are in line with the two injunctions on avoidance of interest and excessive risk in financial contracts. This, it is claimed, makes such a bank more conservative and thus safer for communities participating in such banks. However, the safety can be compromised by poor operational controls, and in many developing countries, there is considerable room for improvement in order to ensure operational risk is controlled.

11.3   Principles of Islamic banking and finance

This section aims to give a very brief introduction to the important operational principles which distinguish Islamic banking from conventional banks. The first of these is the avoidance of interest-based financial transactions. The second is, for some classes of financial transactions, substitution of PLS contracts for interest-based contract terms. The third principle is the widespread use of FBMU in what are termed trade in *non*-financial assets. Examples would be the lease of a submarine, which is a nonfinancial asset, by an undersea exploring firm, or purchase of a commercial office by a company. The final principle is the requirement that the customer is informed of the level of risk of a financial contract up-front, and that this risk is not excessive, resembling the odds of a gamble.

The question of whether humanity should avoid interest in financial transactions has been a topic of great thinkers among men for some 4000 years. Our first record of the prohibition of excessive interest rates – the first usury law – was written in a stone tablet by Hammurabi of Mesopotamia. His prescribed punishment for this malfeasance was execution! He specified a charge of third of the money lent as interest as usurious interest. The Hindu scriptures, particularly the Upanisad, and the Jewish scripture, the Torah, have references to avoiding interest in financial transactions. Christianity has the largest number of scripture-based commandments prohibiting interest in general, not just usurious interest. The Muslim scripture has six key commandments prohibiting financial transactions based on interest. Some scholars actually interpret this prohibition as meaning excessive interest – usurious interest rather than small interest – and for over 1400 years from the advent of Islam there have been scholars who gave permission for small interest. However, all were agreed that excessive interest is not permitted. In the current period, since the mid-1950s, the pendulum has swung the other way and the consensus after careful discussion is that no form of interest is good for society. Since the middle of the twentieth century, a majority consensus has evolved among a majority of Muslim scholars that no interest is permitted in financial transactions, and usurious interest is certainly banned.[5]

The key provision under Islamic laws based on canon law states: "Thou . . . shall not take usury, compounded over and over" meaning that the use of capital by a capital-owning rich person to gain an excessive advantage by indebting a person without wealth is considered an uncharitable act that is forbidden in God's law. Hence, to make a financial gain by lending capital, the lender must share in the risk of the venture of the person putting the money to work, and *subsequently* obtain a share of the pre-agreed profits coming from the venture and not *ex ante* impose interest. Thus is born the legal requirement in canon law that, up front, the borrower reveals the risk of the venture, the lender agrees to partake of the risk *ex ante*, and both parties agree to a ratio of profit share deemed fair for the inherent risk in the financial transaction. Such a contract must be witnessed in writing by a third person.

Hence, a financier providing funds to an entrepreneur building a roadway as a turnkey project, may agree to share 25 per cent of the profits collected as toll charges rather than lending on fixed interest without waiting to ensure that the financier has in fact participated in the risk of building the road. If an entrepreneurial activity is relevant to both entrepreneur and the financier, the act of financing the project cannot be separated from the economic act of building the road. Why should the financing be considered as a matter unrelated to the completion of the project by imposing repayment of the loan without regard to the risk of completion of the project? This is the fundamental principle of the risk-share and profit-share argument as a feature of fairness in contract. Pre-fixing the reward in the form of interest payments unrelated to the completion of the project does not lead to risk-sharing or reward-sharing, and thus places the borrower in an unequal position. If one is to practice this risk- and reward-sharing principle strictly, an alternative mode of financial contracting is needed. That is the niche banking practiced by Islamic banks.

The core banking activities of any bank can be divided into (a) safe-keeping, (b) savings and (c) credit and loans. Safe keeping is an age-old practice that started with pious Catholics going to Jerusalem as pilgrims and leaving their money and valuables in the custody of the Church. Later the Knights Templar took over this role, and continued in it until the King of Portugal brought a false charge of devil worship against the chief Templar in order to force the forfeit of the wealth of the order to pay off his war debt. This brought an end to the Knights Templar acting as a bank, though the Church continued receiving the pilgrims' deposits in financial transactions. Modern banking evolved after 1752 when the Church watered-down its interpretation of a ban on interest, largely as a result of the greater egalitarianism that followed the Reformation and that influenced the longstanding papal position. In fact, some German followers of Luther gave implicit permission to wealthy financiers to take over the lending business by charging interest, from other non-German groups that used to dominate this sector. In modern-day banking, this practice of safe-keeping deposits underlies checking accounts and, more recently, cash cards for the convenience of safekeeping and drawing money from one's own account.

The second and third core activities of a bank are savings for a duration of time in a savings account and credit or loan in advance when non-financial assets such as a house, a car, a submarine or a factory – in general borrowers – are financed by a bank lending money. The bank actually creates credit money using the fractional-reserve to deposit banking principle, which multiplies money creation by banks by the reciprocal of the liquidity ratio of money in deposits.

What reward should be paid to the customers for safekeeping? This case is simple. As was the practice in banking for centuries, money placed in checking accounts does not get any return since the service of safekeeping provided by the bank is sufficient reward provided the principal is returned. So, Islamic banks do not pay a return on cash-safekeeping accounts. For non-money items kept in bank safe boxes, the customers are charged a fee. Since the 1970s, with a change in the banking regulations, conventional banks do pay a return to checking account holders. But the interest paid is a paltry amount – in countries with about 6 per cent interest rates, this is less than 1 per cent – and the banks recover this payment by imposing a minimum sum in checking deposits and a fee on check-clearing. The effect is that the checking account gets almost zero returns in conventional banking.

The savings account is not that simple and the consensus is that account holders should earn a return. There is erosion of value of money over time because of inflation. Also, the bank actually uses this money to create credits for others – recall fractional-reserve money creation – using the fractional banking principle. The permitted practice in Islamic banking as regards savings is for the bank to accept the deposit without promising pre-fixed "return" or interest. Instead, at the end of each month, a return – instead of pre-fixed interest – is declared for the savings account based on the calculation by the bank of the profit share declared for that month. By this practice, the savers get to earn a return commensurate with the profitability of the bank – at least that is the principle – and the use of interest is avoided. Studies have shown that the so-called distribution of profits is just about the amount of interest ruling in the market place in the month before the declaration of the return.

Why the return declared at the end of a month has no bearing on the profitability of the bank remains an unresearched issue, and the accusation leveled at the Islamic banks is that they are actually practicing a pseudo-interest payment, paying a "return" that equates to current interest. Orthodox Muslim scholars have used this as a major weapon, calling Islamic banking a scam by modern-day Muslim countries. This is an important issue in that, as these critiques point out, the practice of banking has to be Islamic-law consistent rather than merely compliant! Merely repackaging interest as a return is not to practice the principle of profit-sharing. This writer believes that the return to savings account holders should be greater than the interest rates if profit-share is actually practiced. The average return to equity in modern-day banks is about 20 per cent. This equity forms at most about 15 per cent of the total assets, meaning that the majority of the assets are based on money created on the fractional-reserve to deposit principle. The average rate of return that depositors have been getting in conventional banks is about half a per cent higher than Treasury yields, which translates as about 5–6 per cent during the last 20 years. Obviously, a move to pin the return to profitability of the bank will yield more than 10 per cent for savings deposit holders if about a third of the profits to shareholders are distributed to the deposit holders.

With modern-day accounting and technology, it is possible for banks to know how much profit they are making in a month and thus base the return to the savings accounts as a ratio of the profits. The bankers point out that the real profits will be known only at the end of the year (accounting standards require this), and so the return cannot be based on such a simple calculation. That is fine, provided that at the end of the year, an adjustment amount should be given to equate the returns to-date to some defined share of the profits of the bank. If the banks really share the profits in a given ratio of profitability, it is highly likely that the return would be larger than the ruling interest rates. At present, this is all that is available to ordinary savers, and the good news is that the returns, though almost tailing the interest in the market, are no worse than that they would have gotten from a conventional bank. Additionally, these savers are sure of avoiding perdition by participating in an Islamic savings deposit. Surveys indicate that

about three out of ten persons in majority-Muslim countries wish to participate in this form of savings deposits. That is the market niche. Add to this
the rich individuals who could tailor-make the profit-share in syndicated
loans in large contracts and earn much higher returns than are possible in
conventional bank-based lending. Firms directly tapping the rich loan
providers under profit shares can also cut off the bank as middlemen and
thus access cheaper loans in this niche market place. This is the incentive
for the big banks offering facilities as Islamic bankers in this new century.

One interpretation of practice relating to ordinary savings deposits in
Iran is expressed in a legal article, which calls for "minimum returns to be
given to the depositors." This is encouraged in Islamic jurisprudence.
Borrowers, however, are not required to give a return (since borrowing is
contingent on risk-sharing and profit share), but the borrower going the
extra mile to give some return above the principal is considered to act in a
benevolent manner. Such behavior – another is donating the interest earned
to charity or forgiving a malfeasant – is considered exemplary in the canon
laws of Islam. Hence, in practice savers do expect to get a minimum
payment by the bank in Iran. Though documented findings are not yet
available, oral evidence suggests that this return has been around the
inflation rate in that country. This ensures that savings preserve the purchasing power of the wealth.

Under the interpretation of forbearance of interest on strictly religious
grounds (there are customers who want to observe this for fear of hell fire
if they receive or paid interest) the PLS contracts ensure that both parties
share in the risk of the venture and that there is a pre-agreed share of the
anticipated profits. This is how the profit-share agreements are made.
Prominent banks and institutions that are making custom-made contracts
using PLS contracts – for example Swiss banks, HSBC and so on – negotiate the profit-share ratios and then custom-make a debenture agreement for
investing large sums in infrastructural and industrial projects. These profit-
share contracts lead, importantly, to (a) sharing in the risk and (b) higher
returns should the project become successful.

This form of indenture agreement under profit-sharing is called the
mudaraba or *murabaha* (there are some differences between the two), but
these are PLS contracts for a term of time. Since Islamic banks are new, not
too large and they operate in developing countries, most of the lending
activities of some 500 such banks are based on the funds in the savings
deposits being made available to traders in goods and services. However,
this form of lending for a very short term on profit share is attractive in a
small community where entrepreneurship can be encouraged by the bank
lending on this basis. The agency problem in a small community of closely-
linked people defaulting on sharing profits or engaging in false contracting

is rather small. However, this form of lending in more developed economies with anonymous borrowers and lenders requires a more formal mechanism that is yet to be invented in order overcome the agency problem inherent in this form of lending. As the Islamic banks become larger new structures will be needed to ensure that the agency problem of false projects being financed by PLS lenders will not incur fraudulent losses.

The core banking activity of financing purchases of real assets requires fee-based and mark-up (FBMU) techniques. A buyer of a property approaches the bank for credit. The bank makes the required amount of money available and charges a mark-up on that purchase cost as the compensation for making the credit. The problem here is to predict the price of the property – say a submarine 20 years from now. The usual shortcut taken by the bank is to consider a mark-up based on the current cost of money in the loan market in conventional banks for that asset. In practice this will lead to a mark-up based on the ruling interest rate. However, once the mark-up is added, and the amortization of loan-plus-mark-up is computed, the Islamic principle requires that the amortization is based upon equal treatment of principal and mark-up payment. Conventional banks recover all the interest payments in the first periods of repayment, leaving equity build-up by the purchaser to a later date after most of the interest is recovered. Typically a 20-year loan will begin to build significant equity in the property after about 10 years of payments. This is not – I should say should not be – the case in amortization under Islamic principle. Under an Islamic mortgage amortization the owner of the property builds equity from the first payment on an equal basis. There are reports that some Islamic banks adopt the conventional banking practice, which, in the opinion of scholars in this area, would be not a fair practice and is not permissible.

Finally, under the board of scholars guidelines, it is a requirement that the party to the contracts must reveal the full extent of risk in a financial transaction. If purchase of a ship is financed by a bank, then the ship owner/operator requiring the finance must reveal the actuarial facts about accident rates in the route taken (apart from the seaworthiness of the ship) and so forth. Thus, all contracts have up-front revealing of material facts to a transaction witnessed by a third party. This is akin to the modern practice – particularly after the Citibank and Enron debacles – in investment advisory services. Further to this is the requirement that the bank – a public institution – does not offer a financial transaction that has excessive risk bordering on gambling. Gambling is not permitted. This injunction fosters conservatism and avoids adventurous financing by banks. In insurance, it is permitted, as there is a way of quantifying the risk and compensating it. Some consider this function of the board of scholars as making community banking safer than it has been under conventional banking. That may be a good thing, especially if the bank operates in communities with low-income customers.

How about other things a bank may do? Banks engage in investment services – a fact today in the UK and USA – in addition to core banking transactions. The requirement is that the securities in which a customer's money is invested are from businesses that do not engage in (a) interest-based majority activities, (b) gambling, (c) production and distribution of intoxicants to humans, and (d) prostitution. The Islamic Dow-Jones Index for example has identified about 40 per cent of the New York Exchange listed firms as those that fulfill these criteria. The principle is that capital should only be made available to community-friendly economic activities and not to activities that place the community (and family) at risk of long-term survival. As long as the returns to the investors are from activities congenial to community welfare, then that investment instrument becomes a permitted Islamic investment. There are increasing numbers of Islamic investment firms – call them mutual funds – operating all over the world. These funds could include in their equity holding the *sukuk* bonds, which are not based on interest but on income from the vested firms – a property-owning firm collecting rent – that owns the bond issue.

It is sufficient in this brief introduction to summarize the main principles of the Islamic banking operations. Participation in risk sharing with full knowledge of the risk of a financial contract is essential in financial transactions; a witness is also required to attest to the truth of the information. This means there should be no asymmetric information. There are a number of ways of promoting this idea. There is no guarantee that one participant in a contract may not bluff his way into the contract (thus perpetrating asymmetric information) despite all these controls, which may well lead to losses. This is a fact of life in societies with large populations, and new control procedures and monitoring devices are needed to ensure that *ex post* the contract, the parties live up to the revelations made *ex ante*. This risk-share and profit-share aspect is not highlighted in the literature, and it is a major principle (a position that is entirely consistent with the modern finance idea that the return-risk paradigm is an increasing function of the amount of risk taken).

Add to that the avoidance of interest, which is based on the principle of PLS, with the sharing ratio depending on the risk of the project and also on the extent to which the lender is committing his time to the project (perhaps as an independent director in the project). Convenience deposits (checking accounts) are merely a depository and no return is given for this deposit. Strictly financial transactions (savings accounts and loans) are based on PLS but with risk-sharing agreements. Finally FBMU as a principle is applied in financing purchases of *non*-financial assets such as a home, commercial office, equipment and so on. It is a lease agreement, but with the provision that eventual ownership is preserved from first payment on equal basis with mark-up payment.

11.4 Financial statements of an Islamic bank

In this section the reader is guided to understand the financial statements of an Islamic bank. Currently, there is an institute based in Bahrain that has come up with several accounting standards for the preparation of the financial accounts of an Islamic bank. This has fostered comparison, with more banks adopting these standards in addition to the usual accounting standards, and international banking accounting practices are wont to converge in the near future to the standards already being adopted. On the banking regulatory side, there is the Islamic Financial Services Board (IFSB), which works closely with the BIS, IMF and World Bank to ensure that the banking standards on capital requirements, non-performing loans, and risk-weighting assets are applied to the Islamic banks as well. Thus, over time, Islamic banks – niche banking without interest rates – will converge to best practice in this area, although at present it is difficult to compare the financial statements of banks operating in places as distant as the Philippines and Switzerland. Islamic banks are in fact not comparable unless they adopt uniform reporting standards.

The first thing to note is that the traditional accounting framework in Islamic banks is the same as in conventional banks. That is, there is a balance sheet, income statement and cash flow statement. There is the asset side to the balance sheet equaling liability plus owner's equity. The income report reports sales, and washes this through costs, depreciation and so on to tax and then computes the net income. The cash flow statement records the sources and uses of capital. Banks also report the statement of retained earnings after paying dividends to the shareholders.

Thus, on the structural side, the financial statements are similar. However, the items recorded in the statements come from only PLS and FBMU activities (and service charges). One should add that Islamic banks often set aside a small part of the profits in each year as contribution to the welfare of the poor in the community. Conventional banks do not have this item, but have an item before tax for promotion of, say, football or art activities; this is recorded as expenses, not as part of the profits set aside to promote sports and arts. The second item in an Islamic bank is a religious contribution – a voluntary wealth tax – that rich people pay into the bank to be mixed with the bank's set-aside profits for the needy. In Iranian jurisdiction, this item is about 1–4 per cent of the total profit of the bank. These two items are strictly after-tax, from bank profits; to that the bank adds the wealth-based charity. It should be emphasized that the last item is a very

Table 11.1   A stylized representation of balance sheet and income statements

(a) Balance sheet

Assets	Liabilities
Cash	Accounts payable
Cash due	Deposits
Securities in	Deferrals
Receivables	Short-term borrowing
Gross assets	Long-term borrowing
Depreciation	Shareholder equity
Net assets	Retained earnings
	Reserves
Total Assets	Liabilities + equity

(b) Income statement

Revenue
   Material cost
   Wage costs
   Depreciation cost
   Overhead cost
   Deposit dividends
Income before tax
   Tax expense

Net income

tiny portion of the income statements, and may be missing in some banks as it is a voluntary contribution.

As can be seen in Table 11.1, the charitable activities are not recorded – there is no compulsion that the bank set aside charity money and some banks may not receive any contribution from the rich as wealth tax. This sum, if any, is contributed to the institutions that take care of the poor and the orphans. All other items are equivalent to items found in conventional bank reports. Examining the income statement, the revenue refers to the income received through PLS and FBMU activities (not interest-based activities). The costs incurred are material costs, wage costs, overhead costs, depreciation costs, and cost of PLS given to the savings depositors. The earnings before tax is the amount on which tax is paid (in most cases there is corporate tax although in some jurisdictions such as Iran there is no tax on corporate income). The resulting number is the net income. Thus, the income statement appears to use the same structure as a conventional bank, but the items entering the statement are not derived from interest-based activities.

The balance sheet can be interpreted in a similar manner. The asset side consists of current assets, including cash, cash owing to the bank including deposits with the central bank, payments due to the bank from PLS and FBMU activities, and an adjustment for non-performing loans. The current liabilities are the accounts payable, tax payable, and cash payable to other parties. Thus, what is missing is the "marketable securities" based on interest (if marketable securities based on profit-share is available, there will be an entry on this item) and loans by banks to be repaid based on interest (if PLS is incurred, this item will be there).

On the asset side, there is plant and equipment with accumulated depreciation and current depreciation, and the book value of loans and investments. The long-term liabilities are items of capital borrowing (Tier-2 capital) items. At the end is the shareholder equity account.

Thus, the financial statements are easily interpretable as in conventional bank reports, although in some cases the same items have different meanings as the item is generated through profit-sharing or fee and-mark-up financial activities. As mentioned, the accounting standards that are increasingly being applied to the preparation of these accounts are those issued by the Bahrain-based institute. The same is the case with banking standards complying with the IFSB schedules. This means that in the near future Islamic bank reports from very diverse economies should be comparable and their relative performance easily evaluated.

11.5 Selection of special terms explained

Here we consider the special meaning of some of the words already used in this chapter, and a selection of other terms that are needed to understand the operation of Islamic banks. In some places, reference has to be made to non-bank activities, such as investments, insurance, and so on since these traditionally non-bank activities have been increasingly undertaken by banks since the 1999 amendments to the anti-trust laws in the USA and similar changes to bank regulations in the UK and other countries. In such places, we also observe Islamic banking activities increasing in this new century.

The debate as to the merits of banking, as we see it in conventional banking practices, has led to three distinct views. Banking is largely viewed as a necessary licensed activity that fosters (a) less risk-taking by the masses – delegated monitoring by banks on behalf of the savers, (b) mobilization of savings at low cost, (c) the promotion of delegated monitoring of users of funds on behalf of the depositors, and (d) ensuring efficient payments to factors of production. Today one may add that a bank also (e) helps economic agents to transfer risk either for the agents or for the bank itself when the bank repackages risky holdings and sells them off to those who want to undertake that risk for a higher return. That these five objectives are consistent with the promotion of community welfare is not a matter of debate, and it is accepted broadly they are worth striving for by a modern society and that resources must be spent to ensure that these objectives are achieved. Is there, however, an alternative to conventional banking?

Whether these objectives can only be achieved through the structure of conventional banking as it has developed over the past four to five hundred years is at the heart of this question. Proponents of free banking – there are very prominent scholars, including Hayek, taking this position – advocate that the regulated nature of banking makes it costly to deliver these society-wide goods. They claim that free banking would lead to greater monitoring of banks by the users of the banks – depositors, savers, borrowers – who will use the market to get information, to punish the bad banks and promote the good ones so that in the end the banks will be able to deliver these functions more efficiently. There will be less opportunity for middle-men, the central banks, and so on, purporting to do good, while actually not doing the right thing for society. They advocate a free trade in banking rather than licence-based banking, where the supra-institutions of central banks and world institutions have failed to create safe banking. Rather this non-free banking has promoted the concentration of wealth in societal elites – worst of all, in developing countries the system has promoted the evil triumvirate of bank-business-political elites working to enrich themselves – and that the world has become indebted through the interest-on-interest based lending practices.

The second view, which can be traced back to Benjamin Franklin, and even Aristotle, is the idea that fractional banking has led to the creation of a wealthy class of banks and their owners and permeated the world with debt so heavy that the citizens are paying a huge price in interest. This is being paid to the bank from the tax collected by politicians who have no qualms about ensuring their re-election through irresponsible borrowing. This line of argument questions why a bank having $1000 can lend $10 000 under fractional bank lending and claims that this is the source of world indebtedness. There are huge figures quoted in the literature on indebtedness in developed and developing countries to bolster this argument. Most of these studies are by well-respected scholars and commentators.

The third point of view is that interest-based banking practices are the source of the problem, and that society will be better off replacing interest with risk and profit-shared lending in financial activities. Islamic banking appears to come from this angle, although the argument for the avoidance of interest is based on Divine revelation in all world religions.

So, there is an ongoing debate as to which form of banking design is best for society. Taken in this context, Islamic banking and finance appear to place the ethical dimension of risk and reward-share at the centre of the argument in favor of this new niche banking (and finance) that has been growing continuously since its formation in 1963. Islamic banking practices were ubiquitous for more than 1500 years, but the last 45 years have seen these practices become formalized. Customers are willing to transact under PLS and FBMU banking as favorable to them, and the banks have responded to the demand. Examples of new entrants are the HSBC, Citigroup, Barclays, and some Swiss and German banks, while a vast number of Islamic banks are found in countries with significant Muslim populations, such as Sudan in Africa, Malaysia in Asia, Bahrain or Iran in the Middle East, or Turkey in Europe (where, however, there are constitutional restrictions on the use of the word "Islamic").

Thus, Islamic banking provides niche banking for special clients. It fulfills the needs of customers who do not wish to participate in harmful activities. To these customers interest-based financial transactions are harmful because of unequal contracting. They also wish their transactions research clear of intoxicant production, gambling, or prostitution. This niche market is there to harness another sources of funds into the broader banking system which the conventional banks will continue to dominate. After all, the assets of all the Islamic banks in the world after 45 years of growth just add up to the total assets of the fourth largest single bank in the world. Under this scenario, one needs to understand how best to operate these new entities.

Over the years, it has come to be accepted that convenience deposits are simply what these are. They will not earn a return, and the deposited money is simply safeguarded for either use by the depositors or withdrawal by the depositors. In conventional banking such deposits attract a very small interest rate and depositors may be required to deposit a sizable amount in order to avoid a service charge. In a sense, even conventional banks appear to treat checking deposits as less than savings, and the return given is paltry. Savings deposits are considered as funds deserving of a reward. In Islamic banking these are considered *mudaraba* deposits and attract a return at the end of each month. There are variations of this and they are referred to by other terms.

On the part of the bank lending on the *mudaraba* basis, the borrower agrees to pay a ratio of the profits from the project or venture to which the borrowed money is put to use. The bank then receives the reward on a regular basis using the ratio of the profits generated by the projects. In such an agreement, the *mudaraba* borrower only parts with that portion of the profits commensurate with the services provided by the bank (or the direct investor if the contract is with a direct lender). If the banker (or the direct lender) actually sits in the project team (for example, a turnkey project for road construction) then there is both a financial service and a management service based on participation in the project management. Thus, the reward to the bank (or the direct lender) will be larger than would be the case if money is the only thing that was lent.

How to vary the profit ratio is a matter that has still not been well-developed even after 45 years, simply because most Islamic banks' funds are used for short-term projects in developing countries, which are more likely to be trade-related than industrial ventures. However, the bigger banks are now directly negotiating larger lending (a German state body borrowed €400 million in 2006) on a particular profit share ratio. As the Islamic banks gather more experience in the area of large-scale lending, there may be some form of categorizing loans according to quality and then varying the profit shares in relation to the quality of the loans. Thus *mudaraba* financiers may take a leading role in facilitating financing, based on better rewards than are at present possible up-front under interest rate arrangements, making this form of lending more attractive.

The other form of financial transaction is the equity share in the ownership of a firm, be it as silent owners or as active owners of the firm. The reward in this case will be the residual income after the debt-holders have been paid their profit share. This reward is the dividends and the retained earnings of the firm. Such contracts are called the *musharaka* contracts, and these are exactly equivalent to the share certificates in conventional practice. As the reward for such financing is decided after the financier has participated in the risk of the firm and before getting a claim to the residual earnings (part being distributed as dividends), this has never been a bone of contention in the anti-interest-rate literature. Thus common stock is a non-interest-based permitted instrument except when the issuer engages in prohibited activities (interest earnings, production of intoxicants for sale to persons, gambling and prostitution).

The last item to be discussed in this section is the *ijaara* contract, which is a buy and lease-back agreement involving buying a property with a mark-up added and then requiring regular payments to recover the up-front payment by a bank while the ownership passes to the borrower from day one. It has been claimed that this is akin to the conventional mortgage except that the equity created in the agreement starts from the first payment in equal proportion to the money paid out. There are reports that in fact the conventional bank's practice of pricing the mark-up on interest rates is contrary to this principle. In addition to these forms of contracts (deposits for safekeeping, savings, lending and shares), Islamic banks are now holding Treasury bonds that are based on PLS contracts, whereby these instruments, called the *sukuk* bonds, are held by a firm that owns assets that generate non-interest income to pay the return to the *sukuk* holders, that is, the bank. This instrument can also be held by an Islamic mutual fund that may wish to add no-risk Treasury bonds to its portfolio of risky securities. *Sukuk* bonds can, in theory, also be designed and issued by private lenders.

There are many other things the bank does. Advisory services provided by banks can be paid for as fees for services, as is the case with an investment bank issuing securities in the primary market. Letters of credit may be given by a bank for a fee, as can the accounts receivable be factored at a discounted price by a factoring company. Thus, there are many areas of financial transactions that require no change in operating principles from those in conventional banks, so long as the instrument is not one that is issued by a firm that engages in intoxicant production, gambling or prostitution or receives its income in the form of interest. For simplicity, only the most common terms have been explained here.

11.6   Future direction
It is debatable whether the world at large will recognize the failure of the fractional-reserve-based banking that has produced, (a) non-risk-sharing lending practices, (b) debt-laden economies and individuals as a result of interest-on-interest-based lending, and (c) institutions such as central banks and world institutions that are largely failing to deliver what they are supposed to for the greater welfare of the human society. In contrast, Islamic banks, based on fractional-reserve banking but eschewing interest-on-interest, appear to discourage loans without the participation in the risk of loss, and not to extend credit to socially-harmful activities.

Despite the ideals of the Islamic banks, they have to date borrowed most of their ideas (except in the areas of forward and futures instruments as these are not permitted as yet by the board of scholars) from conventional banks, adapting conventional contracts to become compliant with the "avoid interest" principle. Some commentators have called this a sheepish practice of making essentially interest-based decisions in which the contract is compliant with the letter of the law rather than with the spirit of true profit-sharing or fair mark-up in lease contracts. An extreme view expressed by one scholar is that this practice has made Islamic banking a $300 billion scam! What is needed is thinking out of the box in order to design instruments and products that are *consistent* with Islamic principles rather than compliant. The well-trained new entrants to the market have enough credibility to move in this way – this writer firmly believes so – and this is the new direction in which change will come.

The second practical issue is how to use derivatives to overcome the riskiness of the banking operations. Here, given the risk-averse nature of the board of scholars, the prohibition on the use of derivatives is a stumbling block to making Islamic banks safer from price change (basis) risk. Unless the *Shari'ah* board members, who are both secular and religious scholars, are educated in the intricacies of these new financial instruments they are likely to treat them as bordering on gambling, and refuse to let this be permitted. New thinking is needed here to interpret what exactly the case laws on risk (*garar* in Islam) have to say about the difference between derivatives and gambling. Believers are required not to take too much risk in life and to avoid risky financial ventures, essentially because the full disclosure is not possible when risk is very high. But then risk pricing is permitted in *takaful* insurance provided the profits of the insurance are returned to the policyholders after all management expenses. Why then is the risk of derivatives considered excessive?

Finally, there is a huge shortage of skilled management personnel in Islamic banks. Only since the start of the twenty-first century have efforts been made to address this. As more trained personnel come on stream, the design of new products will increasingly – if slowly at first – be in the true spirit of the profit-loss-share principle and mark-up principle. This may herald innovations that are not simply seeking to comply with the letter of the law but where the law is at the core of the design. The kind of large players entering the market place have the resources and personnel to achieve these things. With a better trained workforce, and competition in banking, the truly profit-shared lending practices and fair mark-ups in lease contracts may emerge to replace the compliance culture that is pervading practice in Islamic banking and finance.

Notes

1. As at 2007, published reports indicate 67 countries in which Islamic institutions are operating under some form of official licensing arrangements. After the Bank of London amended the UK laws to permit the licensing of Islamic financial institutions, many more countries, including countries with no Muslim population, are rushing to amend their laws to get into this niche banking. The major draw is the large pool of money that is likely to be attracted to this form of banking from customers who would like to lend on the basis of profit-share deposits.

2. The term "Islamic bank" has come to be widely accepted. However, a more appropriate name, and more descriptive of its proper practices is Bank *Mualamat*. This latter term avoids the implication that the bank has something to do with Islam. Apart from the injunction in Islam to avoid interest in financial activities, almost all the instruments are based on pre-Islamic contract terms as these evolved over time to the present day. The only connection that such a bank has with Islam is the doctrine (as was also the case in Catholicism till 1752 AD) that all forms of interest are forbidden by God. There is a wide

body of respectable literature going back to Aristotle, reiterated by Benjamin Franklin and some modern-day thinkers that the debt-based banking system is not conducive to human welfare and that the fractional-reserve banking and the wealth earned by the banking organizers have failed to promote human welfare.

3. Despite this, it is always possible that some errant bankers may engage in practices that are contrary to this oversight function. There was a case of such a malfeasance in Bank Islam Malaysia. An errant officer used some of the funds of the bank to the tune of US$300 million in derivatives positions in an offshore operation, leading to the loss of all the money. This happened because of lack of operational controls rather than sanctioned practice.

4. For a while a Bahrain-based institute was training personnel in Islamic banking. A number of universities have started to offer programs to train graduates in banking with specialization in Islamic banking product design and operations. However, the number of students graduating in this regard is very small. In 2006 two international bodies have been found – INCEIF, which began a certifying program in Islamic banking, and IFCB, which establishes prudential standards in association with world institutions, such as the BIS, on banking norms. In addition the Islamic Development Training Institute conducts intensive training programs around the world – usually in central banks – for regulators and private bankers in Islamic banking. There is no requirement that a student has to be a Muslim to enter any of these.

5. One of the six commandments on interest rates states that lending resulting in two-fold and three-fold in interest is harmful and thus must not be practiced, while other commandments specify that giving the money from interest to charity rather than devouring it is commendable. Except in the Jewish scripture the ban on interest appears to be applicable to all humans: Jewish scripture forbids interest only among the Jewish people.

Bibliography

Divanna, J. (2003), *Understanding Islamic Banking: The Value Proposition that Transcends Culture*, Oxford: Oxford University Press.

Dowd, K. (1996), "The case for financial laissez-faire," *Economics Journal*, **106**, 679–87.

Dowd, K. (2003), "Free banking," in A. Mulleux and V. Murinde (eds), *Handbook of International Banking*, Cheltenham UK and Northampton, MA, USA: Edward Elgar, pp. 173–91.

El-Gamal, M.A. (2006), *Islamic Finance: Law, Economics and Practice*, New York: Cambridge University Press.

Hayek, F.A. (1976), "Denationalisation of money," Hobart Institute of Economic Affairs special paper no. 70, London.

International Association of Islamic Economists (IAIE) (various years), *Directory of Islamic Banks and Financial Institutions*, Jeddah, Saudi Arabia: IAIE.

Iqbal, M. (2006), *A Mini Guide to Islamic Banking and Finance*, Cheltenham, UK and Northampton, MA, USA: Edward Elgar.

Kane, E.J. (1985), *The Gathering Crisis in Federal Deposit Insurance*, Cambridge, MA: MIT Press.

Khan, M.S. and A. Mirakhor (2005), *Theoretical Studies in Islamic Banking and Finance*, Oxford: Oxford University Press.

Miller, M., R. Ippolito and L. Zhang (1998), "Shareholders and stakeholders: human capital and industry," *Economic Journal*, **108**, 490–508.

Mirakhor, A. (1987), "Analysis of short-term asset concentration in Islamic banking," International Monetary Fund working paper no. 67, Washington DC.

Morris, V.B. (2005), *Guide to Understanding Islamic Investing*, New York: Lightbulb Press.

Mullineux, A. and V. Murinde (eds) (2003), *Handbook of International Banking*, Cheltenham, UK and Northampton, MA, USA: Edward Elgar.

Saleem, M., *Islamic Banking: A $300 Billion Dollar Scam*, publisher not listed.

White, L.H. (1984), *Free Banking in Britain: Theory, Experience and Debate 1800–1845*, New York: Cambridge University Press.

Index